Effective Review and Approval of Digital Promotional Tactics, Second Edition

Dale Cooke
President
PhillyCooke Consulting

Jennifer De Camara
With Foreword by
Assistant General Counsel
Johnson & Johnson

FDLI

 ISBN 978-1-935065-85-2

To order additional copies of this publication, please visit our website at www.fdli.org.

FDLI

1155 15th St. NW, Suite 900, Washington, DC 20005
Tel: (202) 371-1420
info@fdli.org
www.fdli.org

Table of Contents

About This Book

Food and Drug Administration enforcement action for promotional activities remains a concern, and digital tactics receive more than their fair share of attention. At the same time, new media consumption habits (of both patients and physicians) make the use of digital tactics imperative. This primer provides a system for reviewing digital tactics. Included in this discussion are the similarities and differences of reviewing digital promotional tactics vs. traditional offline tactics, the value of establishing standard templates for submission of materials, best practices for reviewer comments, a discussion of the role of PDFs in review, a look at the 2253 filing, and some of the key components of continuous improvement of the promotional review process. In addition, sample checklists and templates are provided that can be customized for immediate use.

About FDLI

The Food and Drug Law Institute (FDLI), founded in 1949, is a nonprofit membership organization that offers education, training, publications, and professional engagement opportunities in the field of food and drug law. As a neutral convener, FDLI provides a venue for stakeholders to inform innovative public policy, law, and regulation.

FDLI's scope covers all industries regulated by the U.S. Food and Drug Administration (FDA) and related agencies and authorities in the U.S. and globally, including drugs, medical devices, food, dietary supplements, cosmetics, veterinary, and tobacco products.

FDLI publishes the quarterly, peer-reviewed *Food and Drug Law Journal* presenting in-depth scholarly analysis of food and drug law developments; *Update* magazine, which provides members with concise analytical articles on cutting-edge food and drug issues; and essential reference and educational resources.

About the Author

Dale Cooke is the president of PhillyCooke Consulting, which provides advice and training to companies about developing compliant promotional materials for FDA-regulated products. Dale has worked with more than 40 pharmaceutical and medical device clients and more than 20 advertising agencies around the world. His insights have been featured in the Wall Street Journal's Health blog, The Pink Sheet, MedAdNews, PharmExec, and others. Dale is an active member of the Regulatory Affairs Professionals Society (RAPS), Drug Information Association (DIA), Food and Drug Law Institute (FDLI), the Alliance for a Stronger FDA, and the Google Health Advisory Board.

Dale is regularly invited to speak at industry conferences on topics including FDA enforcement trends, best practices for review processes, global review practices, and life sciences use of social media.

Dale earned his B.A. in philosophy from Southern Methodist University, an M.A. in philosophy from the University of Arizona, and studied epidemiology and biostatistics at Drexel University's School of Public Health and healthcare compliance at Seton Hall University's School of Law. Dale is currently pursuing a law degree at Drexel University's Kline School of Law with anticipated completion in 2019.

Foreword

By Jennifer De Camara, Assistant General Counsel, Johnson & Johnson

For 10 years, I provided regulatory legal counsel on digital and social media issues for the Janssen Pharmaceutical Companies of Johnson & Johnson located in the U.S. During that time, the IMS Institute for Healthcare Informatics recognized Johnson & Johnson as leading other pharmaceutical companies in social media engagement by a significant margin. These accomplishments are particularly notable as they occurred during the period before the Food and Drug Administration (FDA) had issued any draft guidance on social media. Importantly, when finally published, no changes were required to any social media platforms in which Janssen was engaged.

For those of us advising on legal considerations in the early years of social media engagement, FDA's opinions on how to apply drug laws and regulations to social media were not clear. What we learned usually came in the form of enforcement letters. Thankfully, FDA released more draft guidance in 2014, covering character space limitations, post-marketing submissions and correcting misinformation.

While the absence of regulatory guidance made advising on social media and digital efforts challenging, it also afforded opportunities for applying experience and best judgment to reach good solutions. While some companies held back from social media efforts initially, we at Janssen felt it important to communicate to our patients and health care professionals in venues where they sought information about our products and their disease states. We believed it was critical that we find a path forward to engage online because we, as the manufacturer, arguably had the best and most accurate information about our products.

To comply with our analysis we created policies, guidelines, guardrails, and other governance documents and processes that helped us ensure that we had thought through the issues associated with each social media engagement, including ensuring consistency of execution. Chapters I and II of this primer, covering basic review principles and tools extrapolated from a bricks and mortar world to a cyber one, touch on some of the techniques we used.

We also created other tools and resources to ensure clarity and consistency, both within a team and across the Janssen U.S. companies. We routinely, and specifically, considered opportunities to maximize timeliness and flexibility, and to minimize demands on reviewers. That mindset is why the concept of continuous improvement, outlined in Chapter V, is critical to success. Nothing about digital is static—technology constantly changes. Further, platform developers don't base their changes on pharmaceutical industry regulatory considerations. Communication norms evolve, and what we are trying to communicate changes and leads to new issues. A critical part of allowing flexibility is visibility to what actually happens, and an expectation that execution will be evaluated and guidelines enhanced accordingly.

Regarding chapters I and II, although laid out methodically as an almost step-by-step process, readers would be well advised to think of the various principles described in those chapters as tools. Reviewers vary by company, as do copy review steps, reviewer commenting expectations, escalation or executive committee review triggers, and other steps described in those chapters. For example, while there may be a general expectation that reviewers "stay in their lanes" or provide alternative language in providing comments, there should probably also be an expectation that reviewers raise concerns outside of their lanes or raise questions that don't have ready-to-go language suggestions if there are concerns about potential impact to patient safety. Always encourage those discussions.

Along those lines, companies have different litigation-risk profiles that drive considerations that may not even be listed in the chapters, given that the focus is more on drug promotional considerations than the full set of concerns that a copy review team may consider. Looking at these chapters as setting forth options provides a valuable checklist for a company or review team to think about in considering building the steps in its own process, pressure testing their process and analysis approaches, and modifying as appropriate to fit their own needs.

I met Dale Cooke fairly early in my time counseling on social media issues, and had the pleasure of speaking with him on several panels at regulatory conferences. I came to know and admire Dale's engaging and witty speaking style, backed by an encyclopedic command of the regulatory framework applied to the countless details that arise in application to social media. This primer, and its predecessor, channel that knowledge into specific steps and recommendations for marketing teams and reviewers.

Having a methodical framework to approach digital and social projects is key to meaningfully advancing them. Otherwise, projects risk stalling out in concept discussions that don't achieve aligned understanding. Worse yet, an approved project could turn out differently than anticipated. Surprises are seldom welcome in pharmaceutical social media efforts, and it takes exceedingly tight preparation and coordination to avoid them.

As outlined in the preface, Dale has made several enhancements to the original edition, including a new chapter on mobile promotion and a significantly expanded review of search engine marketing. While the 2014 draft guidances have helped answer some questions, there are many that remain, and some key ones are tackled in these new chapters.

The new chapter on search engine marketing is where the primer really shines, because Dale has combined his ability to glean information that is not readily available with his sharp analytical skills. The result is an insightful and fresh analysis of FDA's enforcement posture, particularly in treatment of "reminder-like" boxed warning ads, and not submitting keywords in Form 2253 filings. He lays out carefully constructed analyses to allow reviewers to come to rational and supported decisions about how to proceed—in the absence of assurances and regulatory clarity.

That is where significant aspects of advising on social media remain, despite the areas of clarity provided by the draft guidances. These discussions manifest the kind of experience and judgment that allow companies and reviewers to find paths forward, using best, well-grounded efforts to remain compliant. Considered and robust resources like this primer should be used to full advantage to do just that—build the review platforms, create the tools and resources teams need, do the hard and creative analysis needed to find a principled path forward, and mandate the feedback loop to see what worked, and learn from mistakes. In doing so, we are providing information to the health care community where it is looking: online, in apps, in tweets and in venues we can't even imagine yet, for which hopefully there will be future editions with new chapters.

Preface to the Second Edition

Since its initial publication in 2013, the topic of this primer, how to ensure compliance of digital promotional tactics, has become even more important and complicated. The growth in digital promotion noted in the original has accelerated with a special emphasis on the explosion of mobile devices. More people are consuming more content in more ways than ever before. In addition, the proliferation of new platforms and growth of old platforms has continued apace.

Throughout this, the FDA has not been a mere bystander. Within a few months of the first publication, FDA released the first of its three initial social media guidances (included in the appendices here). In light of these guidances and the overall growth and importance of social media for the marketing of prescription products, a new chapter has been added to address the unique issues associated with mobile promotion and social media. Finally, the appendix addressing search engine marketing has been completely overhauled to reflect guidance (both formal and informal) from FDA and new policies from the search engine platforms themselves. That discussion is now included as a chapter in the body of the primer.

Beyond these revisions, minor changes to (I hope) improve the clarity of presentation have been made throughout.

Introduction

According to Manhattan Research's 2012 Taking the Pulse survey of U.S. physicians, 85 percent of physicians use search engines daily or weekly. In America, 85 percent of all adults have a cell phone, and increasingly, they are using their cell phones for activities other than making phone calls. Indeed, for many people, making phone calls is the second, third, or even fourth most common use of their cell phone. Instead, people are using these portable computers in their pockets to send and receive messages (both SMS and emails), visit websites, and download and use one of the million-plus apps available.

Clearly, people (both physicians and non-physicians) are no longer accessing information in the same way they used to. Pharmaceutical companies and others who produce prescription products have started to provide product information to people via these new channels, but doing so has not been easy.

The Food and Drug Administration's (FDA) position has been consistent. The regulations are essentially media agnostic. If a proprietary name is mentioned, then the established name must also be used, according to 21 CFR 202.1(a)(1). If a product benefit is mentioned, then appropriate risk information must be provided to meet the fair balance requirement of 21 CFR 202.1(e)(1). Ensuring that digital tactics meet all of these requirements has proven especially challenging in certain contexts, such as a message on Twitter, which is limited to 140 characters. In addition, the rapidly evolving nature of digital communications means that reviewers who are experts in law, federal regulation, and medicine are now being required to become experts in the digital channels themselves. This primer is intended to help address this difficulty.

The traditional review and approval process for promotional material was designed around print materials because print was the dominant medium of the day. Digital tactics frequently prove to be the proverbial square peg being forced into the round hole of traditional approval process. This book is structured as a resource to guide users through the complexities of reviewing digital tactics to ensure their compliance. First, the functional roles played by each step in the review process are described, followed by a look at some of the most common digital tactics. Practical advice is provided about what information reviewers need at each stage to ensure that digital tactics are compliant with all applicable laws, regulations, and policies.

A Word about Terminology

Every company has a process for the review of promotional materials. While there are detailed regulations and FDA guidance about the content of promotional materials, there are no regulations or guidance about the review process itself. There is no reason for companies to adopt the exact same process, and in fact, there is significant variety in the nomenclature around the review process and some of the nuances. Despite that variety, there are certain core functions that have to be accounted for as part of any review process. Chapter I provides more detail about the terminology used in this primer to discuss the different stages of review.

Individual companies refer to these reviewing bodies as Promotional Review Boards, Review Committees, Copy Clearance Committees, and other names. Because the committees typically include representatives from the Medical, Legal, and Regulatory capabilities within the company, the terms "MLR committee" and "MLR review" are used throughout.

I refer to "Originators" to mean anyone who is responsible for developing materials that are submitted for MLR review. Originators include, but are not limited to, brand managers and advertising agencies.

What Is a Digital Tactic?

As used here, the phrase "digital tactic" refers to any tactic whose consumption or distribution is reliant on electronic devices such as computers, iPads, or cell phones. Examples of digital tactics include websites, search engine text ads, text messages sent to cell phones, and emails. Note that certain tactics seem to straddle the digital/non-digital divide. Examples of such hybrid tactics include print ads featuring a Quick Response (QR) code that requires a digital device to read the QR code to gain access to additional information.

For purposes of this book, traditional broadcast media of television and radio are not regarded as digital channels, though they share many features in common with digital tactics. The promotional materials (TV or radio ad) become digital tactics when their distribution expands beyond the traditional medium (television screen or radio speaker) to websites or other digital means. Because TV ads share much in common with other digital tactics, one of the appendices discusses the review and approval process for television ads in light of recent FDA guidance on the subject.

Chapter I
The Stages of a Review and Approval Process

A well-designed Medical Legal Regulatory (MLR) review and approval process has distinct stages. At each stage, the originator of a promotional tactic provides information to the MLR team about the desired tactic and solicits feedback from the MLR committee about what can be done compliantly. The stages described in this chapter ensure that the originator of a tactic receives appropriate feedback to prevent wasting resources developing tactics that would not be compliant. The stages also enable MLR reviewers to fulfill their vital role of ensuring tactics are compliant with all applicable rules and regulations, such as the fair balance requirement of 21 CFR 202.1(e)(2), while not adding unnecessary cost to the content development process.

A project could go through up to five distinct stages:

A. Concept Review

B. MLR Committee Review

C. Check Changes Review

D. Executive Committee Review

E. Final Samples Submission

A. Concept Review

The first stage is called the Concept Review. The purpose of a Concept Review is to solicit feedback from the MLR committee early in the development process. The intent is to uncover what constraints the committee is going to impose on a project and uncover what information the committee will need to evaluate the project when it has been developed and is ready for the full MLR Committee Review. Concept Reviews are not usually included for routine projects, such as updating a visual aid or producing a new printed patient brochure. Instead, the Concept Review is reserved for discussing the first time a company (or brand) is incorporating an innovative or unprecedented type of tactic or is developing a brand new line of messaging. As such, Concept Reviews are particularly relevant for digital tactics.

The first time a company launches a mobile app or a Facebook page, for example, the Concept Review can be used to explain to the MLR committee how the technology works and get feedback about what information the committee will want to see at later stages of development. Given that role, it is obvious why not every project warrants a Concept Review. For example, a project originator who is developing a new adherence program that incorporates text messaging, emails, and hard-copy print materials might bring in the overall program for a Concept Review to determine what constraints MLR will put on the space-limited format of a text message or what connections the committee is comfortable with between the different formats. It would, however, be extremely unusual after having brought in the overall program for a Concept Review to then follow up with a separate Concept Review for an individual email or text message included in that program. Instead, those individual items will probably move directly into the second phase of review: the MLR Committee Review.

Coming out of a Concept Review, the originator of the project should have the information needed to develop a project successfully and bring it back to the MLR Committee Review. In some cases, the MLR committee will determine that the company is not comfortable moving forward with the tactic as proposed. In those cases, the reviewing team will either reject the project concept or request significant changes before it moves into development.

So, there are three possible outcomes from a Concept Review:

a) Rejected

b) Move Forward to Development

c) Revise and Re-submit

Pointers

Steps for Ensuring a Successful Concept Review for Digital Tactics

1) Conduct the Concept Review with the same team that will be reviewing the developed project.
2) Devote adequate time to educating the committee about the relevant technology, its capabilities, and its limitations.
3) Bring prototypes and/or examples of similar projects produced by other brands or companies.
4) Develop a tactic description detailed enough to elicit meaningful feedback—but don't spend too much of your budget before you start developing content.
5) Be prepared to discuss source references and the types of claims that might be made.

B. MLR Committee Review*

The MLR Committee Review is the place where the originator presents a developed project for the MLR committee to evaluate its compliance. Whereas a Concept Review is a discussion about what the project originator would like to do, but has not yet done, the MLR Committee Review carefully assesses the details of exactly what has been developed. This is the stage where all of the references for claims are provided and where the final layout can be reviewed.

There are four possible outcomes from the MLR Committee Review:

a) Rejected

b) Approved

c) Approved with Changes

d) Revise and Re-submit

* Note that although this is referred to as an "MLR Committee Review" nothing in this description requires that the review include all members of the committee or that the review be conducted as an actual committee meeting. Many companies segment different types of tactics and review processes in an attempt to streamline this review. The description here is compatible with such variations.

Projects that are rejected will be terminated. Projects that are approved will move immediately to the Check Changes Review. Projects that are Approved with Changes will go back to the originator to incorporate requested revisions before moving to the Check Changes Review. Under some circumstances, the MLR committee might require that the project be re-submitted for review by the full committee before proceeding. That is the Revise and Re-submit verdict.

Pointers

Improving the Process

Very few projects should be rejected at the MLR Committee Review stage. If the project was likely to be rejected, then it should have gone through a Concept Review, and coming out of the Concept Review the originator should have developed the material in a way that avoided the rejection. If many projects are being rejected at this stage, that shows that either Concept Reviews are not being conducted or they are not being conducted effectively. There are several possible reasons for this failure. First, the committee is not providing clear feedback. Second, the originator(s) are not providing enough information to elicit actionable feedback from the reviewers to avoid rejection. Third, the originator(s) are not developing their projects according to the feedback provided. Regardless of its root cause, one metric for evaluating the efficiency of a review process is how many projects are rejected at the MLR Committee Review stage.

C. Check Changes Review

The purpose of a Check Changes Review is to ensure that all of the changes that were required by the MLR committee are incorporated. Because the sole purpose of this review is to check that the required changes have been made, the possible verdicts at this stage are:

a) Approved

b) Revise and Re-submit for Check Changes

c) Re-submit to MLR Committee

Approved projects move to the next stage in the review process. If some changes were not incorporated or were incorrectly made, originators are required to revise the project and re-submit after correcting those errors. Under certain circumstances, the check changes reviewer might require that a project go back to the full MLR Committee Review. An example of when this might be necessary is when a label update has happened between the time the project was initially reviewed by the MLR Committee and the time the project is submitted to the Check Changes Review.

Pointers

Who conducts the Check Changes Review?

Depending on a company's size, volume of promotional materials, and overall staffing and structure, this review can be conducted by a dedicated proofreader (or group of proofreaders), one of the members of the MLR committee, or even by the brand manager responsible for the project. Regardless of who conducts the review, the purpose is the same.

Deviation Reports

Originators must incorporate all direction provided by MLR reviewers to ensure tactics are compliant. The check changes stage of review is intended to ensure that all such direction is correctly incorporated. Reviewers, however, occasionally make mistakes of spelling, grammar, or consistency (sometimes via an inconsistency within the same project or an inconsistency across multiple projects). Under such circumstances, originators should not be obligated to blindly incorporate such errors, but there has to be documentation about why any deviation from MLR reviewer direction is occurring. For these reasons, companies often incorporate a Deviation Report into the Check Changes Review. Originators who believe an MLR review comment was mistaken must provide the requested change, the deviation from the requested change, and a reason for the deviation. Such reports enable originators to avoid multiple re-reviews going back to MLR committees to have comments updated, while providing a complete audit trail indicating exactly what was done and why. A further refinement of the process requires that a submitted Deviation Report receive approval from one member of the MLR committee before being permitted to be used by the Check Changes Reviewer.

D. Executive Committee Review

An Executive Committee consists of higher-level executives who are not reviewing compliance of the tactic itself, but instead have been brought in to the review and approval process for a different reason. Membership of an Executive Committee might include the company's Chief Medical Officer (in place of a Medical Reviewer), Chief Counsel, and Head of Regulatory Affairs. Typically, there are three reasons a project undergoes an Executive Committee Review:

1) The company is using a new type of tactic or platform (e.g., Facebook) for the first time, and the company has decided that in addition to being approved by the relevant MLR Committee, such tactics must also receive executive sign-off.

2) There is disagreement among MLR committee members about whether a tactic is appropriate, and the review has been escalated to executives to resolve the disagreement.

3) The tactic is so high profile (e.g., a television commercial) that the tactic is being escalated as a matter of course to ensure executive sign-off.

E. Final Samples Submission

All product promotional materials must be submitted to FDA under cover of Form 2253 prior to use. At this stage of the approval process, the materials are being reviewed to ensure that they match what was approved at the earlier stages and are in an appropriate format for submission to FDA.

Consequently, the only possible verdicts are:

a) Approved for Distribution

b) Revise and Re-submit

c) Re-submit to MLR Committee

Projects that are received in the appropriate format are submitted to FDA and then the originator is notified that they are approved for distribution, though of course, other tasks (such as training a sales force on appropriate use of a tactic) might be warranted before the tactic is actually distributed. On the other hand, if the piece is not submitted correctly, then the originator must revise and re-submit final samples. In rare circumstances, such as when a label update has been received between the Check Changes Review and the Final Samples Submission, it might be necessary to re-submit materials to the MLR committee.

Pointers

The submission of product promotional materials is itself a regulatory requirement. Consequently, there should never be any confusion or miscommunication about whether a piece is approved for distribution. Most companies make use of an electronic system for the review and approval of materials, such as Veeva's Vault or Vodori. Such systems can be implemented so that as soon as the 2253 submission has occurred an email is sent to notify the originator that the promotional materials may be used. With more companies adopting the Electronic Common Technical Document (eCTD) for the submission of promotional materials via the FDA Gateway, it is possible that the actual 2253 submission is no longer being handled by a company's ad-promo regulatory group, but is instead being managed by a publishing group.

Regardless of who handles the 2253 submission, and regardless of what system (if any) is used, there should be a clear, unambiguous communication to the project originator that the promotional material in question may be used. And of course, under no circumstances should materials be used prior to receiving such a communication.

F. Additional Review Types

The above description of the review process focuses on the review of product promotional tactics from conception through submission to FDA. That process is distinct from the review of disease awareness communications and the quarantine review.

Disease Awareness Communications Review

Disease awareness communications must also be reviewed to ensure that such materials are not being used for product promotion. The only significant difference in the process for disease awareness communications is that because they are by definition not product promotions, they are not required to be submitted to FDA under cover of Form 2253 prior to distribution. Consequently, at the final samples stage of the review and approval process there will often be variation. However, there should still be a clear step where the final disease awareness materials are submitted to the company and the originator receives clear indication that the materials may be used.

Quarantine Reviews

All materials are approved for use only for a specific period of time. Typically, the approval lasts for one year, but in some cases, it is only valid for six months (such as when the word "new" is used). As the material nears its expiration, a decision must be made about whether to continue its use or whether to withdraw the material from use. If the decision is made to continue its use, the material must go back for a Quarantine Review. The exact nature of that review varies by company, but typically, it is some version of an MLR Committee Review. Digital tactics can create particular challenges when it comes to the Quarantine Review.

Rarely does a digital tactic such as a website go completely unchanged for an entire calendar year. Indeed, frequent updates to websites are quite common. This can complicate the Quarantine Review because each update typically receives a separate review and becomes tracked as a distinct piece with its own date for quarantine. The best practice for dealing with this issue is to set at a digital tactic's inception its anniversary and require the entire website (or other tactic), including any updates that have occurred in the interim, to go through Quarantine Review prior to its anniversary date. In practice, what this typically means is that one of the updates to the website turns into a complete review of the full website prior to its expiration.

Pointers

Commenting Procedures

Proper commenting procedures save time and money. Below are some best practices reviewers should follow when providing comments on a project.

1) Questions for other reviewers should be explicitly directed to another reviewer and distinguished from comments for the originator of the project.

   For example,

   "For legal, is this the right privacy policy?" is correct;

   but

   "Is this the right privacy policy?" is incorrect.

2) Queries must be resolved before distributing comments.

   It is perfectly acceptable for a reviewer to note the need to confirm certain information within a review document (e.g., "Need to confirm phone number with call center."). However, distributing a PDF with such comments can cause confusion because originators might not know how they are supposed to deal with such queries and whether they are being asked to confirm such information.

3) Comments should be directive and specific.

   Originators often are not present for a review committee meeting (if one is held), and even if the originator is present, he or she might not remember the details of the discussion days or weeks later when attempting to address the comment. In addition, the person responsible for checking changes might not be the same as the person making the comment. Consequently, there should be no ambiguity about how to address a comment.

   For example,

   Bad Comment: "This sentence is unclear."

   Good Comment: "Change this sentence to read, 'The product…'"

4) Reviewers should keep to their functional roles.

   Even after many years of sitting on a review committee together, a lawyer is not transformed into a medical reviewer, nor is a regulatory reviewer transformed into a lawyer. It is certainly appropriate to ask questions of colleagues on the committee, but as a rule of thumb, when reviewers stray outside their area of expertise, they introduce uncertainty about whose direction to follow.

5) Reviewers should review the tactic, not the PDF.

   The PDF plays a very specific purpose in the review process. Specifically, it is a place where reviewers can provide their comments to originators. It is very easy to become confused and begin to review the PDF itself. For example, during PDF creation, certain imagery might become pixelated. So long as the tactic itself is clear, that is not an issue on which to comment. Relative sizes of items can also change in a PDF versus in the tactic itself. The focus should be on the digital tactic under review, not on the appearance of the PDF itself.

6) There should be a clear communication of the outcome of the review and next steps.

   There are at most four possible outcomes of any given review: 1) Approved, 2) Approved with Changes, 3) Revise and Re-submit, and 4) Rejected. One of these four verdicts should clearly be indicated at the top of the reviewed document, and there should be clearly defined next steps depending on the stage of review (e.g., "Approved" from a Concept Review = Develop tactics and submit for MLR Committee Review).

Chapter II
Taking a Digital Project through Approval

The stages of review described in the previous chapter are tactic-channel agnostic. In theory, a print ad or core visual aid goes through the same review process as a mobile app, iPad eDetail, or Google search ad campaign. In practice, the process outlined in the preceding chapter was designed for printed promotional materials, and taking digital tactics through that process can seem like fitting a square peg in a round hole. This chapter outlines some of the key principles that ensure digital tactics are reviewed correctly.

First, we discuss the reviewers' understanding of the technology. People can't review what they don't understand. Unfortunately, there is a tendency among marketers and advertising agencies to assume that because they have been using a particular technology for years that it is fully understood by MLR committees. Many delays in reviews are created by reviewers who are not comfortable with the underlying technology, rather than by the particular promotional tactic that is being submitted for review.

Second, different types of projects should be reviewed at different stages of development. In this chapter, we look at some of the most common digital tactics (websites, banner ads, emails, search engine text ads, and video) and discuss the appropriate stages for review and what reviewers need to see to ensure compliance.

That leads us to the third topic, which is the use of submission templates for standard digital tactics. Templates can significantly enhance review quality. Among the benefits of submission templates are consistent presentation of information. This enables reviewers to examine materials faster and with greater confidence because they are familiar with layout. And because templates direct originators about what to present as well as how to present it, reviewers can fulfill their responsibility with confidence that they are seeing all of the necessary information to ensure compliance. Submission templates also enhance the efficiency for originators by eliminating the need to expend effort determining what to present for review and how to present it. Instead, they can spend their time developing promotional tactics. This section includes several sample templates for some of the most common digital tactics.

Fourth, we discuss the role of the PDF in the review process. Within the past ten years, electronic review and approval systems (such as Zinc Ahead, Veeva Vault, and Vodori) have been widely adopted within the industry. Very few companies still conduct their reviews on paper. This transition can have significant benefits in increased efficiency, lower costs, and improved compliance. Such systems typically require that tactics (whether digital or non-digital) be converted to a PDF before being submitted into the system. In this section, we look at the role of the PDF and some of the best practices for utilizing PDFs in the review process.

Fifth, we discuss the 2253 filing of digital tactics for product promotion. When the promotional material is, for example, a printed brochure, it is very clear what to submit for the 2253 filing. Companies simply take a stack of the final, printed piece, and send them to the Office of Prescription Drug Promotion (OPDP) under cover of Form 2253. Digital tactics do not fit that model. This chapter includes specific recommendations about what to provide to OPDP for some of the most common digital tactics.

A. Understanding the Technology

Reviewers cannot review technology that they do not understand. When they are asked to do so, the process will frequently be delayed as reviewers request changes that are simply not possible.

Concept Reviews for new technologies can help avoid these pitfalls. The purpose of such Concept Reviews is to explain how the technology itself works and permit reviewers to ask questions about different aspects of the technology. When relevant, prototypes or actively functioning staging environments can be extremely useful for such Concept Reviews.

Reviewers should focus on the following areas during these Concept Reviews:

1) What is under the company's control?

2) How do the items/features that are outside the company's control function? Is it possible to influence items/features that are not directly under the company's control?

3) What (if any) are the offline analogues for this technology? For example, a video on YouTube is analogous to a television commercial and similar issues must be taken into account for both.

Let's consider how these principles play out in the case of a YouTube video.

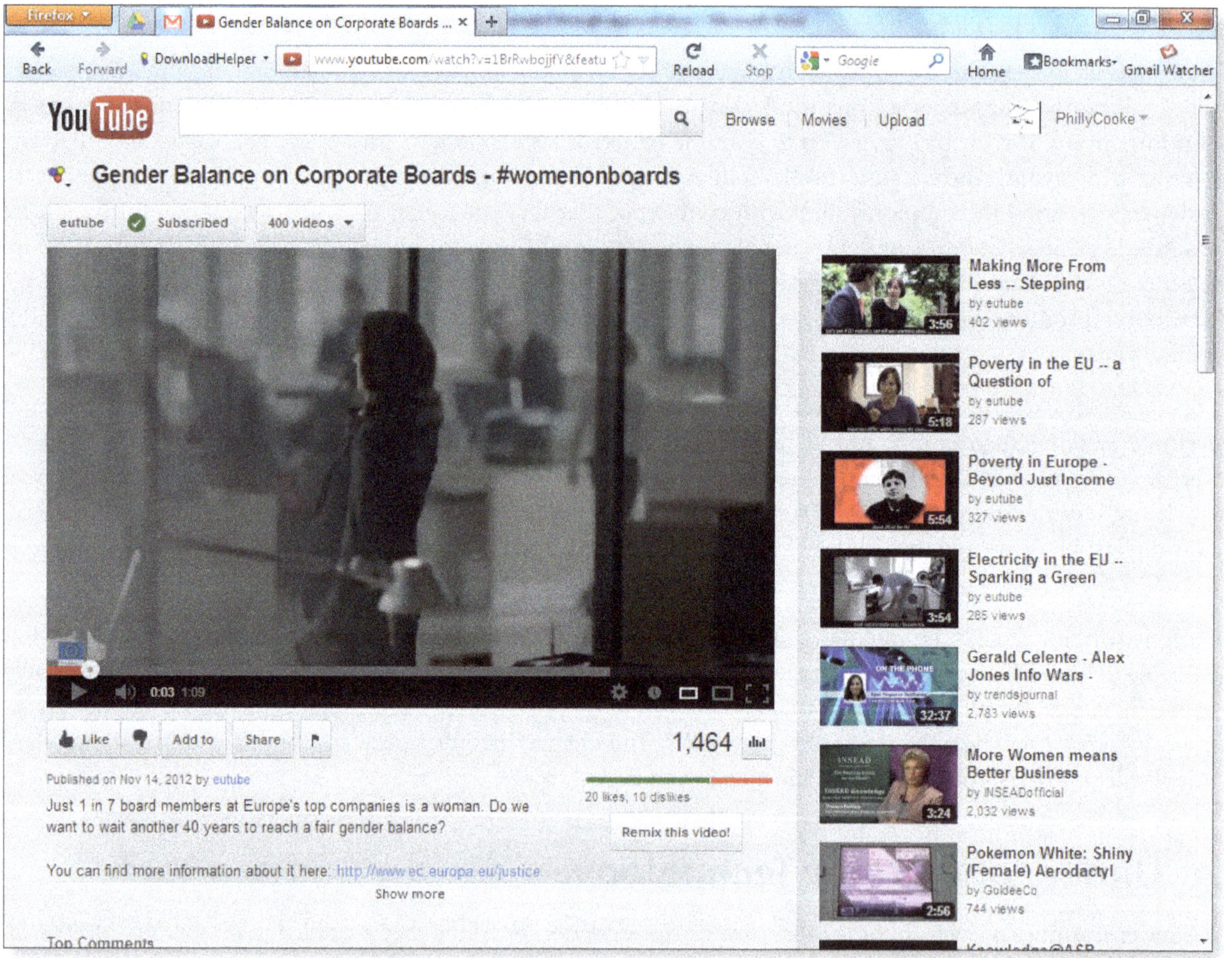

Sample YouTube Video

In this case, the video itself, the name of the video, account name, and the description are fully under the company's control.

YouTube Video Highlighting in Green Features Entirely under Company's Control

By contrast, YouTube's core functionality, the functionality of the player itself, and the suggested other videos (or advertising videos if applicable) are outside the company's control. However, people who upload videos to YouTube can have some influence over what functionality appears. For example, when a video is uploaded, users can choose to permit commenting without moderation, allow only approved comments to appear, or disable commenting; voting also can be permitted or disabled.

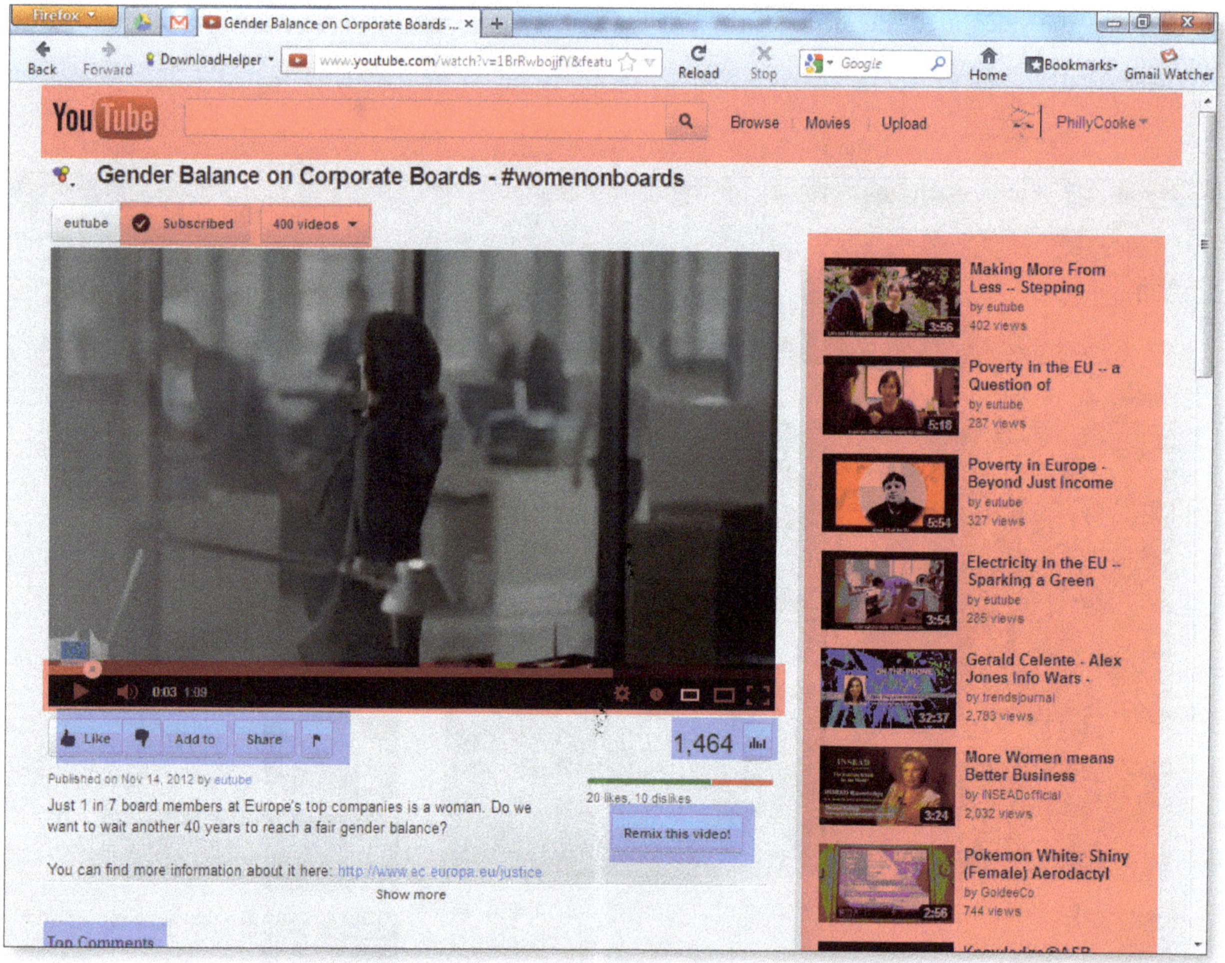

YouTube Video Highlighting in Red Features Outside Company's Control & in Blue Features Company Can Include or Exclude (but not change)

The Concept Review should provide opportunities for reviewers to see all of this information and have discussions about what options are available. The platform itself should be monitored regularly because platforms will change, sometimes without notice. New options will be added; old options will be deleted. For example, the closed captioning functionality of YouTube has recently been updated.

Reviewers need to understand all of these options and what decisions they will be asked to make when the tactic is submitted for MLR review. In the case of reviewing and approving a video for use on YouTube, that means reviewers must ensure that they review all of those items that are completely under the company's control: a) user name, b) video itself, c) video's name, and d) video description. Reviewers must also make decisions about those factors that can be influenced by the company, such as whether to allow unmoderated commenting, allow moderated commenting, or prevent commenting.

It is also extremely helpful to integrate use of certain technology (such as iPads and other mobile devices) into reviewers' everyday work flow. If all reviewers have iPads and need to use their iPads as part of their everyday work, then it will be much easier to discuss how an eDetail on an iPad works than if the reviewers have never used this device. People who need to review technology ideally should be familiar with that technology, and that includes establishing comfort with technology outside of the review itself.

B. What to Review When

Certain digital tactics create challenges for reviewers because it is unclear what they should be reviewing and when they should be reviewing it. For tactics that undergo a Concept Review, this can (and should) be one of the items for discussion. In some cases, however, neither reviewers nor originators have a clear idea of exactly what should be brought to a Concept Review. Below are suggested items to review at specific stages for some of the most common digital tactics.

1. Digital Tactic: Websites

Websites remain the backbone of almost all digital marketing efforts. One of the first activities when a brand name is under consideration is checking to see whether **BrandName.com** is an available URL. That is essential because both consumers and healthcare professionals (HCPs) will frequently simply type that into their browser when they want information about a prescription product.

Stage of Review: **Concept Review**

Content outline identifying categories of content to be covered and the content's arrangement

Design comps showing the layout for the home page, section landing pages, and interior pages

Site map showing the complete content plan for the site

A fully developed site map is a very different document from the site map that is visible to the public on a website. The site map that is visible to the public is better referred to as a site index. The site index might include as little as half of the actual site content. The site map that should be submitted for review at a Concept Review should document every page of content, pages requiring people to enter data (e.g., to sign up for updates), and hidden pages (e.g., error states) that a user might see on a website.

Wire frames showing the functionality that is intended to be implemented. Wire frames are particularly useful when complex interactivity is being proposed (e.g., chat functionality that enables site visitors to have live discussions with a company representative), and the originator wants to receive feedback about the MLR committee requirements related to this technology before spending developer time writing code. In some cases, a prototype can supplement or replace wire frames for purposes of a Concept Review.

Stage of Review: **MLR Committee Review**

PDF of the Entire Site showing every page of content and every possible state of each page (e.g., error states and drop-down menus). Depending on the site being developed and the overall project plan, the PDF of the site that is submitted for MLR Committee Review can either be created by snagging screen shots of a staging location, which is available for the MLR committee to review, or by creating design comps in a page layout program prior to building the site. There are benefits and drawbacks of both methods. Staging locations tend to take longer but should look and function like the actual site when it is live. Design comps will always have some differences from the finished site but often can be produced faster than the functioning site. If the site is already on a staging location, then that staging location information is also provided to the MLR committee.

Metadata includes information that is for the most part not visible to users but enables search engines, such as Google, to "index" the site and make pages of the site available for users looking for specific information provided by the site. Metadata includes the title of pages that appear in the Internet browsers, Alt-tags for images that are provided to the visually impaired, keywords that help search engines categorize websites, and page descriptions that further help search engines determine whether an individual Web page has the information a user seeks.

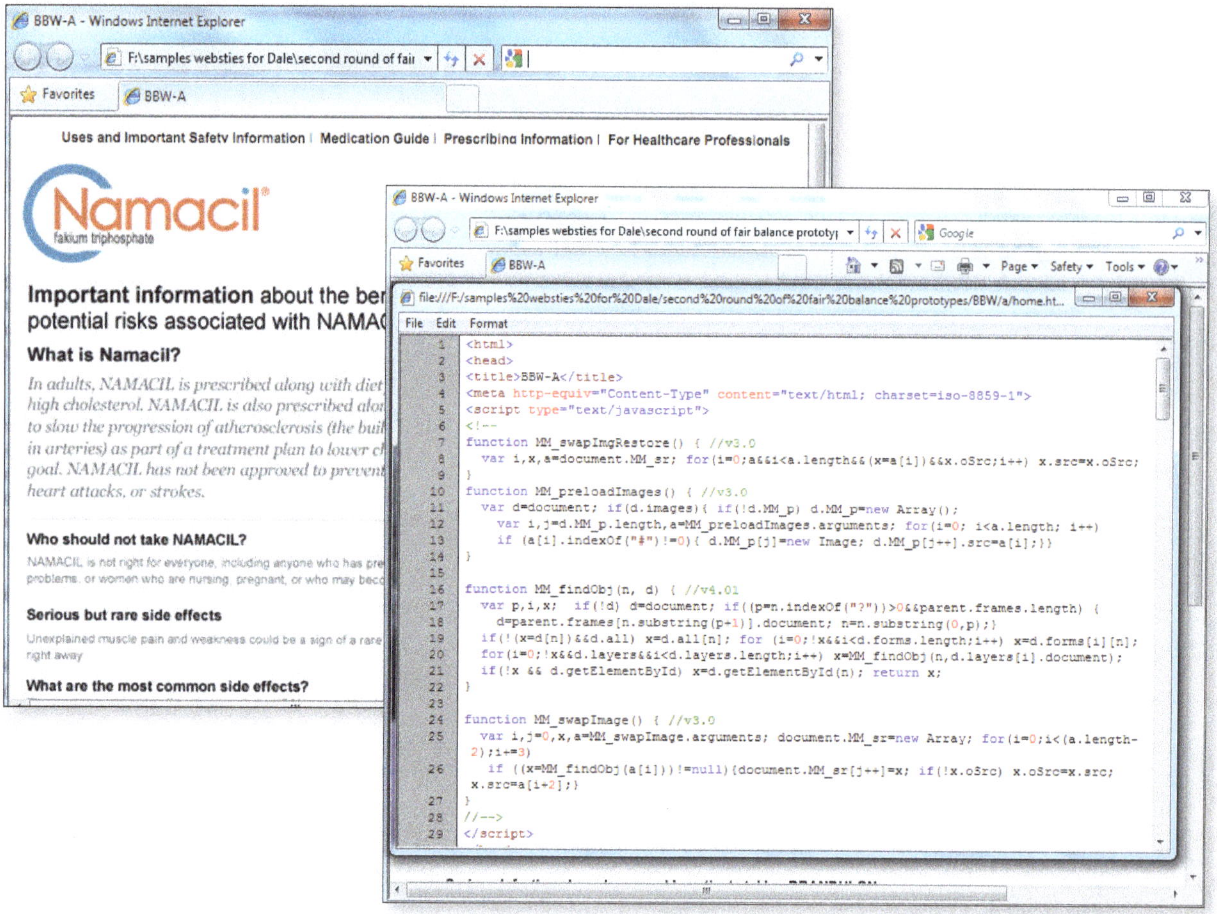

Sample Website Pages and Source Code

Most metadata is only viewable as source code in the final website, but MLR committee members should review page titles, keywords, page descriptions, and Alt-tags as part of their review of any website. Page titles are visible in the top of the browser bar on each page. FDA has indicated in enforcement actions that the presence of certain words in metadata can indicate intended off-label promotion. Reviewers should ensure that no metadata implies an unapproved use.

Site map showing the complete content of the site. The site map is often submitted along with the PDF of the site to assure the MLR committee that every page of content is included and to provide a road map to the site content as submitted.

Pointers

Why No Manuscript Review?

Several years ago, MLR committees regularly reviewed manuscripts of websites before the manuscript was placed into layout. For the most part, that practice has ended. MLR committees used to think of websites as analogous to TV commercials where they would need to review the manuscript before the script was filmed. For websites, this proved detrimental. Many changes will be required in moving from a manuscript to a website in layout simply because copy will have to be adjusted to fit the final layout or to match imagery. Because it is necessary to track every change that is made at the direction of the MLR committee and ensure that those changes are incorporated in the final site, manuscript review proved to be overly cumbersome. Consequently, almost all companies have eliminated the manuscript from the MLR Committee Review and instead only require the "final" site in layout for MLR Committee Review.

Stage of Review: **Check Changes Review**

PDF of the Entire Site showing every page of content and every possible state of each page (e.g., error states and drop-down menus). Except under very rare circumstances, the Check Changes Review is a review of the functioning site on a staging location. So, the PDF of the entire site is generated from screen shots of the staging location. The PDF, in its entirety, should match every page (and every state of every page such as error states and drop-down menus) that was provided to the MLR Committee.

Pointers

Why No Functional Review?

These recommendations do not include a Functional Review as a distinct stage in the approval process. That does not mean that the MLR committee is not responsible for ensuring that functional materials (as opposed to the design comps of the materials) are compliant. Some companies have incorporated the Functional Review as a separate stage. When used, the purpose of this stage of review is for the MLR committee or some subset of that committee to review the functioning site and ensure that everything works. The assumption behind that review is that non-functioning materials (such as PDFs of a site built as design comps) are being reviewed by the MLR committee and only later is the functioning tactic reviewed. While that is one way to approach such a review, the MLR committee must see the functioning materials at some point and thus it is taken for granted that one of the MLR Committee Reviews (or re-reviews) will include a review of the fully functioning materials. In addition, separate technical quality controls are occurring behind the scenes to ensure that the materials are functioning correctly as they move from one development stage to another.

2. Digital Tactic: Flash Banner Ads and Web Pages

Banner ads are the billboards of the Internet, and they remain a key component of most online media campaigns. Flash is an optional feature of Web browsers that is widely used on desktop and laptop computers. Flash enables certain additional functionality in websites that has otherwise been difficult or impossible, such as very complex animation. Because it is extremely useful, most people install Flash on their computers, and many computers even have Flash pre-installed at the factory. Flash, however, is not available on every computer. Most famously, Flash has never been installed on iPhones or iPads, and Adobe announced that it was discontinuing the development of Flash for mobile devices. Consequently, although Flash is still widely used for development of banner ads and some Web pages, it is always necessary to know what people without Flash will experience. Failing to provide a backup available for non-Flash users can result in a blank box appearing where the Flash module is supposed to be. If, for example, that Flash module contained risk information, the non-Flash version of that module could present an unbalanced message that would violate FDA regulations.

Stage of Review: **MLR Committee**

PDF of the Full Banner Ad or Website showing every frame of the banner if it is animated

Static Backup Banner or Web Page indicating what users who do not have Flash on their computers will see

In the case of banner ads, there does not need to be any connection between the content of a Flash banner ad, and its static backup. Indeed, quite often the static backup will be completely unrelated, such as being an ad for the company instead of for any specific product. This is often done because the limited functionality of the backup often makes it difficult to provide appropriate balance for any promotional message.

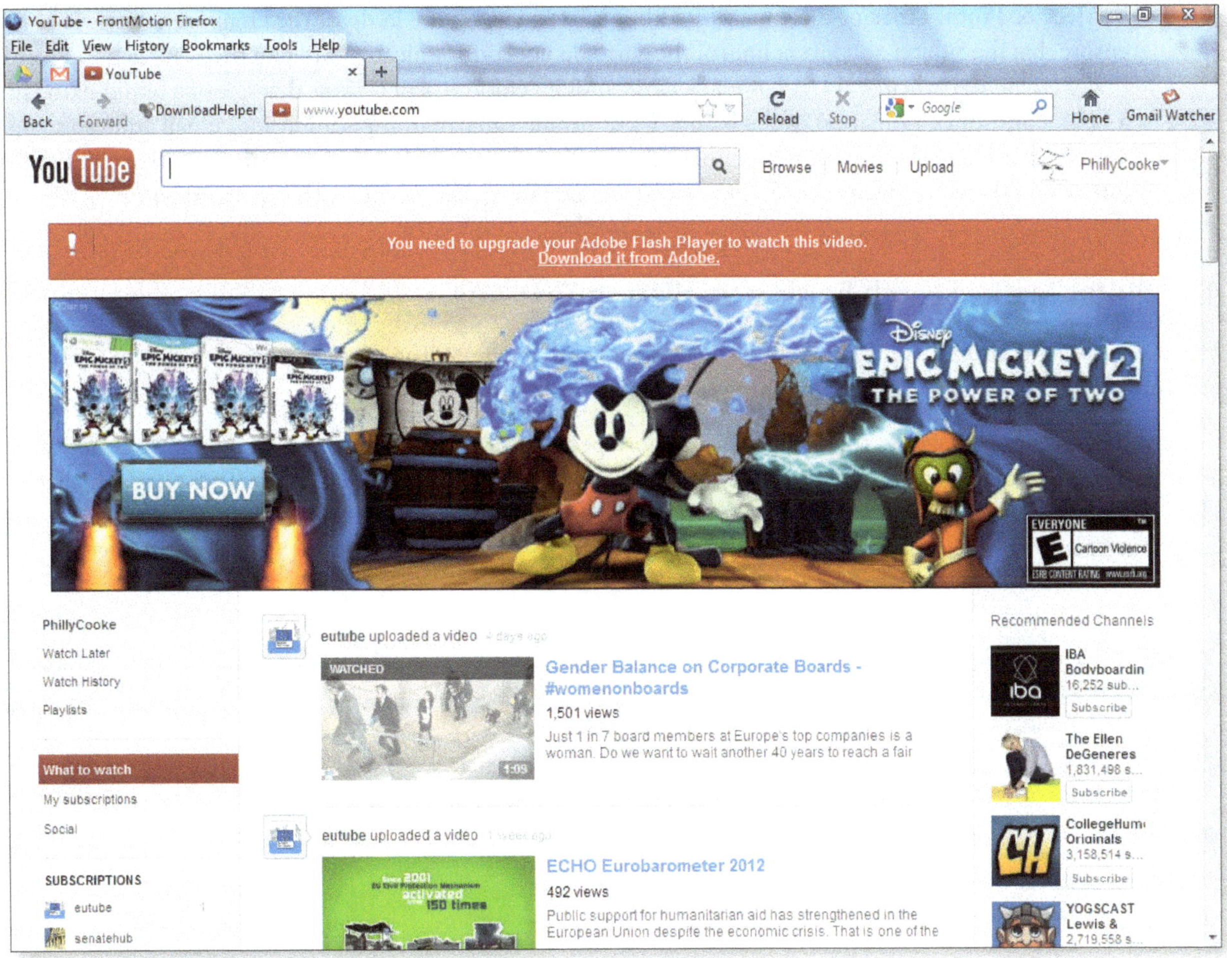

Web Page without Flash

This page shows a message that indicates that Flash is not operating. If this alternative messaging is not developed and deployed, the resulting page would display with a blank box where the Flash module should be.

3. Digital Tactic: Emails

Email communication is now standard for almost all audiences, and adherence campaigns always include a significant component of messaging that is delivered via email.

Stage of Review: **MLR Committee**

HTML, Text, and Web Page versions of the email. Some users will accept emails sent as HTML files; others will only accept text versions. The HTML version of the email will be able to display graphics and have certain functionality (such as including a hyperlink in the body of the email) that is not available to users who only accept text versions. Consequently, email communications must be developed both as HTML and text versions. Because of the large variety of email utilities, many companies also develop a separate Web page version of the email and make that accessible to recipients via a link at the top of the email. If the Web page version of an email is developed, it also must be submitted for review.

Subject & From: Lines of the email. In addition to reviewing the body of the email, reviewers need to ensure that the Subject and From: lines of the email do not communicate a different message than the body of the email. In particular, FDA has made clear through enforcement actions that use of a brand name in a URL constitutes a mention of the brand. Most people carry that implication into email addresses and assume that if an email is sent from either XXXX@Brand.com or Brand@Company.com that the From: line would therefore violate the requirement to include the generic name with the brand name.

4. Digital Tactic: Search Engine Marketing Text Ads

For most people (consumers and HCPs alike) entering a word or phrase into Google is the first step of trying to find information about any subject, including prescription medicines.

Because a search on Google is the beginning of most people's search for information on the Internet, and because FDA has taken dramatic enforcement action about Search Engine Marketing Text Ads, which the FDA called sponsored links on search engines, chapter IV of this primer provides additional information on developing compliant search engine marketing materials.

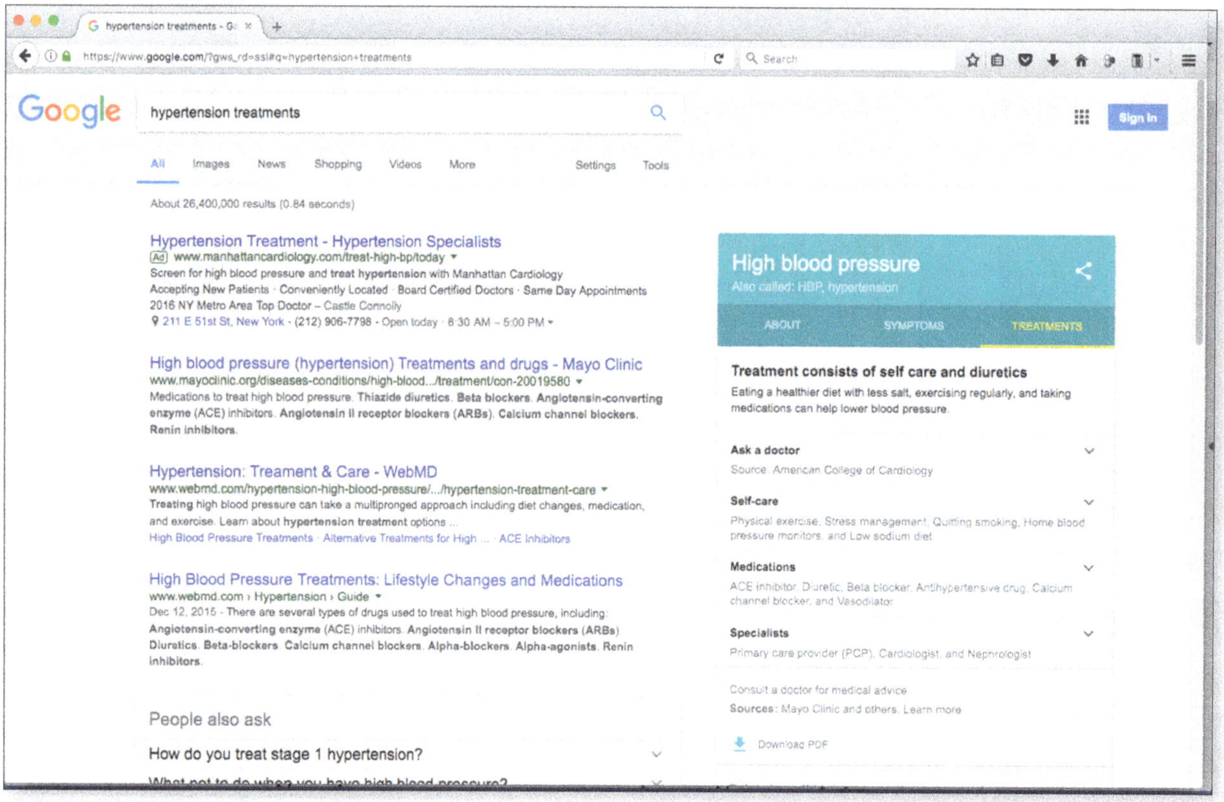

Stage of Review: **MLR Committee**

Keywords indicate what terms people are searching for that could trigger your advertising message to appear. Special care should be taken to ensure that marketing messages are not targeted at people who are looking for information about well-known off-label uses for your product.

Ad Copy comprises a Headline, Description Copy, and a Display URL. These few lines of copy are the entirety of the promotional message that will be seen by users who see your search engine marketing text ads.

Destination URL determines where users will be sent when they click on the ad. Frequently, the actual Web page that a user is sent to has a different URL from the page displayed in the ad itself. Reviewers need to see both the display URL and the destination URL for any ad copy.

Negative Keyword Lists prevent your ad copy from appearing if users type in certain search terms. Reviewers should check negative keywords. Although FDA has not explicitly provided any guidance or taken any enforcement action related to keywords or negative keywords, it is regarded as a best practice to include common off-label uses of your product in the negative keywords list. This will help ensure that your promotional messages do not appear for users who are searching for information about an off-label use.

5. Digital Tactic: Video

There is nothing about video per se that makes it a digital tactic, but the proliferation of broadband as the primary means for accessing the Internet has led to an explosion of video content online. In addition, the later expansion of 3G and 4G broadband networks for cellular devices has compounded the complexity of developing compliant video promotional materials as online videos are viewed on a variety of devices and screen sizes. Consequently, this section discusses the review of video content in general. Appendix B of this primer provides additional information about the review and approval process specifically for television commercials as FDA has released guidance about this topic, and the review of television commercials shares many features in common with review of video for digital distribution.

Stage of Review: **First MLR Review**

Script & Storyboard should be presented to MLR before any filming. The video treatment should include a discussion of casting as many companies have strict policies about the use of actual HCPs and patients in video programs (as opposed to actors portraying HCPs and patients).

Intended Devices for distribution of the video should be discussed at the initial MLR review. Device screen sizes vary, so while information presented in super-imposed text on a desktop computer might be perfectly acceptable, the same text might be illegible when the program is viewed on a smaller screen (e.g., a smartphone). Consequently, MLR reviewers might request that information be presented differently depending on the device on which it is intended to be consumed.

Stage of Review: **Second MLR Review**

Rough Cut Video Accessible by Target Devices should be reviewed before the finished video file is compiled to ensure that the direction provided in the initial review can be incorporated in the finished production.

Stage of Review: **Third MLR Review**

Final Cut Video Accessible by Target Devices should be presented to the full committee after all post-production work has been completed and the finished video is available for distribution. Again, only in context of the intended distribution can it be determined whether the finished video will be compliant.

C. Submission Templates

The preceding section makes clear that MLR reviewers evaluating digital tactics need to understand a significant amount of information above and beyond the copy and imagery in the final promotional tactic itself to ensure that tactics are compliant with FDA regulations, guidelines, and relevant company standards. Given the tremendous variety of tactics, and the enormous volume of material that reviewers must evaluate, streamlining the process is of utmost importance. Well-designed submission templates can play a valuable role here.

The key to developing effective submission templates is understanding that templates serve two purposes. Templates indicate what information to present and how to present it. In addition, two audiences will use the templates: reviewers and originators. It is important that they are developed with both audiences in mind.

To meet the needs of content originators, templates should eliminate all ambiguity about how to prepare materials for review, while not requiring any elaborate (and expensive) development of separate materials solely for review and approval. Ideally, the templates should be as close to the actual materials being developed as possible.

For reviewers, templates should be easily scannable to provide assurance at a glance that all of the necessary information is provided. It is a tragedy for a reviewer to get 30 pages into a 50-page document only to realize that key information is missing and the entire project has to be resubmitted.

Below are some sample templates that illustrate these principles of effective template design.

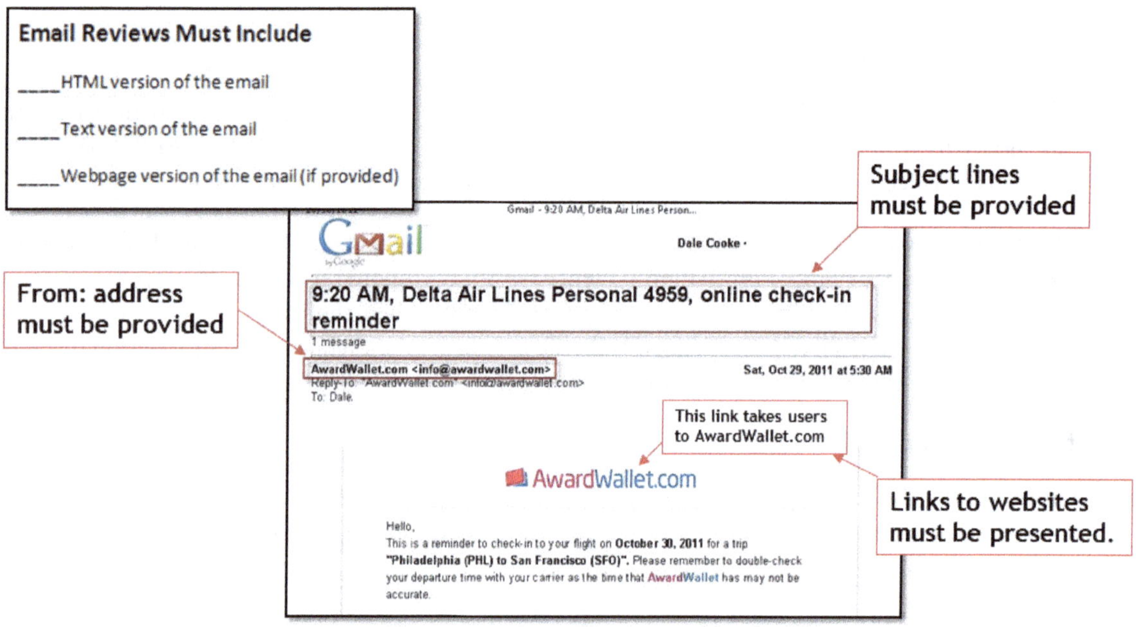

Email Template

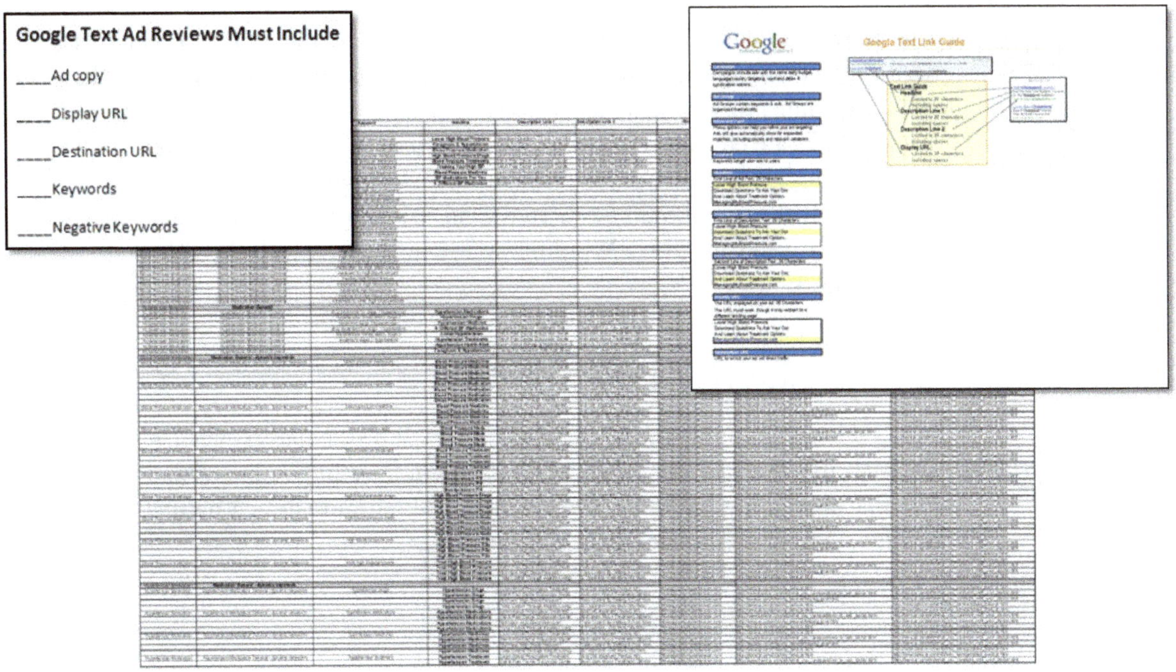

Google Text Ads Template

D. Role of the PDF in a Review

The file that is submitted for review of digital tactics is rarely identical to the final file. Consequently, there is a separate, dedicated process required to create the submission file. It is important to understand the purpose of that file.

The first thing to note is that the file in question is almost always a PDF. Adobe's PDF format is firmly entrenched both in pharmaceutical marketing and in other industries as the standard format for sharing documents that were originally created in different programs but which need to be shared and reviewed by people who are not all using the same software. Most promotional materials electronic review and approval systems either use PDF files directly or use systems that mimic Adobe Acrobat's PDF format.

Purposes of the PDF:

1) To provide a static snapshot of the tactic at a moment in time

   Digital tactics are notorious for their shifting features and appearance. This is both a virtue and a vice. It is a virtue because a digital tactic such as a website can be updated far more easily than updating a printed brochure. It is vice because it becomes difficult to keep track of what was previously available as updated files simply replace the older versions, which often are deleted into oblivion. The PDF provides a snapshot of what the digital tactic looked like at a specific point in time, when it was submitted for review, or when it was submitted to FDA.

2) To convey information back and forth from originators to reviewers

This is undoubtedly the most important function of the PDF. Originators need to supply tangible content, details, and descriptions to reviewers. PDFs include commenting tools that facilitate that communication. For the same reason, PDFs are efficient vehicles to deliver direction from the reviewers back to originators. It is much easier for a reviewer to highlight text in PDF and indicate that the text should be deleted than it is to copy and paste the same copy from a Web page into a Word file and then send a Word file with a series of such directions.

3) To provide a record of directions

Both reviewers at subsequent stages of review and originators when revising materials use PDFs to keep track of all of the individual comments and make sure that everything has been incorporated. This also provides a natural audit trail for tracking the development of content.

4) To provide clear direction on next steps

Immediately upon completion of a review, the PDF capturing all comments should be supplied to the originator, so the project can continue its development. The first question for every originator is, "What's next?" The PDF should clearly indicate on the first page what the verdict from that round of review was, and either the PDF or the process itself should leave zero ambiguity about what to do next.

These are the key purposes of the PDF. Frequently, though, companies and/or individual reviewers treat the PDF as if it had other purposes. This can lead to unnecessary expense and even risk compliance violations if, for example, the actual tactic provides risk information in a way that differs from the PDF.

1) The PDF is NOT the final tactic

Reviewing the PDF alone does not suffice for ensuring compliance. For example, if a PDF of a video has screen shots of the frames of the video and a transcript of the audio, that PDF might be compliant even though the video itself is not, because the audio track presenting risk information is read too rapidly or at a different volume or with distracting music in the background. Reviewers are not determining compliance based on the PDF. They are reviewing the digital tactic and using the PDF to tell the originator what changes need to be made to the tactic itself.

2) Complicated PDFs are expensive to create

Reviewers should get all of the information they need in the file presented to them. When reviewers begin requesting elaborate PDFs, such as PDFs of large websites where every hyperlink on the original website is recreated as a separate hyperlink within the PDF itself, that adds dramatically to the cost of the PDF creation. We need to remember that the PDF is not the final tactic. It is simply a means for conveying information between originators and reviewers. So, any incremental expense to create an elaborate PDF is money spent to create a file that will sit in a review system and never be seen by consumers or HCPs.

3) Complicated PDFs create compliance risk

Beyond the significant costs associated with creating elaborate PDFs, such files create significant compliance risk. Originators should be permitted little latitude in deviating from the direction provided by reviewers. The more elaborate the PDF, the more information that must be checked and verified by the reviewers. When originators create elaborate PDFs, that introduces the possibility of more error than if they create simpler files. And if the project undergoes multiple rounds of review, then more elaborate files created for review are more likely to differ in small ways. All of this introduces increased risk of non-compliance.

E. The 2253 Filing of Digital Tactics

There are no definitive standards established by FDA for what constitutes a complete 2253 filing for digital tactics. For traditional print materials, the answer to this question is fairly straightforward. The 2253 filing for a print brochure should include copies of the printed brochure. The originator literally grabs the first few copies off the press and sends them to FDA under cover of Form 2253.

Obviously that cannot happen the same way for digital tactics. There is no "press" that spits out Google text ads or websites, and the literal item that exists is often an electronic file that resides on multiple servers spread across the country. In addition, as we saw during the discussion of what to review at the different stages, a significant amount of information has to be reviewed that is quite independent of what is actually seen by any consumer, HCP, or caregiver who sees the final digital tactic itself. What among all of this must be sent to FDA to comply with the 2253 filing requirement?

This section sets out some best practices for complying with the 2253 filing requirements for a variety of digital tactics. In determining these requirements, reliance is placed both on standard practice throughout the industry as well as guides provided by FDA in other scenarios (such as the detailed discussion of submitting television ads for advisory comments provided on FDA's website and various enforcement actions) and the recent FDA guidance on the submission of promotional materials (which is provided as Appendix H).

1. Websites

A website comprises every page that could possibly be seen by a consumer or HCP. It also includes metadata and other information, some of which is visible by site visitors, and some of which cannot be seen except under exceptional circumstances. How much of this information must be submitted to FDA to comply with the 2253 filing requirement?

Obviously, every page that could be accessed directly by a site visitor must be submitted. In addition, every possible error state, and drop-down menu must be submitted, as FDA has made clear in guidance that the information provided in drop-down menus is important in determining whether promotional content on websites is compliant. Finally, in August 2010, FDA sent an enforcement action to Novartis for its use of a Facebook sharing widget. That enforcement action was landmark in that it was the first action taken specifically related to Facebook. It also was the first enforcement action to directly deal with metadata because the violations cited by FDA related to the metadata supplied by Novartis to the Facebook sharing widget on its Web pages.

Consequently, 2253 filings for websites should include:

1) Screen shots of every Web page that could be accessed by site visitors
2) Every drop-down menu and error state on the pages of the site
3) Metadata provided by the company that is intended to be seen and shared by site visitors. This metadata would include page titles and page descriptions but does not include keywords, Alt-tags, or other information that is not intended to be seen by site visitors.
4) A link to where the live site will be accessible after the 2253 filing

2. Flash Banner Ads

Banner ads that promote products clearly require 2253 filing. That filing should include screen shots of every frame of animated banner ads. As noted in the earlier discussion of Flash banner ads, such files require development of separate backup files seen by users who do not have Flash installed on their computers. By definition, users will either see the Flash content or the non-Flash content. If the backup banner ads are not themselves product promotions, then the static backup ads do not have to be submitted under cover of Form 2253.

3. Emails

Because all three versions of emails (HTML, text, and Web page) contain promotional messaging and the three versions are very similar but not identical, all three versions should be supplied to FDA under cover of Form 2253 at the time of initial dissemination.

4. Google Text Ads

FDA sent 14 letters to 16 companies (including joint venture partners) on March 26, 2009, for violative Search Engine Marketing Text Ads. One of the striking things about these letters was the promotional materials referenced by FDA in the letters. As is its standard practice, FDA makes available a copy of the violative promotional materials. Most often those materials appear to be identical to or simple photocopies of the promotional materials supplied by the companies to FDA on a 2253 filing.

In this case, FDA did not do so. Instead, FDA provided screen shots of actual Web searches conducted on a user's computer. It would have been literally impossible for any of the companies in question to have supplied such screen shots to FDA as the 2253 filing because ads can only appear in search results after they are live, and ad copy cannot be made live until after the 2253 filing with FDA.

In addition, the violations found by FDA included only discussion of the ad copy used in the search engine marketing. None of the violations mentioned any of the keywords typed in to bring up the resulting ad copy. Also, none of the violations discussed the destination URL, only the display URL.

Based on this landmark event in FDA enforcement, this author concludes that the 2253 filing requirement for Google text ads is for all ad copy that is displayed to users but does not include keywords, negative keywords, or destination URLs.

Chapter III
Issues Unique to Social Media and Mobile Promotion

Since 2010, total time spent with digital media has continued to increase, reaching 48% of all time spent consuming any media in 2017.[1] However, the total time spent on digital media on desktop and laptop devices has actually decreased over the same period. (see **Figure 1**) This has happened because people have shifted some of their digital consumption to mobile, and the total time spent consuming media on mobile devices has grown significantly. A major contributor to the growth in mobile is the growth in social media, which is disproportionately consumed on mobile devices.

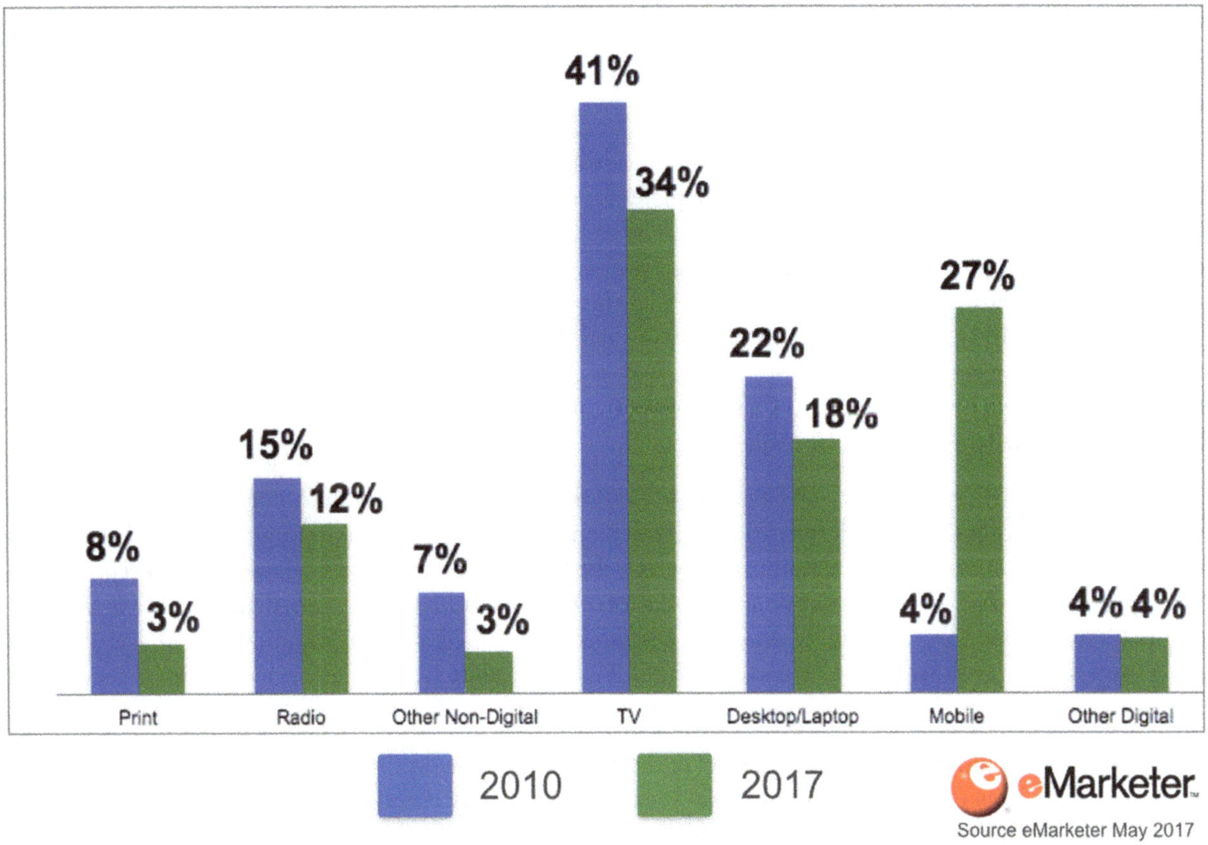

Figure1: *Total time spent with media by channel*

Consequently, mobile promotion has moved from the periphery to the mainstream, and not surprisingly the second half of 2016 was the first time that total spending on mobile media surpassed desktop/laptop media.[2] For the MLR Committee this means an increasing amount of mobile promotional content is being developed and submitted for review.

What special issues do mobile and social promotional tactics bring above and beyond the issues already discussed for other digital tactics?

Mobile Promotion

First, the devices themselves are very different with a whole range of new functionality. There are no clicks or hover states associated with a mouse and trackpad. Instead, users touch, tap, press, and swipe. While some of these interactions have their analogue in a desktop/laptop setting, none of them are exactly the same. And just as effectively reviewing digital tactics in a desktop/laptop setting required familiarity with the underlying technology, the same holds true for the mobile arena. Reviewers need to learn a new set of tools and should dedicate the same training to these devices. In addition, device variability presents another set of issues as screen sizes change annually with subtle impacts on presentation.

Second, users interact with mobile devices very differently than desktop/laptop computers. Few people spin their laptop from a landscape to a portrait orientation and back as they are browsing the web, but mobile users do so with such frequency, that they sometimes don't even notice it, and because mobile devices are mobile, they're taken into settings where the desktop/laptop rarely ventures.

Establishing Standards

Some of the same principles that were effective for reviewing other digital tactics can be applied to address these mobile differences. Beyond merely creating templates for submitting materials, MLR Committees can develop standards for the devices for which communications are being created. For example, a committee can specify that its target device is an iPhone 7 Plus running a particular version of iOS and develop all of its materials for that device's specifications, while understanding that there will be some variation for individual users who do not have that specific version of the hardware or software. The choice of target device should be dictated by the target audience and the most likely experience as well as choosing something that is likely to be representative of the experience on other equipment. Of course, these standards will need to be updated on a regular basis to keep pace with the latest from Silicon Valley.

In addition, this device variability will have implications for the presentation of information, most importantly the legibility and prominence of information presented on screen. While it is tempting to assume that all users will be accessing promotional communications using the biggest screens, MLR reviewers must keep in mind the experience of users on older and/or smaller devices. While it is highly unlikely that someone is using an original iPhone from 2007, the use of standards shouldn't be confused with the assumption that everyone will use a large screen; and even those accessing promotional messaging on smaller devices must be receiving a compliant message.

Yet another consideration is the full integration of the device's functionality. In a desktop/laptop environment it is not unusual to rely on a user's location (usually actively supplied by the user rather than passively collected), but on a mobile device, location is just the beginning of the device functionality with which communications can be integrated. Such communications can initiate reminders to refill a prescription or pick up lab results, dial a phone number to make a doctor's appointment, set up a calendar event for that appointment, and text information to health care professionals or caregivers. While reviewing mobile tactics, MLR committee members need to understand what (if any) of this integration is playing a role in the messaging.

Mobile Apps

Mobile apps add an extra layer of complexity to the review of promotional materials. First, the classification of a mobile app as advertising and promotional labeling is often unclear. Many uses of mobile apps seem to be medical devices subject to that distinct regulatory framework. The Federal Trade Commission in partnership with the Food and Drug Administration and other federal agencies has created a tool to help businesses determine the applicable legal and regulatory framework for any given set of functionality.[3]

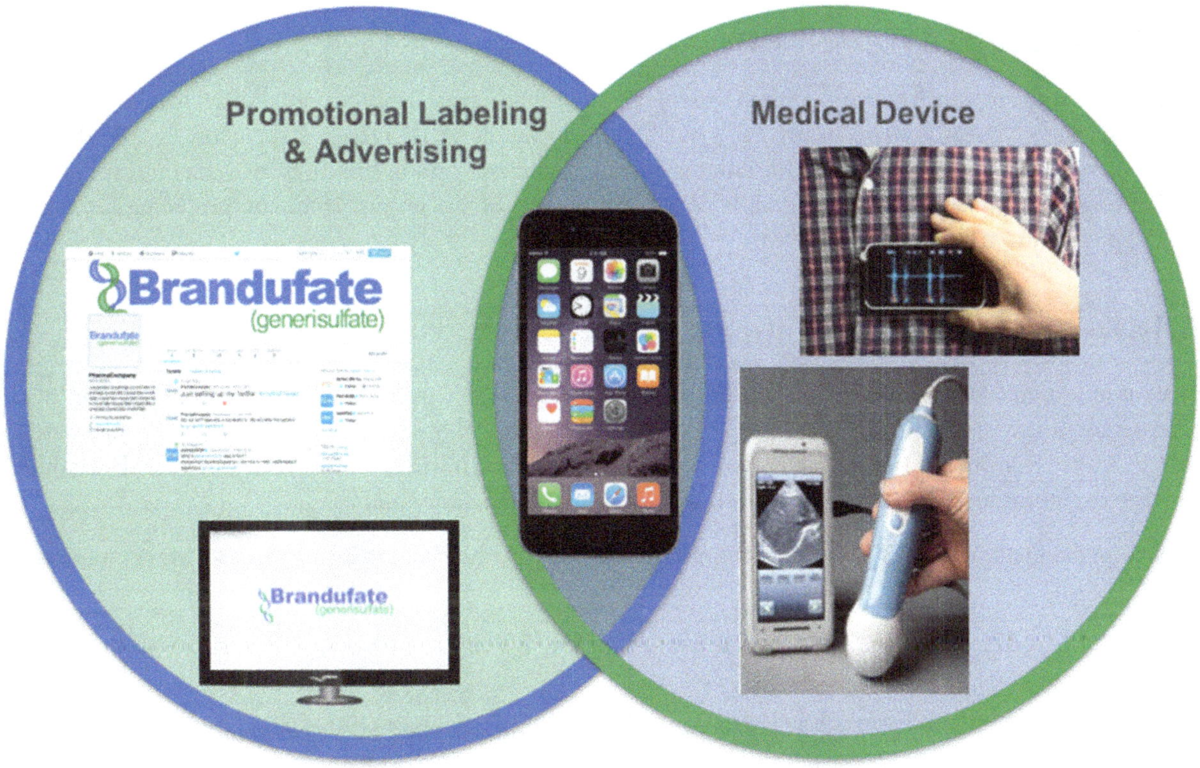

Figure2: *What are you reviewing?*

Assuming the mobile app has been determined to be promotional labeling and not a medical device based on the app's core functionality,[4] MLR reviewers need to remember that the messaging around the app and what it does has the potential to impact that classification. The way the app is described and the claims made about the effects from using the app will continue to affect the app's status because they could be statements of its intended use.

With that in mind, in addition to understanding and reviewing the functionality and all of the different parts of the app itself (screen icon, notifications, registration process, etc.), at some point, the messaging to promote the app must be reviewed. This would include the app store description for both the Apple store, and the various Android environments, as well as any emails or promotional messages posted online or offline to encourage people to download the app. If the app itself is a piece of promotional labeling, it is quite likely that this additional messaging will also qualify as promotional labeling.

Speaking of the app store and its Android counterparts, there is no way to prevent users from reviewing and commenting on the app. That turns these locations into forms where people can provide feedback to the company, and they will need to be regularly monitored for any potential adverse event and product quality reports.

And when developing an app, MLR Committee members need to understand the lifecycle of the app. How will updates be handled as the device software is updated? How often will they need to resubmit the materials supporting the app because of changes to the environments, and what is the plan for keeping the app up to date with the latest product label and other information?

As if this isn't enough to consider regarding mobile apps, remember that mobile apps are not merely vehicles that are created by prescription product marketers, they are also frequently third-party platforms that house promotional messages. Whether those promotional messages are private communications analogous to emails, mini-banners, or text placements, the same rules apply as any other promotional labeling.

Social Media Involvement

As mentioned above, much of the growth in time spent on mobile devices is dedicated to social media. According a leading market research firm, nearly 80% of all time spent on social media is spent on mobile devices.[5] Consequently, when any social media initiative is evaluated, the assumption should be that a significant portion of that engagement will happen on mobile platforms, and all of the lessons from the preceding section on mobile promotion need to be considered.

Addressing the 2253 Filing

As with any digital project, a very early starting point should be determining how to handle the 2253 filing of materials at the time of initial use. In the case of social media with interactive elements, we are fortunate to have guidance from the FDA on exactly that topic.[6] The guidance provides recommendations for determining whether to submit materials, and what to submit (if submission is warranted).

Regarding the first question of whether to submit materials, FDA states that there are three sets of circumstances in which companies have a 2253 filing requirement:

1) The companies own, control, create, influence, or have the site operated on their behalf[7]

2) The companies create interactive promotional content placed on a third-party site (and possibly also must submit the pages on which it is housed)[8]

3) The content is posted or created by employees and other agents of the companies who are acting on behalf of the company.[9]

Regarding the second question of what to submit (assuming a submission is required), FDA splits its recommendation in two: for sites that are publicly accessible and for sites that are not publicly accessible (because for example, they are behind a password log-in). For publicly accessible interactive discussions, FDA recommends that companies submit the static elements of the communication (such as the profile page) at the time of initially beginning to communicate on the platform, the initial communication itself (e.g., "Hello World"), and on a monthly basis to provide the locations (URLs) where the company is engaging in real-time interactions. The FDA does not require that the actual interactions be submitted.[10]

However, if the interaction is behind a log-in, then FDA suggests that in addition to the elements listed above, the companies should include screenshots or other representations of the interactions that are happening on the platform, along with sufficient direction and context to enable FDA to understand the interaction.[11] For example, if there is a physician-only discussion platform on the brand's website, that is not open to the public, then the sponsor should submit the website at its launch along with annotations explaining the nature of the discussion forum. Every month (so long as the discussion is live), the sponsor should include the URL for the forum on its list of locations where real-time interaction is occurring. In addition, because the interactions are not publicly accessible, the 30-day submissions should include screenshots showing the various interactions that have happened. If an HCP logged in as "DocSmith" and asked a question that was answered by the company employee "NurseDavis," then the screenshot should identify that NurseDavis is the company employee and that her responses were provided in response to DocSmith's questions. This process should repeat every 30 days as long as the forum is active, and when it is stopped, FDA should be notified of that via a 30-day submission or separately.

Profile Page

Part of the process of setting up an account is creating a user profile. The exact requirements of each social media platform will vary, but there will always be certain elements in common. Every profile will include:

- An avatar or profile picture
- User name, which will have specific character count and other limitations (such as not including special characters)
- Account name, which might have separate requirements from the user name, and which might be used differently on the platform
- A description of the user/account
- A header image, which often has requirements limiting the amount of copy that can be presented
- The ability to post links to a product page or other area
- Pinned or permanently prominent messages that can remain as the first message people see from the account

Figure 3: Social media profile

As mentioned previously, this profile page will be submitted to the FDA with the initial communication to meet the 2253 filing requirement. The profile page is important, and each element will be carefully crafted. It is, however, equally important to remember that very few people will ever visit a profile page; and even among those who do visit that page, they are unlikely to return. The nature of social media participation is that most people follow various accounts, and then see updates from the accounts within the stream of other content they are following. It is the rare exception that a social media post generates sufficient interest for someone to click through to see the full profile. Because of this, the individual posts are at least as important as the profile page.

Individual Posts

Whether sending out inspirational messages, posting patient testimonial videos, demonstrating how to use a product, or providing other content, each individual message needs to be carefully crafted and evaluated to ensure its compliance. And to make explicit the implication from the preceding discussion about the profile page, sponsors cannot rely on information provided via a profile page to meet their requirements in each individual post.

The nature of the platform and the purpose of the account will determine exactly what gets posted (how-to videos, tips on a healthy lifestyle, diary reminders, etc.). Regardless of these types of accounts, individual posts tend to have the same components:

- Headline
- Description (sometimes both a brief and expanded one)
- Shareable version should others wish to pass along your content to their followers
- Hashtags

The templates discussed earlier should be created for each platform to show originators what information the MLR Committee needs to review each post and how to submit the information so that reviewers know exactly what each piece is. Throughout this process, both originators and reviewers need to keep in mind the variety of means people will use to access this content (both on mobile and desktop/laptop environments).

Engagement

Having established a presence, begun communication, and built up a following, the next issue that must always be addressed in social media is engagement. The expectation on most platforms[12] is that accounts won't simply push out a steady stream of content, but that they will also participate in an ongoing dialogue about the topics. That participation can be as simple as acknowledging a positive response, or as complicated as assisting a patient get access to a prescription product.

The challenges of doing this are the same across all platforms and use cases. Social media participants expect responsiveness. In many cases, the assumption is that responses will be received in minutes or hours, whereas most traditional review and approval processes are designed to take days or weeks. Assuming any comments are received, those comments will need to be monitored for any off-label discussions and for any possible adverse events or product complaints.[13] The monitors, whether employees of the company or third-party vendors, will have to be trained on how to process and address these issues.

Fortunately, this process is not foreign to most companies, as they already have internal expertise via a call center that is accepting phone calls from the public and has developed systems for ensuring compliance. These processes and systems can be adapted to the world of social media, but there will be places where the unique nature of social media requires adaptation.

Endnotes

1. According to eMarketer data, April 2017. Report available at https://www.emarketer.com/Article/US-Adults-Now-Spend-12-Hours-7-Minutes-Day-Consuming-Media/1015775
2. Internet Advertising Bureau report, April 26, 2017, available at https://www.iab.com/news/internet-advertising-revenue-first-time-ever-total-digital-ad-spend-hits-landmark-72-5-billion-2016/ last accessed May 5, 2017
3. For the FTC's interactive tool, visit https://www.ftc.gov/tips-advice/business-center/guidance/mobile-health-apps-interactive-tool last accessed on May 2, 2017. For FDA guidance about mobile apps and whether they qualify as medical devices, see Guidance for Industry and Food and Drug Administration Staff: Mobile Medical Applications https://www.fda.gov/downloads/medicaldevices/deviceregulationandguidance/guidancedocuments/ucm263366.pdf last accessed on August 5, 2017.
4. Of course, the app could also be part of a disease awareness communication rather than being either a medical device or promotional labeling.
5. 2017 U.S. Cross-Platform in Future in Focus, comScore, March 22, 2017, available at https://www.comscore.com/Insights/Presentations-and-Whitepapers/2017/2017-US-Cross-Platform-Future-in-Focus last accessed May 5, 2017.
6. Guidance to Industry: Fulfilling Regulatory Requirements for Postmarketing Submissions of Interactive Promotional Media for Prescription Human and Animal Drugs and Biologics, available at http://www.fda.gov/downloads/Drugs/GuidanceComplianceRegulatoryInformation/Guidances/UCM381352.pdf last accessed May 5, 2017. Hereinafter, "Postmarketing Submissions Guidance." A copy of this guidance is provided in the appendices of this primer. Of course, this guidance does not apply to promotional efforts for restricted devices, and the Center for Devices and Radiological Health is not a signatory to the guidance. For a summary of this guidance, see Cooke, Dale, DH Regulatory Alert: 2253 Filing Requirements for Social Media available at https://www.scribd.com/document/199434412/DH-Regulatory-Alert-2253-Filing-Requirements-for-Social-Media last accessed May 5, 2017.
7. Postmarketing Submissions Guidance, page 3.
8. Postmarketing Submissions Guidance, page 4.
9. Postmarketing Submissions Guidance, page 4.
10. Postmarketing Submissions Guidance, page 6.
11. Postmarketing Submissions Guidance, page 7.
12. I would write all platforms, but I think YouTube might be an exception to this.
13. FDA has provided guidance on how it recommends that companies address one particular type of comment, called unsolicited requests for off-label information. The guidance from FDA on that topic is provided in this primer as an appendix and is available online at https://www.fda.gov/downloads/drugs/guidances/ucm285145.pdf last accessed May 6, 2017.

Chapter IV
Using Search Engine Marketing Compliantly

Author's Notes: Portions of this chapter were previously published as Developing Compliant Search Engine Marketing Campaigns in the September 2014 issue of *Regulatory Focus. In addition, several sections draw heavily on previous blog posts posted at http://regulatoryrx.blogspot.com.*

The infamous 14 letters sent in 2009 by the FDA's Division of Drug Marketing, Advertising, and Communications (DDMAC[1]) to 14 pharmaceutical companies (plus two joint venture partners) for violations related to paid search engine listings (also known as search engine marketing or SEM) began the industry focus on how makers of prescription products[2] could meet their regulatory obligations in space-constrained contexts. The importance of determining a way to do so for SEM cannot be overstated. Google and other search engines are the primary starting point for most people when they are looking for information online, and the Internet has now become one of the most important means of gaining health information overall.[3] Consequently, using SEM compliantly is extremely important to sponsors of prescription products.

Since that initial, landmark enforcement activity in 2009, there have been several important developments. FDA has provided additional information about SEM via subsequent enforcement, public comment, and guidance. Google has changed its ad formats for SEM. Finally, the rise of mobile has created yet another area of concern with slightly different requirements. These changes require a new look at this fundamental aspect of prescription product marketing.

This chapter provides an overview of the 2009 enforcement actions and applies the lessons from that combined with the subsequent developments to create a framework for using SEM compliantly, including a discussion of areas where FDA guidance is still unavailable or unclear.

Anatomy of a Search Campaign

Google's home page and, even more importantly, search results page functions as the beginning of the Internet for most people when they are looking for information online. The search engine results page (SERP) (see **Figure 1**) is divided into three main sections: paid ads, organic search results, and a knowledge graph. (see **Figure 2**) Organic results are the items that Google's independent algorithm has determined are most likely to contain the information the user is looking for based on the words the user entered in the search box. Paid results (SEM) are the items that various advertisers have sponsored intending to attract people who are searching for certain information. The knowledge graph is content compiled by Google that is intended to answer the question prompting the search query.

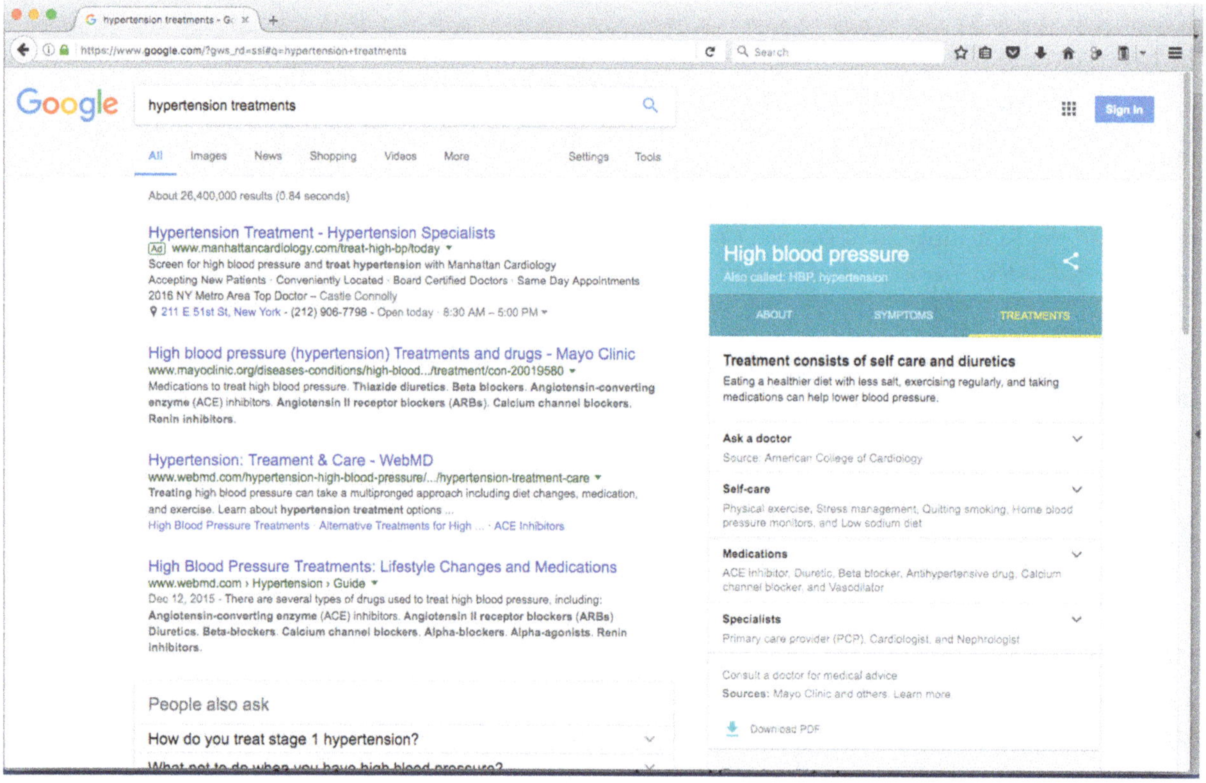

Figure 1: *Google Search Engine Results Page (SERP)*

The exact way Google has identified the distinction between these parts of the page has varied over the years. Different shading, headlines, and other mechanisms have been used to alert users that they are seeing different types of information on the SERP.

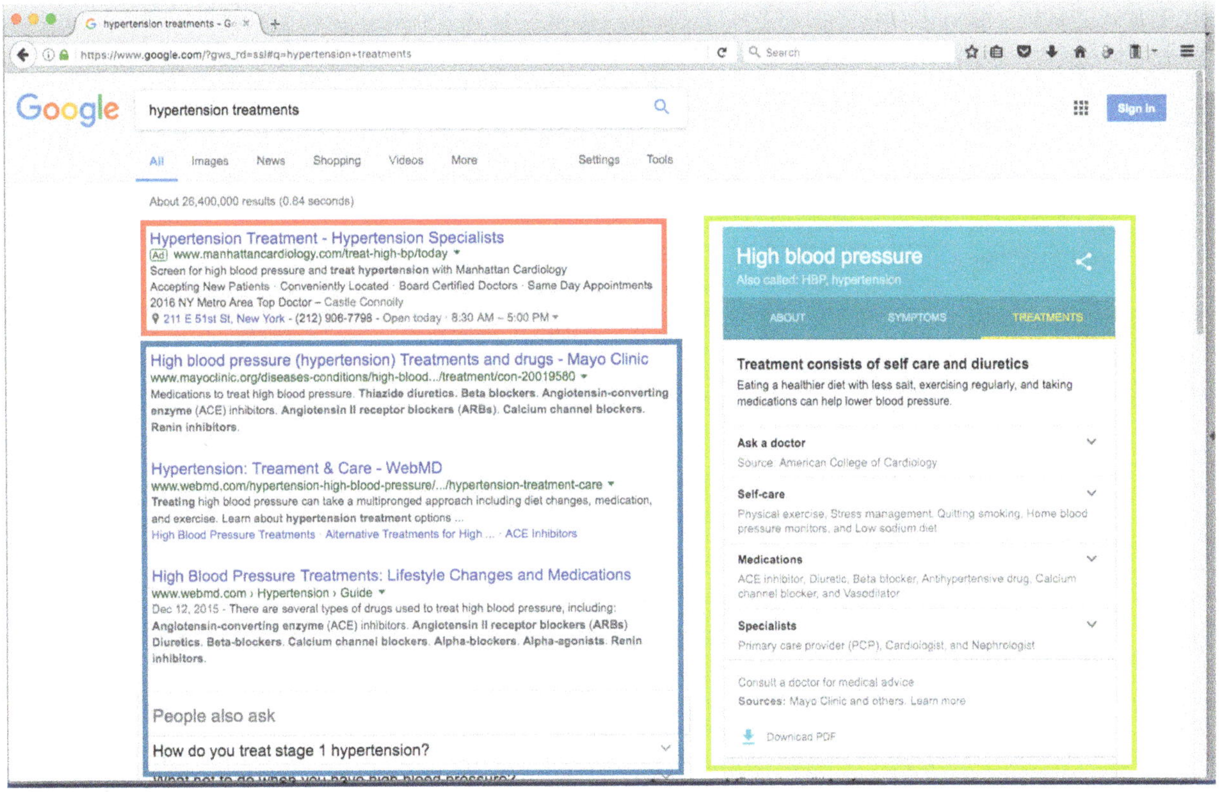

***Figure 2:** Google SERP with paid ads in red box, organic results in blue box, and knowledge graph in green box*

There are various techniques website developers can use to improve their chances of appearing in the organic results and to improve their positioning within those results, but at the end of the day, whether a page will appear and what information from that page appears in the organic listing is ultimately controlled by the search engines.

By contrast, the content of the SEM is entirely under the control of the advertisers.[5] Advertisers place bids in an auction format against other potential advertisers to have their SEM ads appear, and the highest bidder[6] receives the top spot, followed by the second highest bidder, etc. What the advertisers are bidding on are called keywords. The keywords are the terms that users enter that determine the results that appear.[7]

When setting up a campaign on Google, advertisers determine which keywords they want to cause their ads to appear. In this way, keywords are analogous to the media plan used for traditional print and broadcast advertising. In those traditional media, the media buyer determines which programs and magazines attract the audience demographics that the advertiser seeks to reach (e.g., 18-35-year-old women). Analogously, by choosing certain keywords, advertisers are making their ads appear before users whose behavior (i.e., typing a certain keyword into a search engine) makes advertisers believe that the user is interested in the product information.

Google requires advertisers to determine the keywords that will cause their ad to appear, and Google also permits advertisers to supply negative keywords. If a negative keyword appears in a user's search query, then the ad will be prevented from appearing. Google does not require that advertisers specify any negative keywords for their campaigns.[8]

The ads themselves have various components each with different constraints. The headline is the first line of copy. It is hyperlinked. Users clicking on it are taken to the destination page. The description displays as either one or two lines of copy, informs users of what they will see or learn at the destination, and entices users to click on the ad. The display URL is the webpage destination that users see in the ad (see **Figure 3**).

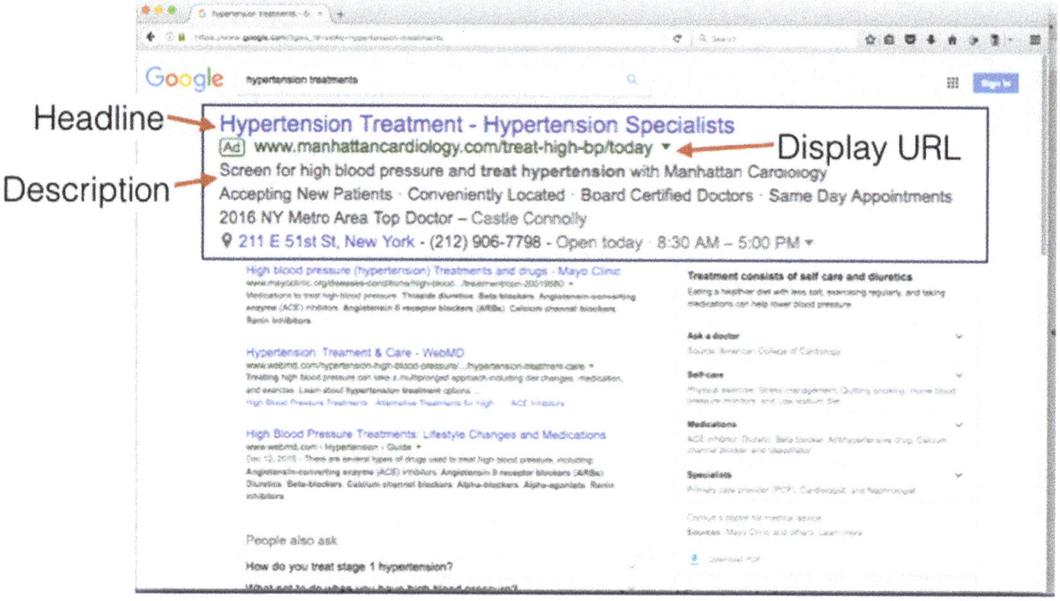

***Figure 3:** Components of a search ad*

In addition, there is a destination URL that is not seen by users in the ad itself. The destination URL is frequently not identical to the display URL. URLs for webpages are often not set up specifically for a given advertising campaign, and the actual destination URL might be unwieldy or otherwise inappropriate for a given ad, so instead of showing a URL such as

Brand.com/HCPs/PatientResources/Downloads/Checklist

in the ad itself, the ad might instead use as the display URL:

Brand.com/Checklist

However, when users click on the ad, they are actually taken to Brand.com/HCPs/PatientResources/Downloads/Checklist.

In addition, Google permits advertisers to include additional links in their ads that direct users to specific pages on their site; for example to the hours that a restaurant is open or to a page with contact information. These additional links within the main site are called sitelinks, and in addition to the links themselves, advertisers can include a brief description of the content on the sitelink pages (see **Figure 4**).

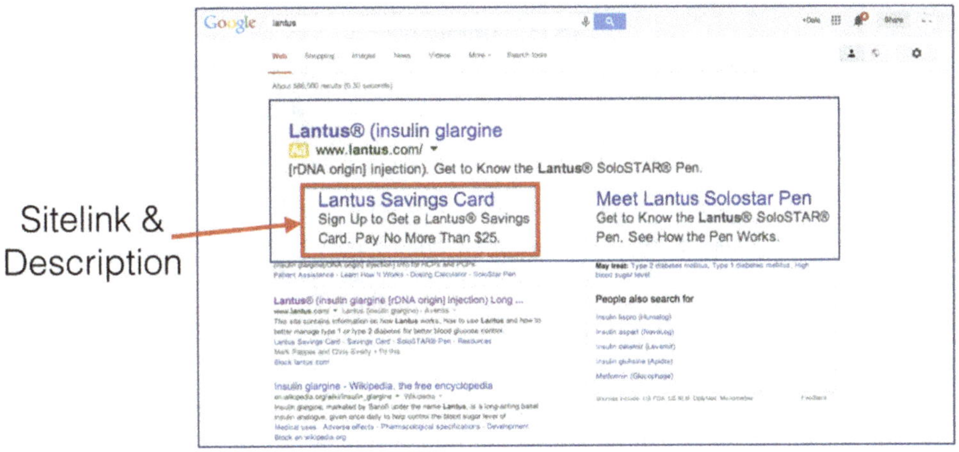

***Figure 4:** Sample Ad Showing Sitelinks*

Sitelinks are an optional feature of ads, and if an advertiser chooses to use sitelinks there are important limitations that they need to be aware of.[9] First, sitelinks will not always appear. The only way sitelinks will appear in an ad is if the ad has the highest bid in the auction for that particular appearance. Although advertisers can raise their bids to try to ensure that their ads always win the auction, it is not entirely within an advertiser's control where an ad appears. Hence, ads with sitelinks might not display with the sitelinks.

In addition, an advertiser can have up to six different sitelinks with corresponding descriptions associated with each ad. Which of the six sitelinks and their specific arrangement is also not entirely under an advertiser's control.

SEM behaves slightly differently on mobile, and those differences are important for ensuring ads are compliant.[10] First, fewer ads appear. Second, although sitelinks can be used for mobile advertising, in addition to all of the restrictions applying to sitelinks on desktop advertising (e.g., that they might not appear and that their order might change), there is a further restriction on mobile sitelinks. Specifically, sitelinks will not include the description when displaying on mobile platforms (see **Figure 5**).

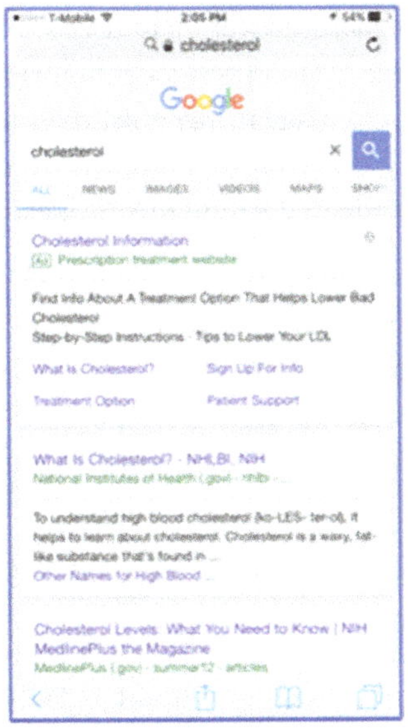

***Figure 5:** Sample mobile ads showing headline, display URL, and sitesinks*

SEM Terminology

Keywords: Words selected by an advertiser to prompt their ads to appear.

Negative Keywords: Words selected by an advertiser that will prevent their ad from appearing.

Headline: The first line of copy of an SEM ad.

Description: The one or two lines of copy below the headline that describe the destination page's content to entice people to click on the ad.

Display URL: The URL that is seen by the person conducting the search.

Destination URL: The URL for the page that a user will actually arrive at if they click on the ad.

Sitelinks: An optional feature of an ad that permits advertisers to include subpages within a site that appear as part of the ad. Sitelines are NOT guaranteed to appear with the rest of the ad.

Sitelink Descriptions: The copy that appears beneath Sitlinks and describes these pages. Sitelink Descriptions will NOT appear on SEM ads on mobile devices.

The 2009 Violations

DDMAC identified four types of violations in its 2009 enforcement action:

1) Omission of Risk Information
2) Inadequate Communication of Indication
3) Overstatement of Efficacy
4) Failure to Use the Required Established Name

Omission of risk information means that the ads did not include risk information. Not all prescription advertising is required to include risk information; however, if a product promotion mentions (or implies) a specific product and includes information about that product's usage or benefits, then it is required to include risk information to meet the fair balance requirement. (21 CFR 202.1(e)(5)(ii)) This is the only violation that was cited in every letter, and thus the apparent trigger of this unprecedented simultaneous issuance of 14 letters citing 48 drugs.

Inadequate communication of indication is familiar to readers of FDA enforcement letters, and most often relates to the failure to make clear restrictions on the intended use of the drug. For example, the Google paid search listing that was cited by the FDA for Flomax included the phrase "Learn About Treating Prostate Problems."[11] According to FDA, that implies a broader intended use than contained in Flomax's Prescribing Information, which states that Flomax is indicated specifically for treatment of the signs and symptoms of benign prostatic hyperplasia. More than half of the 48 drugs cited were found to have impermissibly broadened the indication.

Only one drug (Mirena) was alleged to have overstated efficacy by "failing to reveal that Mirena is only indicated for up to 5 years of use before replacement."[12]

Failure to use the established name refers to the inclusion of the generic (aka "established") name of the drug. Forty-two of the 48 cited drugs failed to include the established name (see **Figure 6**).

			Safety Profile		Violation Committed				
Pharmaceutical Company	Brand	Indication	Black Box	Medication Guide	Omission of Risk	Failure to Use Established Name	Inadequate Communication of Indication	Overstatement of Efficacy	Use of Brand ONLY in URL
Bayer (Schering)	Levitra	Erectile disfunction			X	X			X
Bayer	Yaz	Oral contraceptive	X		X	X	X		
Bayer	Mirena	Intrauterine contraceptive			X	X	X	X	
Biogen Idec	Tysabri	MS			X	X	X		X
Boehringer Ingelheim	Spiriva	COPD			X	X			
Boehringer Ingelheim	Flomax	BPH			X	X	X		X
Boehringer Ingelheim	Mirapex	Restless leg syndrome			X	X			
Cephalon	Fentora	Breakthrough pain in cancer	X	X	X	X	X		
Cephalon	Treanda	Chronic lymphocytic leukemia			X	X			
Forest Laboratories	Bystolic	Hypertension			X	X			
Forest Laboratories	Campral	Alcoholism			X		X		
Forest Laboratories	Lexapro	MDD	X	X	X	X			
Forest Laboratories	Namenda	Alzheimer's dementia			X	X	X		
Genentech	Avastin	Metastatic carcinoma of colon	X		X	X	X		
Genentech	Lucentis	Macular degeneration			X	X	X		
Genentech	Rituxan	non-Hodgkin's lymphoma	X		X		X		
Genentech	Xolair	Asthma	X	X	X	X	X		X
Genentech	Herceptin	Breast cancer	X		X		X		
Genentech	Pulmozyme	Cystic fibrosis			X	X			
GlaxoSmithKline	Avandia	Diabetes		X	X	X	X		
GlaxoSmithKline	Avandamet	Diabetes		X	X	X	X		
GlaxoSmithKline	Avandaryl	Diabetes		X	X	X	X		
GlaxoSmithKline	Avodart	BPH			X	X	X		X
GlaxoSmithKline	Coreg CR	Hypertension			X	X	X		X
GlaxoSmithKline	Tykerb	Breast cancer			X	X	X		X
Hoffmann-La Roche	Boniva	Osteoporosis			X				
Hoffmann-La Roche	Pegasys	Hepatitis C	X	X	X	X	X		
Hoffmann-La Roche	Xeloda	Colon cancer	X		X	X	X		
Johnson & Johnson	Prezista	HIV			X	X	X		X
Eli Lilly	Cymbalta	MDD	X	X	X				
Eli Lilly	Evista	Osteoporosis	X	X	X	X	X		
Eli Lilly	Gemzar	Lung cancer			X		X		
Merck	Januvia	Diabetes			X	X	X		X
Merck	Propecia	Hair loss			X		X		X
Merck	Singulair	Allergies			X	X			X
Merck	Emend	Nausea for cancer patients			X	X	X		X
Novartis	Femara	Breast cancer			X	X	X		X
Novartis	Diovan	Hypertension	X		X	X			X
Novartis	Exforge	Hypertension	X		X	X			X
Novartis	Exjade	Chronic iron overload			X	X	X		
Novartis	Gleevec	Chronic myeloid leukemia			X	X			
Pfizer	Aromasin	Breast cancer			X	X	X		
Pfizer	Caduet	Cholesterol & Blood pressure			X	X			
Pfizer	Chantix	Smoking cessation		X	X	X			
Pfizer	Detrol LA	Overactive bladder			X	X			
Pfizer	Lyrica	Fibromyalgia		X	X	X			
Pfizer	Celebrex	Rheumatoid arthritis	X	X	X	X			
Sanofi-Aventis (Bristol-Myers Squibb)	Plavix	Atherothrombotic events			X	X			

Figure 6: *2009 FDA Enforcement Action Categorization of Offenses*

Compliant Ad Formats

In light of this action, there appeared to be three options open to manufacturers of prescription products for using SEM: disease awareness ads, reminder ads, and redirecting ads.

1. Disease Awareness Ads

Disease awareness communications "discuss a particular disease or health condition, but do not mention any specific drug or device or make any representation or suggestion concerning a particular drug or device."[13] FDA has no authority over properly developed disease awareness communications because they do not promote a prescription product. Consequently, companies are free to use SEM (or any other technique) to promote disease awareness communication efforts, so long as they do not suggest or imply any particular drug or device.

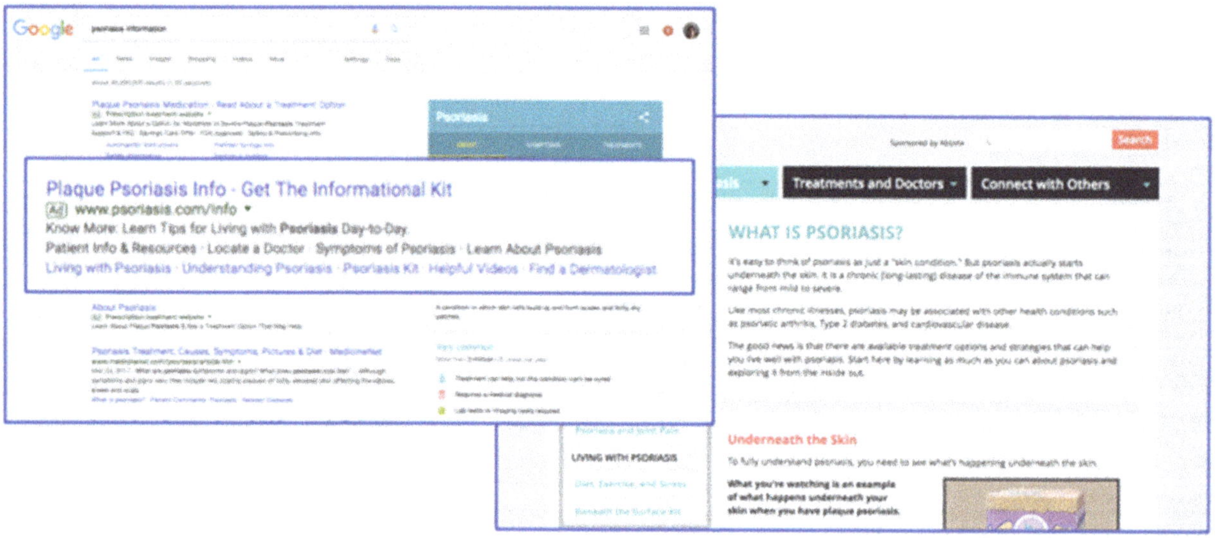

Figure 7: *Sample SERP with disease awareness ad highlighted and disease awareness destination page shown*

Disease awareness SEM ads share the following features (see **Figure** 7):

1) The destination URL is a disease awareness website

2) The body of the ad does not mention or imply any specific product or device

Of course, this means that such communications, by definition, are not product promotions, and while manufacturers of prescription products want to raise awareness of conditions for which they make treatments, they also want people to be aware of those treatments themselves and to provide information about the treatments. So, while disease awareness SEM ads might be one component of an overall communication strategy, it will rarely suffice as the sole component.

2. Reminder Ads

A reminder ad is defined in 21 CFR 201.100(f), and 202.1(e)(2)(i) as an ad (or related promotional item) "which calls attention to the name of the drug product but does not include indications or dosage recommendations for the use of the drug product."

Quoting from 21 CFR 202.1(e)(2)(i), such advertisements:

> "shall contain only the proprietary name [i.e., brand name] of the drug product, if any; the established name [i.e., generic name] of the drug product, if any; the established name of each active ingredient in the drug product; and, optionally, information relating to quantitative ingredient statements, dosage form, quantity of package contents, price, the name and address of the manufacturer, packer, or distributor or other written, printed, or graphic matter containing no representation or suggestion relating to the advertised drug product."

So, the mandatory elements of a reminder ad are

1) The brand name (if any)
2) The generic name of the product and/or active ingredients (if any)

All other elements are optional. Those optional elements may include

1) Quantitative ingredient statements (e.g., 20 mg)
2) Dosage form (e.g., tablets or capsules)
3) Quantity of package contents (e.g., 30 pills per bottle)
4) Price
5) Name and address of the manufacturer, packer or distributor
6) Other information so long as it makes "no representation or suggestion" about the product use

The category of "other information" has been interpreted to include the phrase "FDA-approved"[14] as well as other language that does not describe the product, such as a call to action along the lines of "Click here to learn more."

As applied to SEM, the reminder labeling provision would lead to ads with the following format (see **Figure 8**):

Brand Name

(Established Name)

Click here to learn more about this FDA-approved product.

Display URL (with or without the drug name)

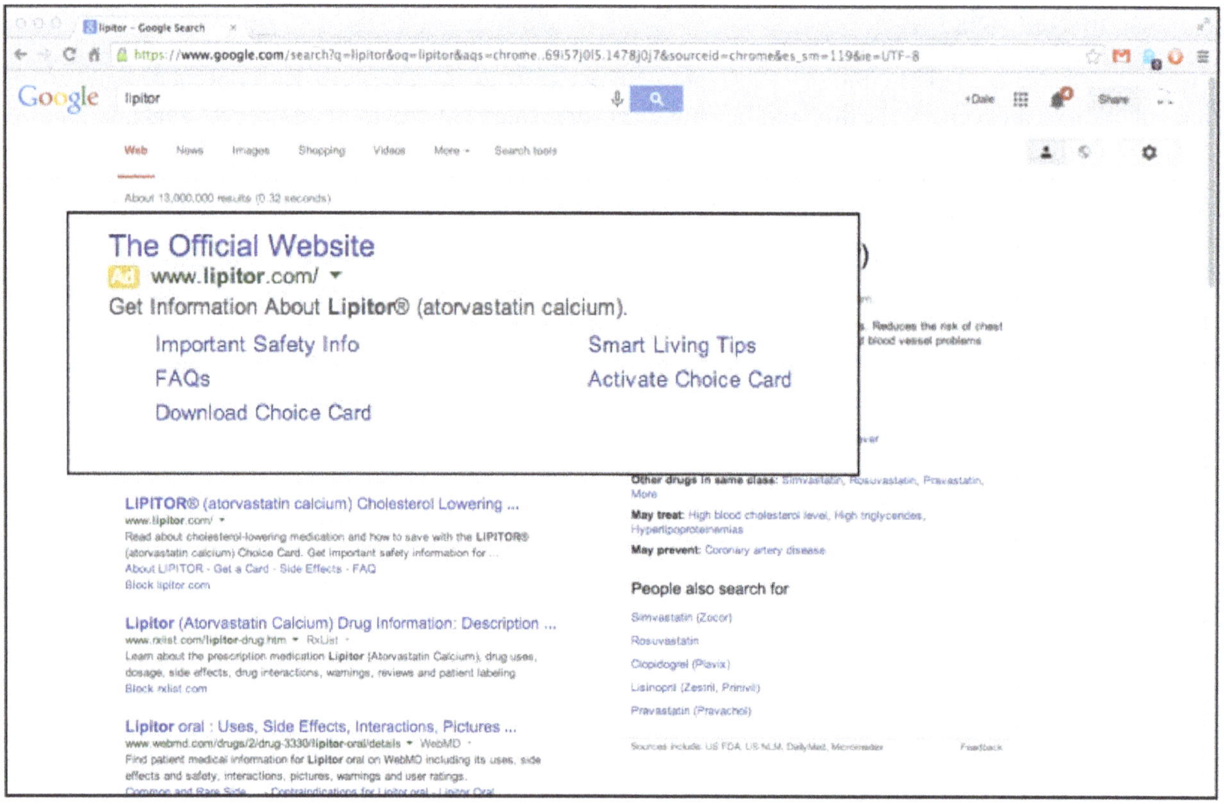

Figure 8: *Sample Reminder Ad Showing Sitelinks*

Importantly, both 21 CFR 201.100(f) and 202.1(e)(2)(i) note that "[r]eminder labeling...is not permitted for a prescription drug product whose labeling contains a boxed warning...." Nothing in these letters indicates either that FDA intended to permit SEM as an exemption to this requirement or that FDA would completely disallow SEM for black box drugs. Fourteen of the drugs receiving a letter contained boxed warnings.

3. Redirecting Ads

Redirecting ads have not received explicit comment or endorsement from FDA; however, they were present in the 2009 enforcement action. FDA frequently posts samples of the violative materials along with its letters, and the same happened in 2009. The nature of the materials posted by FDA was revealing. First, FDA's posted materials were simply screenshots of Google search results.[15] Consequently, it was possible to see the search result that a particular user saw on her computer on some day prior to the issuance of the letters (see **Figure 9**).

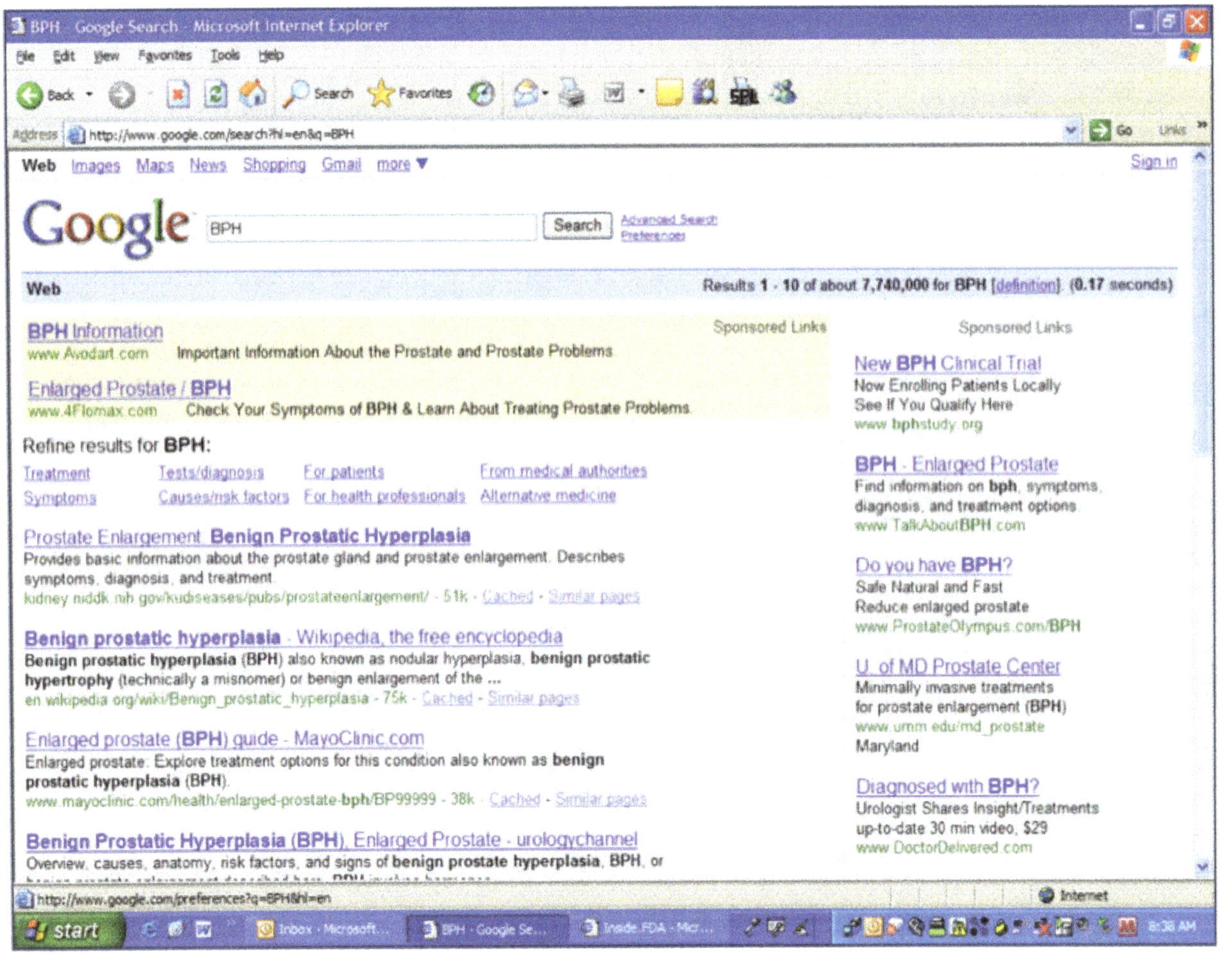

Figure 9: *Violative Promotional Materials from 2009*

That meant that in addition to the violative ads cited by FDA, we could see what other ads were running that day. Sprinkled throughout the violative materials were redirecting ads such as the following (see **Figure 10**):

> BPH – Enlarged Prostate
>
> Find information on bph, symptoms, diagnosis, and treatment options. www.TalkAboutBPH.com

Users who clicked on this ad, or who entered "www.TalkAboutBPH.com" into their browser bar were taken to the product website for Uroxatral.[16] Uroxatral was not cited by FDA as engaging in inappropriate promotional activity, and this ad was far from alone.

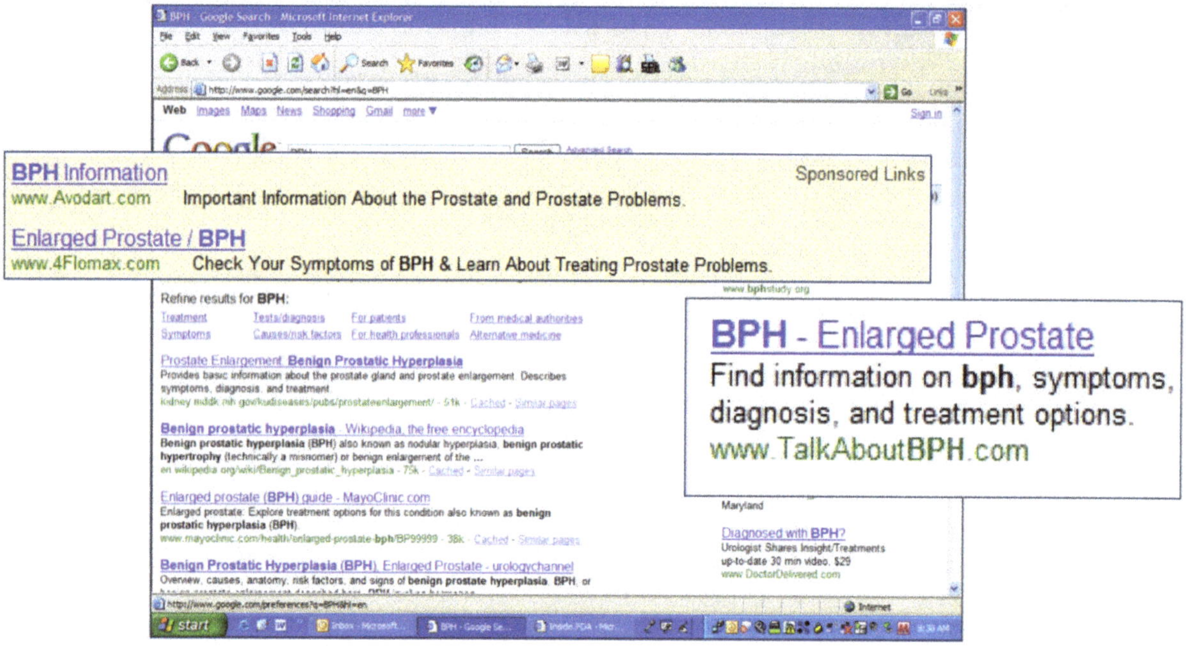

Figure 10: *Violative Promotional Materials from 2009 Showing Redirecting Ad*

The author refers to ads of this type as redirecting ads because they have the following characteristics:

1) Nothing in the SEM ad mentions or implies a specific product
2) The display URL redirects to a distinct destination URL[17]
3) The destination URL is a product-specific promotional website

Google's Vanity URL Policy

Google has recently changed the way it treats redirecting ads, and those changes limit prescription product marketers' options. Google has long had a policy prohibiting ads where the destination URL differs dramatically from the display URL.[18] Such advertising is not limited to the pharmaceutical industry, and while it is sometimes done by reputable, legitimate advertisers, it is also a practice that is shared by many unsavory practitioners. That is why Google has strictly forbidden it across the board, except for the pharmaceutical industry.

This exception was maintained because in many cases, the reminder ads discussed above do not seem appropriate. For example, if a user doesn't already know the name of the prescription product, then a straightforward reminder ad might be at best worthless for the user who by definition is not being reminded of anything since she is not already aware of the product. And depending on the specifics of the case (for example, whether the user is aware that there are prescription treatment options for her condition, or whether prescription drugs frequently advertise without describing their uses), such a reminder ad might actually seem less appealing than other ads (for example, for over the counter or homeopathic treatments that describe the product's name and use).

To reach such people, prescription product marketers have been using the redirecting ads, but beginning in April of 2016, Google no longer permitted advertisers to use their own vanity URLs (such as "PrescriptionTreatmentforConditionX.com") that redirect users to a website (e.g., BrandY.com) that promotes a specific treatment. Instead, prescription product marketers have two options for the display URL.

First, they are permitted to have a Company Name URL appear. (see **Figure 11**) About this option, it should be noted that the URL that is displayed must be an actual company-owned, and accurate URL. So, if, for example, the company's name is BigPharma Company, but BigPharma Company's URL for its website is BigPharma-US.com, then the URL that displays in the ads using this option must be BigPharma-US.com. They may NOT be BigPharma.com. However, although this limitation applies to the display URL, the destination is still entirely under the control of the marketer. The SEM ad on Google that shows BigPharma-US.com as its display URL can have as the destination URL a product page, such as BrandName.com/HCP/Resources.

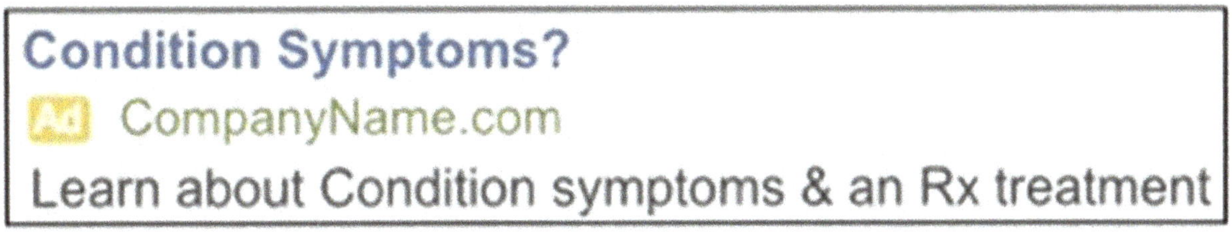

Figure 11: *CompanyName.com Option*

The second option prescription product marketers have on Google is to select from one of six Google options that are available in English and Spanish. (see **Figure 12**)

Prescription treatment website	Sitio de tratamientos con receta
Prescription device website	Sitio de dispositivos con receta
Medical device website	Sitio de dispositivos médicos
Preventative treatment website	Sitio de tratamientos preventivos
Prescription contraception website	Sitio de anticonceptivos con receta
Prescription vaccine website	Sitio de vacunas con receta

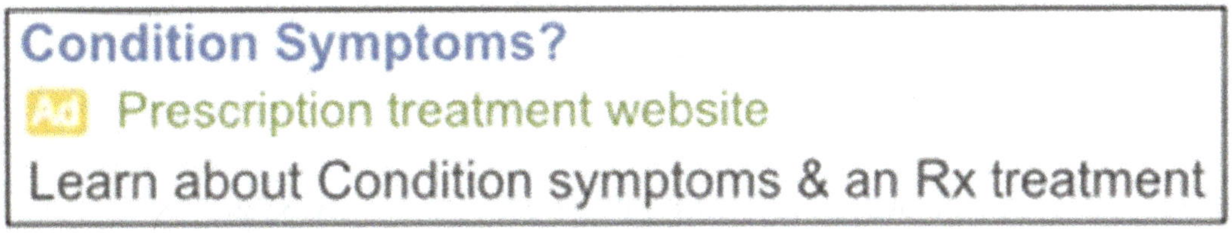

Figure 12: *Google's options*

Note that whereas the CompanyName.com option is a template, and the actual URL that appears will differ, for the Google options, these words are not a template. The actual words "Prescription treatment website," etc. will appear in the ads. This does mean that in some circumstances, more than one ad will appear with the exact same display URL. (see **Figure 13**) However, just as with the CompanyName.com option, the actual destination URL is still entirely under the control of the prescription product marketers.

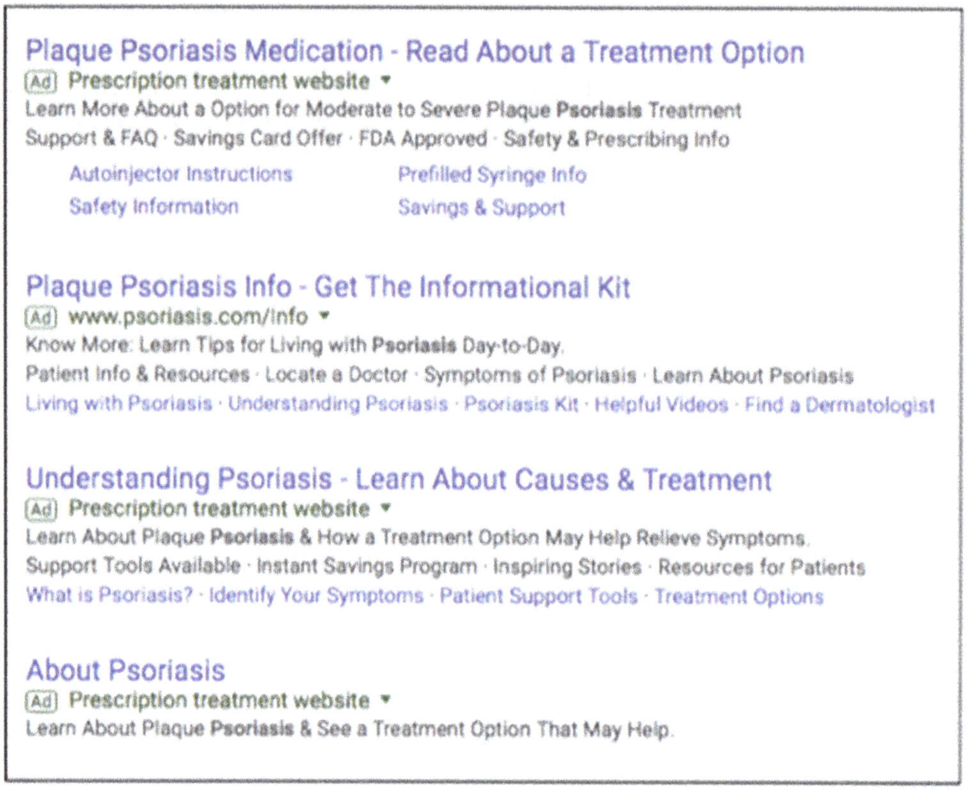

Figure 13: *Google's options in practice*

Black Box Drugs

Fourteen of the products receiving an enforcement action in 2009 had a black box (see **Figure 6**), but none of the infractions cited a product for making use of an otherwise-compliant reminder ad format by a black box product. Subsequent comments from FDA, including the 2014 guidance on presenting benefit and risk information in space-limited contexts, have explicitly disavowed any intention to provide additional information on the topics of reminder advertising in general, and the applicability of reminder advertising to black box drugs in particular.[19]

However, at the September 2014 Food and Drug Law Institute Advertising and Promotion conference, FDA made a subtle, but vital, clarification in the context of discussing the scope of its guidance on space-limited contexts.

The clarification came on the penultimate slide (see **Figure 14**) of FDA's presentation about the space-limited and correcting misinformation guidances. On that slide, and during that portion of the corresponding presentation, FDA noted that the guidance explicitly set aside any discussion of reminder advertising, and addressed the prohibition for use of the reminder ad format by sponsors of black box drugs.

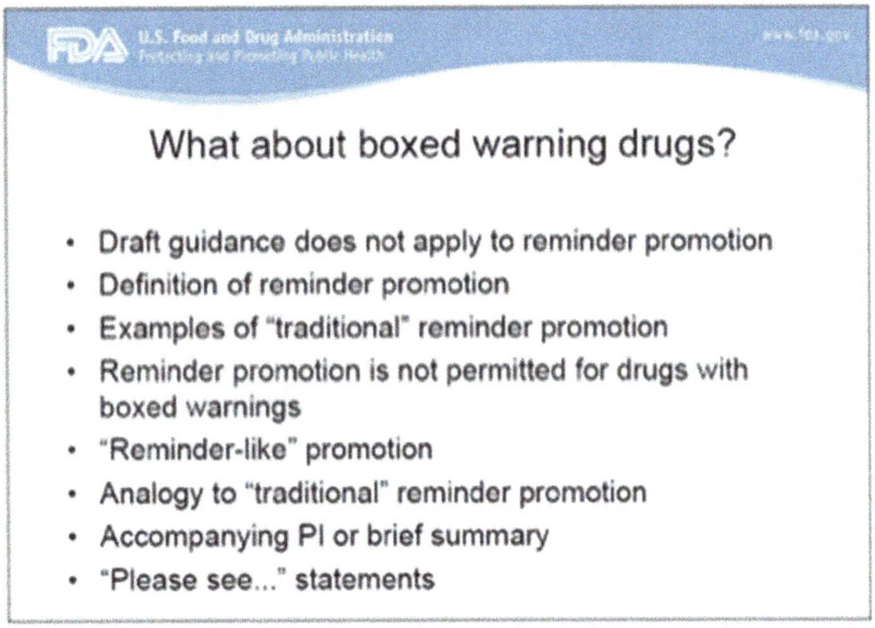

***Figure 14:** FDA Slide from 2014 FDLI Advertising & Promotion Conference*

FDA then proceeded to note that although reminder advertising and promotion is prohibited for black box drugs, FDA has long recognized in traditional (i.e., offline) communications the ability of sponsors of black box drugs to engage in "reminder-like" promotion.

The key distinction for reminder-like promotion vs. reminder promotion is that reminder-like promotion must have an "[a]ccompanying PI or brief summary" and a statement to "Please see..." the accompanying PI. Reminder promotions do not have such requirements.

FDA acknowledged via this presentation the existence of a separate category of communication with a distinct set of requirements. For reminder-like promotion, the required elements appear to be:

1) Brand name (if any)
2) Generic name of the product and/or active ingredients
3) "Please see..." statement directing people to the PI or Brief Summary
4) Provision of a PI or Brief Summary accompanying the advertisement

This presentation was a welcome clarification for many reasons. Perhaps the most important reason is that many people in industry have been concerned that FDA's guidance provisions made it impossible for sponsors of black box products to engage in communication channels with space limitations such as search engine marketing.

After the 2009 enforcement action, Google introduced a new advertising format that was available exclusively to black box drugs. This ad format differed from the standard formats in that it had a dedicated line of copy that informed users that the product being advertised was a black box drug. This dedicated line of copy read, "Click to see full safety and prescribing information, including boxed warning. More info" (see **Figure 15**). The words "More info" were hyperlinked and took users directly to a page dedicated to the product's risk information.

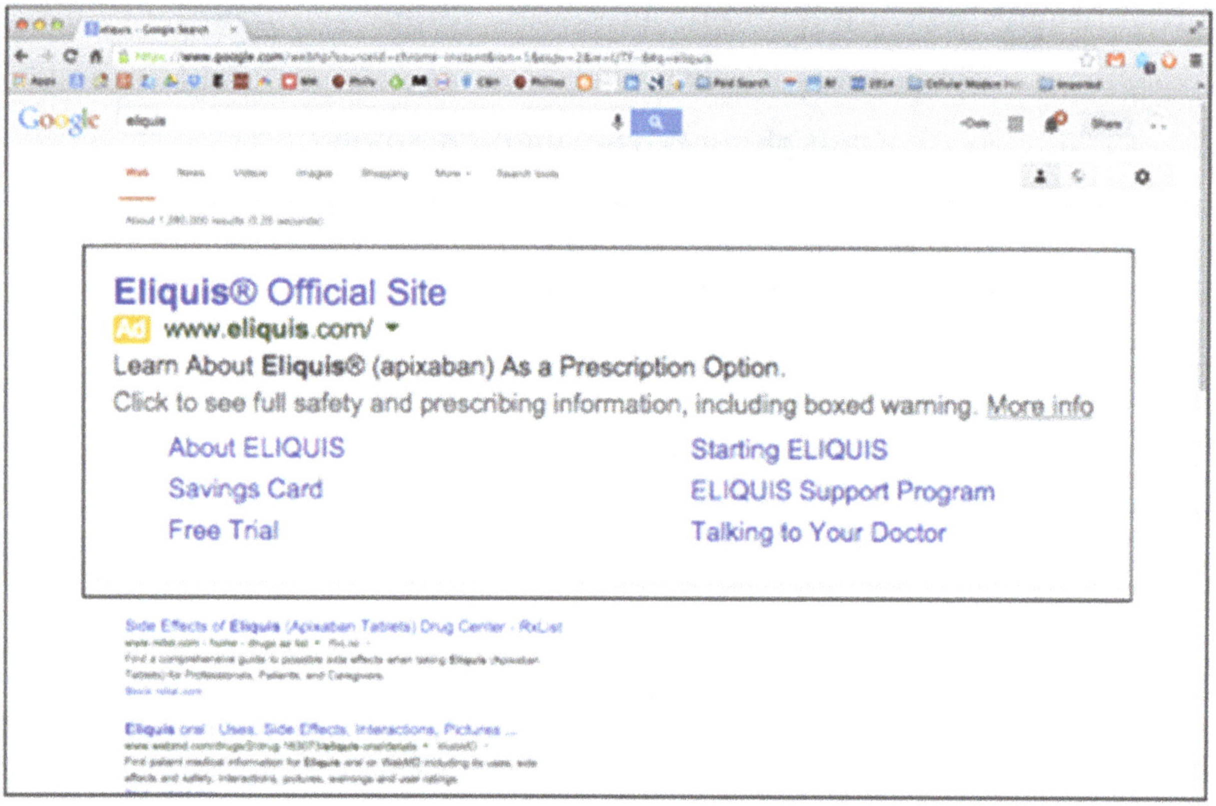

Figure 15: *Google's discontinued black box ad format*

FDA never publicly commented on this ad format, but it would seem to meet the criteria provided for a Reminder-like ad. The line of mandatory copy fits the concept of a "Please see..." statement, and the dedicated link could have as its destination any page, including a page dedicated solely to housing the PI.

From the day Google's black box ad format was introduced, there were limitations to it. First, it never worked on mobile devices, only desktop and laptop searches. Second, because the dedicated line of copy could not be altered, there was concern about whether consumer-directed campaigns were affected, as very few consumers know what a boxed warning is.

In 2015, Google discontinued its support for this ad format. Instead of using this dedicated format, marketers of black box drugs had to use Google's standard ad format. Though this provided some consternation for marketers and MLR Committee reviewers who had grown accustomed to the black box ad unit, it seems possible for most products to create a compliant reminder-like ad in the standard format. (see **Figure 16**)

Figure 16: *Standard reminder-like ad format*

The primary open question in terms of FDA compliance is whether it suffices to have the accompanying PI be provided via a second hyperlink from the destination page as opposed to having a separate dedicated hyperlink in the original ad. The FDA's presentation and comments about the provision of a PI for reminder-like ads was silent on this question.

It is worth noting that in FDA's guidance about providing risk and benefit information in space-limited context, FDA considered it acceptable to provide the PI via a hyperlink from the destination page as opposed to having a separate dedicated link to the PI.[20]

Of course, that guidance did not directly address reminder-like promotion, and in fact, explicitly exempted all reminder ads from its scope.[21]

Nonetheless, it is not too far fetched to believe that if the PI can be provided via a hyperlink from the destination page when the ad itself contains product benefit and risk information, then it would also be acceptable to have the PI provided in the same fashion for a reminder-like ad that does not contain any representation about a product's usage.

In addition, many companies that were using Google's dedicated black box ad format just provided a link to a webpage with risk information (not a direct link to the PI) from the "More info" link, and none of those ads were cited by the FDA as being violative.

One benefit for pharmaceutical companies of this change is that the black box ad format never worked on mobile phones. Consequently, some black box drugs were already adopting the standard ad unit for their mobile campaigns making use of the reminder-like ad format without having the black box ad format available (see **Figure 17**), and again, none of those ads were cited by the FDA as violative prior to this change or since.

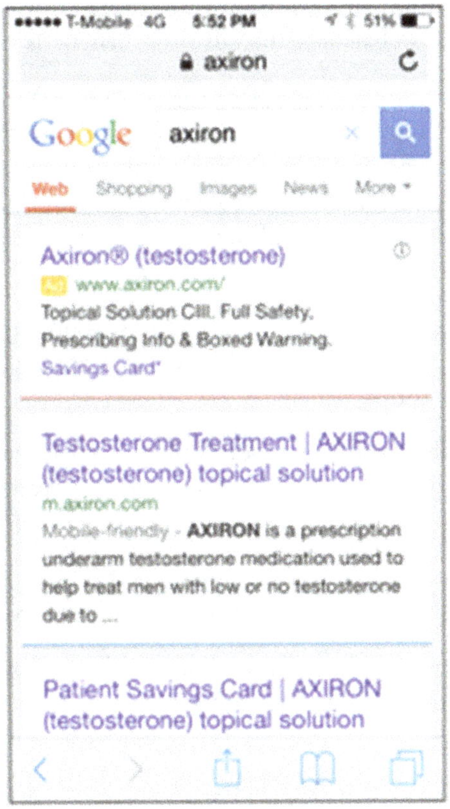

Figure 17: *Sample mobile ad for black box drug*

Incorrect FDA Guidance on Sitelinks

FDA's guidance about presenting risk and benefit information space-limited contexts included a lengthy discussion of the use of sitelinks for the presentation of risk information. That discussion was incorrect, and following the recommendations of that guidance could result in sponsors running ads that would replicate the omission of risk information violation cited by the FDA in 2009.

FDA's specific example and recommendation for the ad is shown in **Figure 18** (numbers in brackets represent character counts supplied by FDA):

Headhurtz (ouchafol) *[20/25]*
www.headhurtz.com *[17/ 35]*
For severe headache from traumatic brain injury *[47/ 70]*

Boxed warning *[13/25]*	Warning *[7/25]*
Potential for brain swelling *[28/35]*	Potentially fatal drug reaction *[31/35]*
Warning *[7/25]*	Risk information *[16/25]*
Life-threatening drop in heart rate *[35/35]*	Important safety information *[28/35]*

Figure 18: *FDA example using sitelinks*

About this example, FDA writes, "FDA would not intend to object to this sponsored link format."[22]

In this example, the benefit information "For severe headache from traumatic brain injury" requires corresponding risk information to be balanced because the benefit is combined with the product name (Headhurtz).

FDA accomplishes that risk presentation via the various sitelink descriptions "Potential for brain swelling," "Life-threatening drop in heart rate," etc. Importantly, the words in the sitelinks themselves "Boxed warning," "Warning," and "Risk information" do not themselves constitute risk information, just links to risk information. Consequently, those links in themselves do not suffice to provide the risk information, and simply providing those links would not enable the sponsor to meet its fair balance requirement according to FDA's guidance.

The first problem with FDA's recommendation is that FDA is assuming that a product manufacturer can guarantee that their ads have the sitelinks and the link descriptions appear when they run the ad, but as noted earlier, advertisers do not have that control.

Google does not guarantee that sitelinks will ever appear. In fact, Google has a page about extensions dedicated to the topic of how to make the sitelinks more likely to appear in paid search campaigns.[23]

That's a problem because if an ad is running with benefit information presented in the body of the ad, the ad requires the risk information to meet the fair balance requirement. If an ad displaying the benefit information does not include the sitelinks, then the ad would violate the fair balance requirement.

So, if the maker of HeadHurtz were to actually run the ad that the FDA provides as an example, there's a chance that the ad would actually appear as follows (see **Figure 19**):

Headhurtz (ouchafol) [*20/25*]
www.headhurtz.com [*17/ 35*]
For severe headache from traumatic brain injury [*47/ 70*]

Figure 19: *FDA example that might be seen*

This ad would definitely be violative because as we learned in 2009, and as FDA reiterates in the June 2014 guidance, if the product name and benefit information is presented, then FDA requires that some risk information be presented at the same time with comparable prominence as the benefit information.

So following the FDA's provided example could result in violative promotional activity. Moreover, even if the sitelinks appear, there's a chance that the sitelink description would not appear. But again, the sitelinks provided in the example ("Warning," etc.) do not in themselves provide risk information. So, just providing the sitelinks would not meet the fair balance requirement.

Further compounding the problems with the FDA's example is that the order and number of sitelinks provided varies without complete control by the advertiser. So, if all four sitelinks were not provided, there's a chance (based on FDA's guidance) that the advertiser might not be complying with the fair balance requirement because FDA might deem it necessary to provide ALL four sitelinks to meet that requirement.

As if these problems were not enough, there's one more difficulty: mobile devices. If this ad were enabled for display on mobile phones (which is not required for Google ads but is encouraged), then you would definitely not have all four sitelinks presented, and as mentioned earlier none of the descriptions of the sitelinks would be presented.

Appropriate Use of Sitelinks

Given everything that has been said about sitelinks, it should be clear that a few principles should govern their use in ads that mention a prescription product. First, the sitelinks (and their descriptions) should not include any information that is necessary to ensure the ad's compliance, such as the generic name. Second, sitelinks (and their descriptions) should be developed on the assumption that users might not see all of the information or any specific combination of sitelinks. Each sitelink and its description should be compliant, without need for other sitelinks or descriptions to be understood. Third, all information in sitelinks for SEM ads that mention prescription products should fall within the reminder ad category of "other information" that does not describe a product. Typically, prescription drug manufacturers use descriptions such as "Adverse Reactions," "Savings Card Info," and "Dosing & Administration" as sitelinks because these descriptions reveal nothing about the specific use of the product, and they also provide deep links into a site to some of the most frequently accessed pages (see **Figure 15**).

Making Benefit Claims in SEM Ads

The FDA guidance about presenting benefit and risk information in space-limited contexts, did offer the theoretical possibility of doing so. Specifically, FDA stated that if a brand were to make benefit claims in an ad in a space-limited context, the ad itself should include[24]:

1) Brand name
2) Generic name and/or active ingredients
3) A non-misleading but possibly abbreviated indication statement
4) Abbreviated risk info (with ALL life-threatening risks and contraindications other than mere hypersensitivity to the active ingredient)
5) A link to a page solely containing risk information, which has
    a. Full risk information
    b. Dosage form
    c. Quantitative ingredient information
    d. Full label

In practice, no brand has attempted to making product benefit claims in SEM ads. The practical consequences of this guidance has not enabled any additional types of ads for prescription product marketers. As a consequence, there are only four types of ads in SEM campaigns:

1) Reminder ads
2) Reminder-like ads
3) Redirecting ads
4) Disease awareness ads

Compliant SEM Ad Formats

Disease Awareness Ads neither mention nor imply any specific product and take users to a disease awareness website. These are not subject to FDA regulation when properly executed.

Reminder Ads include brand and generic names with no representation of usage.

Reminder-like Ads for black box products cannot describe product usage or population.

Redirecting Ads include no mention or implication of a specific product, but redirect to a product website.

Other Search Engines

Much of the discussion above focuses on Google. That is appropriate for several reasons. First, Google dominates search with approximately two-thirds of all search traffic.[25] Second, in general, because Google is such a large player, the other search engines follow Google's lead on many practices. However, it is important to note that there is no reason to assume that is true.

And since marketers cannot afford to ignore the one-third of searches happening on other search engines, that means regulatory reviewers must also review materials for use on these other search engines, and ensure that they comply with FDA regulatory requirements. Neither Bing nor Yahoo! has yet adopted Google's templates for redirecting ad URLs, and there are other differences that will have to be considered when the campaigns arise, such as the use of imagery or character count variations. (see **Figure 20**)

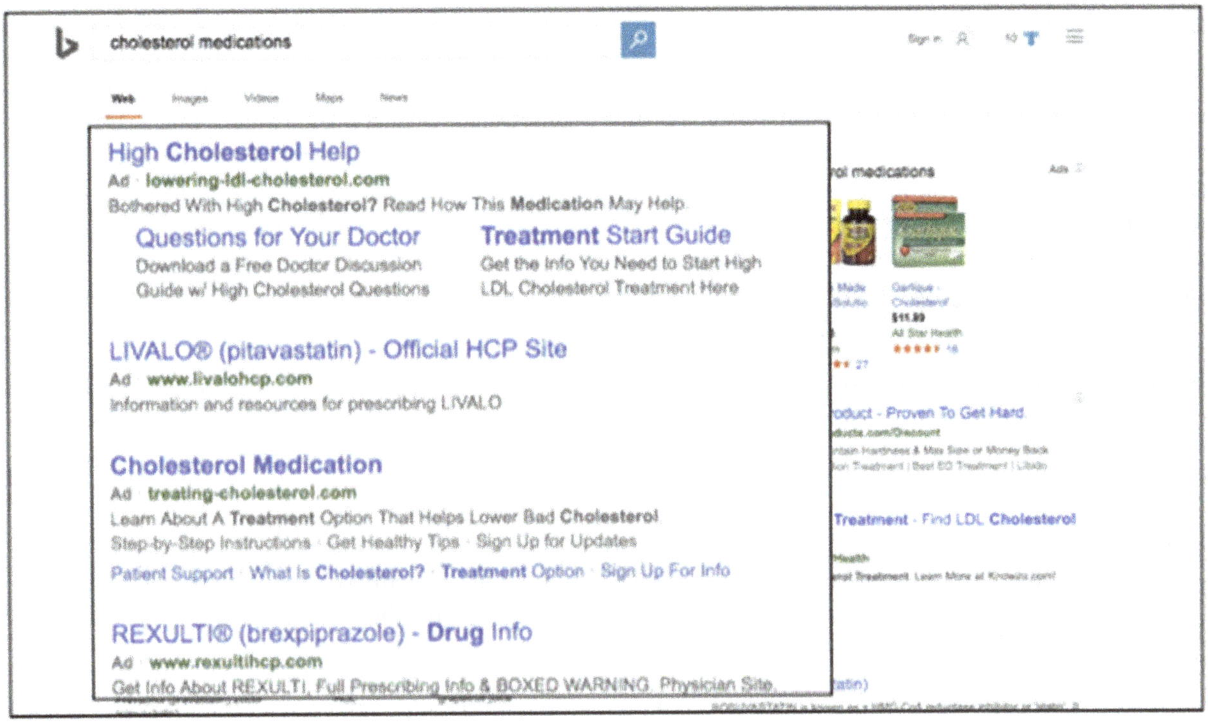

Figure 20: Bing SERP

Going Beyond the Ad

Advertising and promotional specialists know that FDA takes into account factors beyond the contents of an ad itself when determining compliance. For example, FDA mentioned in its "Help-Seeking" Communications guidance that a compliant reminder advertisement might be deemed out of compliance if it is paired with an otherwise-compliant disease awareness communication by being too close in time, space, or visual appearance.[26] In addition, there are other organizations beyond FDA that pay attention to promotional activity, such as the Office of the Inspector General (OIG). There is a need to consider what other factors outside of the characters in an SEM ad should be evaluated when developing such campaigns.

Keywords

As noted above, keywords play an analogous role to the media buy for traditional offline advertising campaigns, in that the keywords selected determine when an SEM ad will appear. And just as a perfectly compliant print ad placed in an inappropriate publication can be used as evidence of the intent to promote a product for off-label uses, so also could FDA or OIG see the appearance of an SEM ad in response to a search for information about an off-label usage as evidence of intent to promote the product off-label. Consequently, keywords should be reviewed to ensure that all targeted placements are on label, and a robust negative keyword strategy should be developed to minimize the appearance of the SEM ads against queries for off-label uses. It is also worth noting that although keywords should be reviewed to ensure that the placement of the ad is compliant, FDA has indicated (as discussed further below) that the keywords themselves do not have to be submitted as part of the 2253 filing.

Combining Ad Formats

FDA has made clear via enforcement action[27] and guidance[28] that individual communications can be appropriate as standalone disease awareness or product promotional messages, but can become inappropriate when combined in certain ways. Specifically, FDA calls out perceptual similarity, use of similar storylines and taglines, and physical proximity as being key elements that it evaluates when determining whether two independently compliant messages are intended to be understood as forming one combined message that itself might not be compliant. Consequently, when engaging in any disease awareness or other communications that do not include complete product risk information, it is important to evaluate how the combinations of communications function as a unit.

Best practice for SEM ads is to ensure that disease awareness ads are not served up in combination with any of the other ad formats discussed above (reminder ads, redirecting ads, or reminder-like ads). This can be accomplished either by using distinct keywords for the targeting or by blocking the ads from appearing simultaneously via backend targeting parameters.

In addition, prudence would suggest that redirecting ads (which again do not include any mention of a specific product) should not run in conjunction with either reminder ads or reminder-like ads to ensure that the combination of messages does not form an unintended joint message that falls out of compliance.

Because SEM ads do not generally include imagery[29] or other visual elements, there is less concern about visual similarity causing two messages to be combined; however, the cautious approach would certainly be to evaluate the text and key phrases used in all SEM ads to ensure that similar, product-specific words are not used in multiple ad types. Obviously, there would be little concern about using universally applicable language such as "Dosing & Administration" in both a reminder ad format and a redirecting ad, but if there were a unique tagline used repeatedly with a product's reminder ad formats and then carried over to a redirecting ad format, there might be concern that the two ads (even if not served up simultaneously) could be construed as forming a single message.

The 2253 Filing

FDA has not provided any direct, written guidance about the requirements for meeting the 2253 filing requirement for SEM campaigns. As noted above, FDA provided sample violative materials as part of its 2009 enforcement action, and those materials were notable for several reasons. First, they were screenshots of actual search results from a user's monitor.[30] That is important because, of course, such results could not have been the actual submission from the product sponsors. Such results can only be generated AFTER the campaign has launched, and thus the sponsors would have been guilty of launching their promotional materials prior to their 2253 filing if they had submitted these screenshots as their 2253 filing. Yet, none of the 14 letters mentioned the failure to submit under Form 2253 as a violation.[31]

So, sponsors submitted something other than screenshots, yet when FDA took action, they only posted the screenshots. There is no reason to believe that all of the sponsors would have submitted the same thing for their 2253 filing, as absent explicit guidance, each company has been left to its own devices. We can, however, note that FDA was clearly holding companies accountable only for the words that appeared in their SEM ads. Nothing in the letters mentioned, for example, any of the keywords that caused the ads to appear as constituting a separate violation. We can also again use the analogy of a print ad. When submitting a print ad under Form 2253, companies only submit the ad itself, without including the media plan behind the ad or the publications in which the ad will run; and as noted earlier, the keywords in an SEM campaign function analogously to the media plan for a print campaign.

Providing further clarification about the 2253 filing of SEM ads, FDA held a webinar in August of 2013, during which the speaker was asked whether keywords needed to be submitted under Form 2253. The speaker responded that keywords did not need to be submitted.[32] Statements made in such webinars do not constitute formal advice, guidance, or regulation, but the off-hand nature of the comment and lack of any elaboration would lead one to believe that this was not regarded by the speaker as a controversial area but rather settled policy.

Based on this evidence, it seems reasonable to infer that a complete 2253 filing for an SEM campaign promoting prescription products by name includes the following:

1) Text of the ads themselves, including any optional components that might appear
2) The destination URLs corresponding to the ads if they differ from the display URLs

Note that redirecting ads discussed above do not count as product promotions since they do not include the name of the specific product, and of course, disease awareness campaigns are not product promotions and do not require 2253 filing.

Key Lessons

Summarizing the discussion above, sponsors would be well served to take the following steps to ensure their SEM ads are compliant:

1) Submit all product promotion ads under cover of Form 2253 prior to use
    a. All copy that will appear in the SEM ads themselves, including any optional copy that might not always appear such as sitelinks and sitelink descriptions
    b. Destination URLs, if they differ from the display URLs
    c. Do NOT include keywords
2) Do NOT submit disease awareness SEM ads under cover of Form 2253
3) Do NOT submit redirecting ads under cover of Form 2253
4) SEM ads for drugs with black box warnings should make use of a reminder-like ad format

5) If using sitelinks, then take the following additional steps:

   a. Ensure that all regulatory requirements are met in the body of the ad itself, not in any sitelink or sitelink description

   b. Ensure that the sitelink and its description is compatible with the body of the ad (i.e., if the main ad is a reminder ad, then the sitelink cannot imply the product usage; if the main ad is a redirecting ad that omits the product name, then the sitelink cannot imply or name a specific product)

6) Ensure that all keywords are on label

7) Ensure that negative keywords for the most common known off-label uses are implemented

8) Avoid combining ad formats that mention a product with ad formats that do not mention a product

Conclusion

Although there are still questions that FDA has yet to answer about Internet advertising, search engine marketing is a well-established space with well-defined parameters for what sponsors may do. Given the importance of search for people looking for health information online, it is vital that marketers of prescription products use this space and do so compliantly.

Endnotes

1. DDMAC has been re-organized into the Office of Prescription Drug Promotion since issuing the letters, and the FDA has redesigned all of its websites, and many of the old URLs no longer function. The new page where people can access these letters is http://www.fda.gov/Drugs/GuidanceComplianceRegulatoryInformation/EnforcementActivitiesbyFDA/WarningLettersandNoticeofViolationLetterstoPharmaceuticalCompanies/ucm055773.htm#more, accessed July 9, 2014.

2. "Prescription products" is being used here and throughout this chapter as a shorthand for all the products (prescription drugs, biologics, vaccines, restricted medical devices, etc.) over which FDA exercises authority for their advertising.

3. According to the Pew Research's Internet Project, 77% of people accessing the Internet for health information started at a search engine such as Google, Yahoo!, or Bing. Last accessed August 25, 2014, from http://www.pewinternet.org/fact-sheets/health-fact-sheet/

4. Note that although Google is discussed below, many of the same points apply mutatis mutandis to Yahoo!, Bing, and other search engines.

5. Please note the crucial caveat to this control that applies to SEM in the case of "enhanced" SEM using sitelinks that is discussed below.

6. This is a slight oversimplification of the process as Google also takes into account the performance of an ad (how many people click on it, whether the people clicking on it immediately return to conduct the same search again, etc.) in determining ad placement. For more on the factors

determining the appearance of an SEM ad, see http://www.wordstream.com/articles/what-is-google-adwords last accessed May 4, 2017.

7. Again, this is a slight simplification of Google's functionality. Users' search history, location information, and other factors also determine the results that appear. For a more nuanced discussion of the search results, see this page from Google: https://support.google.com/webmasters/answer/70897?hl=en last accessed May 4, 2017.

8. This discussion of keywords omits the important distinctions between broad, exact match, and other match types. For more on these distinctions, see this page from Google: https://support.google.com/adwords/answer/2497836?hl=en last accessed on May 4, 2017.

9. The following discussion of the limitations of sitelinks draws upon the main Google page discussing sitelinks: https://support.google.com/adwords/answer/2375416?hl=en last accessed August 28, 2014, as well as private correspondence with Google representatives.

10. Advertisers are not required to have their ads appear on mobile devices; however, the explosive growth of mobile usage makes it increasingly important that people make information available there. In addition, Google is encouraging advertisers to make their ads mobile-friendly and giving preference to advertisers who use mobile advertising. Not using mobile advertising hurts advertisers on their desktop advertising's quality metrics.

11. See page 3 of letter sent March 26, 2009, to Boehringer Ingelheim for MACMIS #17308. Last accessed from http://www.fda.gov/downloads/Drugs/GuidanceComplianceRegulatoryInformation/EnforcementActivitiesbyFDA/WarningLettersandNoticeofViolationLetterstoPharmaceuticalCompanies/UCM143499.pdf on August 28, 2014.

12. See page 3 of letter sent March 26, 2009, to Bayer for MACMIS #17307. Last accessed from http://www.fda.gov/downloads/Drugs/GuidanceComplianceRegulatoryInformation/EnforcementActivitiesbyFDA/WarningLettersandNoticeofViolationLetterstoPharmaceuticalCompanies/UCM143477.pdf on August 28, 2014.

13. Draft Guidance for Industry "Help-Seeking" and Other Disease Awareness Communications by or on Behalf of Drug and Device Firms, page 1. This guidance has been withdrawn by the Agency but continues to remain important for regulatory professionals. An archived version of this guidance is available at https://drive.google.com/file/d/0Bz2keqj7ej5IMThsNnJDQXduNms/view last accessed May 4, 2017. Hereinafter, "Disease Awareness Guidance."

14. Note that the Food and Drug Administration Modernization Act of 1997 permitted the use of the phrase "FDA-approved" for advertisements of products that have received FDA approval. For more on this, see http://www.fda.gov/BiologicsBloodVaccines/DevelopmentApprovalProcess/AdvertisingLabelingPromotionalMaterials/ucm117616.htm last accessed on August 28, 2014.

15. Thirteen of the 14 letters mentioned only Google searches. One letter (to sanofi-aventis and BMS for the marketing of Plavix) mentioned Yahoo! but the posted materials made clear that this was not in fact an SEM campaign. Instead, it was an organic search campaign that FDA misidentified as paid SEM. For the Plavix materials, see http://www.fda.gov/downloads/Drugs/GuidanceComplianceRegulatoryInformation/EnforcementActivitiesbyFDA/WarningLettersandNoticeofViolationLetterstoPharmaceuticalCompanies/UCM166249.pdf last accessed August 28, 2014

16. As of May 4, 2017, the URL www.TalkAboutBPH.com takes users to the product label for Uroxatral. In 2009, the URL redirected to Uroxatral.com.

17. It is important to note that FDA's announcement of its 2009 hearing on the Internet explicitly discussed the type of use of hyperlinks that is described here. As of the writing of this piece, no guidance from FDA has been received on this topic; however, there was an item listed on the CDER guidance agenda for 2016 about providing guidance on the use of hyperlinks. It is possible that the FDA guidance on the use of hyperlinks, when available, will contravene the recommendations provided here, but until learning otherwise, the recommendations provided here seem sound and have attracted large agreement across the industry.

18. See Google's AdWord policy on Destination URLs at the following page: https://support.google.com/adwordspolicy/answer/6008942?hl=en&ref_topic=1626336#pra last accessed May 4, 2017.

19. "This draft guidance does not apply to those *reminder* promotions (labeling or advertising that calls attention to the name of a drug or device but does not include indications, dosage recommendations, or other information) that are exempted by regulation from the requirements under the FD&C Act for the disclosure of risk information," page 4n10 in Guidance for Industry: Internet/Social Media Platforms with Character Space Limitations—Presenting Risk and Benefit Information for Prescription Drugs and Medical Devices, available from http://www.fda.gov/downloads/Drugs/GuidanceComplianceRegulatoryInformation/Guidances/UCM401087.pdf last accessed on August 28, 2014. Hereinafter "Space-limited Guidance."

20. Space-limited Guidance, page 10.

21. Space-limited Guidance, page 4, note 10.

22. Space-limited Guidance, page 15.

23. For Google's discussion of sitelinks see https://support.google.com/adwords/answer/1704420?hl=en last accessed on May 4, 2017.

24. Space-limited Guidance, pages 6-14.

25. According to search engine rankings from comScore, Google had 64% of all desktop search activity in March of 2017. https://www.comscore.com/Insights/Rankings/ last accessed May 4, 2017.

26. Disease Awareness Guidance, page 5-7.

27. See for example, page 1 of the letter sent August 18, 2000, to Schering for MACMIS #9224. Last accessed from http://www.fda.gov/downloads/Drugs/GuidanceComplianceRegulatoryInformation/EnforcementActivitiesbyFDA/WarningLettersandNoticeofViolationLetterstoPharmaceuticalCompanies/UCM166052.pdf on August 29, 2014.

28. Disease Awareness Guidance, pages 5-7.

29. Note that search engines do offer enhanced advertising options that offer the use of imagery and video, but the standard format is text-only and discourages (or prohibits) use of emoticons and other elements to enhance the visual appeal.

30. Again, the letter to sanofi-aventis (and BMS) for Plavix stands out. The materials presented included both organic search engine results on Yahoo! and information about the metadata from the websites themselves that appears to have been submitted to FDA separately.

31. Note that the only FDA enforcement action targeting SEM since 2009 was a 2014 letter to Gilead for Viread. That letter did cite the failure to submit under Form 2253. For more on that enforcement action, see http://regulatoryrx.blogspot.com/2014/07/another-google-search-letter.html last accessed August 28, 2014.

32. FDA has not made the complete transcript of this webinar available. For a contemporaneous report of this comment and its implications, see the Coalition for Healthcare Communications article http://www.cohealthcom.org/2013/09/03/fda-states-keywords-do-not-have-to-be-reported-on-form-2253s/ last accessed on August 28, 2014.

Chapter V
Continuous Improvement

It is the nature of any discussion about digital topics that it is impossible to be comprehensive. There simply are too many variables, permutations, etc. But even if it were possible to provide a comprehensive discussion of the review and approval of digital tactics, someone will create something new next week, and then the initial discussion is no longer complete.

Rather than attempting to provide the impossible, this primer has attempted to provide a framework for ensuring that digital tactics can go through the review and approval process smoothly, and while some specific sample templates and checklists have been provided, the key takeaway should be about the need to develop such items.

Ideally, this becomes an ongoing process rather than a one-time investment because there will be changes needed and new templates and checklists. One way to incorporate this into the review and approval process itself is to include the checklist of what needs to be submitted and a template for how to provide it as part of the outcome of the Concept Review any time a new technology is being reviewed. Those items then provide direction not merely to that project's originator but to everyone who originates that type of project in the future.

Many large companies with multiple review committees and reviewers have instituted learning sessions for the reviewers to compare challenging issues and their resolution. These sessions also provide a great opportunity for sharing tips about how to review digital tactics, to roll out new templates, and to solicit feedback about the usefulness of existing practices.

Regardless of the mechanism, the only certainty in this arena is change. Someone will create a new way to consume information, and people will want to access health information on it. When that happens, makers of prescription products have a choice. Provide the information, and establish review and approval procedures to ensure that the material is compliant. Or fail to provide the information, and let the resulting information vacuum be occupied by others.

Appendices

A. Presenting Risk Information on Web Sites

B. Reviewing Television Commercials

C. Where Things Stand on FDA Guidance about Social Media

Relevant FDA Draft Guidances

D. Draft Guidance on Presenting Risk Information

E. Draft Guidance on Post-marketing Submissions of Interactive Promotional Materials

F. Draft Guidance on Character-space Limited Promotions

G. Draft Guidance on Correcting Misinformation on Third-party Sites

H. Draft Guidance on Submitting Promotional Materials in Electronic and Non-Electronic Format

I. Draft Guidance on Television Commercial Pre-dissemination Review

J. Draft Guidance on Responding to Unsolicited Requests for Off-label Information

Appendix A.
Presenting Risk Information on Web Sites

Presenting Risk Information on Web Sites

By Dale A. Cooke

On October 17, 2011, Otsuka Pharmaceutical received an untitled notice of violation letter from the Food and Drug Administration's Office of Prescription Drug Promotion (OPDP) for the promotion of Busulfex® (busulfan) on Busulfex.com. OPDP is the new office responsible for enforcing promotional compliance that replaces the Division of Drug Marketing, Advertising and Communications. The letter noted several violations, one of which was the omission of material facts as presented via the Important Safety Information (or ISI) on a webpage.

In the absence of specific guidance from the FDA about the presentation of risk information online, certain conventions have taken root. One is the use of the ISI. This article addresses what companies can learn about correctly presenting risk information via the ISI based on FDA guidance and enforcement actions, including the most recent one regarding Busulfex.com.

A Caveat

It's important to note that simply not doing things that FDA has previously cited as infractions does not in itself ensure compliance with FDA requirements. However, it is certainly prudent to at least avoid making the same mistakes others have already made.

The Requirement

Promotions for prescription drugs are required to "present a fair balance between information relating to side effects and contraindications and information relating to effectiveness of the drug."[1] FDA has elaborated on that requirement in draft guidance for industry.[2] In that document, FDA emphasized that the net impression of a piece taken as a whole (the effect created by the presentation of the risk information and the benefit information) dictates whether the piece accomplishes its fair balance requirement. FDA saw the need to present a guidance specifically addressing the presentation of risk information because studies have shown that risk information is poorly presented and minimization of risk continues to be "the most frequent violation of the regulations."[3]

The ISI

Most prescription drug websites[4] present risk information via an ISI that appears on every page of the website.[5] There is variation in how this is done, but the standard technique is to have a persistent block of copy headlined "Important Safety Information" or "Important Safety Information for Drug X" at the bottom of the webpage. Usually, there are prominent links to the ISI in the top and/or left navigation, and the ISI also resides as a separate page of the website.

On consumer sites, this copy is typically an abbreviated, consumer-friendly version of the information provided in the risks, contraindications, warnings and precautions, and adverse reactions sections of the Prescribing Information or a condensed version of the FDA-approved Patient Prescribing Information or Medication Guide.

The ISI itself is not referred to in any federal law or regulation. The copy that is presented there, though certainly reviewed by the FDA as part of advisory comments submissions, does not itself have the same canonical status as the Prescribing Information, Patient Prescribing Information, or Medication Guide. The specific language in all of those documents is reviewed and explicitly approved by the FDA and is part of any official label update issued by the FDA.

Enforcement Actions Involving the Provision of Risk Information Websites

The FDA has taken numerous enforcement actions for omission or minimization of risk information on websites. From these letters, it is possible to discern certain principles regarding the provision of risk information on a website, and apply those principles to how the ISI is used.

First, risk information should be included on every page along with a link to the full ISI. Going back at least to a 2001 letter to Braintree Laboratories[6] for its website promoting MiraLax (polyethylene glycol 3350 NF Powder) FDA established the principle through its enforcement action that risk information must be provided on every page of the website. This principle has been reaffirmed in numerous enforcement actions over the years, including as recently as March 2010.[7, 8]

Second, other letters note the additional violation of not including a link to the full risk information when abbreviated risk information is provided on the page itself. This violation was noted in a letter from 2004 to Bradley Pharmaceutical and again in 2010 to Eli Lilly.[9]

The next lesson regards the use of signaling. FDA evaluates the use of appropriate signals, such as headlines and subheads, to see how information is being conveyed and whether it achieves balance. In the guidance, FDA noted that "beginning the presentation of risk information with unrelated information," such as the indication statement "can also minimize the risks."[10] This has played out in enforcement actions including a 2010 letter to Novartis and a 2011 letter to Cephalon.[11]

Another part of the guidance discussed the font size and styles and the importance of treating the risk information in a manner "comparably noticeable" to the benefit information.[12] In enforcement actions[13], this has been applied to both the formatting of the ISI and the links to the ISI.

Finally, we turn to the recent letter sent to Otsuka for its promotion of Busulfex.[14] This action calls attention to another item discussed in FDA's guidance on risk information. Specifically, FDA elaborated on the need to include "material information about a product's risks… even if the piece devotes similar space or time to risk and effectiveness presentations."[15] In other words, mere inclusion of a prominent ISI on every page does not guarantee that the presentation of risk information is sufficient. There might be risk information that is materially relevant to specific claims that is omitted from the ISI. In the letter to Otsuka, FDA indicated that information about adverse events specific to a pediatric population was lacking from a discussion of pediatric dosing and that there needed to be more information about premedication to address the large prevalence of nausea and vomiting associated with Busulfex.[16]

Recommendations

Based on this review of FDA's guidance and enforcement actions, the following recommendations can be offered for providing risk information via an ISI on websites:

1. Include the ISI on every page of a web site.

2. Include a link to the ISI on every page.

3. Do not separate the risk information from the headline by inserting the indication statement or other non-risk information between the headline and the beginning of the risk information.

4. Ensure the overall presentation of the risk information (font size, color, spacing, etc.) and links to the ISI is reasonably comparable to the presentation of the benefit information.

5. Check your ISI against the discussion on the page. Ensure that all of the materially relevant information is added to the page, if it is not present in the ISI. ▲

Mr. Cooke is the Vice President/Group Director, Regulatory Review at Digitas Health

1. See 21 CFR 202.1(e)(5)(ii)
2. Draft Guidance for Industry Presenting Risk Information in Prescription Drug and Medical Device Promotion ("Presenting Risk"). Last accessed November 28, 2011, from http://www.fda.gov/Drugs/GuidanceComplianceRegulatoryInformation/Guidances/ucm064956.htm
3. Presenting Risk, page 3.
4. This article focuses on using the ISI on websites, but the ISI is used in many other communications. It originated in print advertising and is also used in emails, banner ads, patient education materials, and other places. Many of the same issues discussed here affect those uses as well.
5. In a review by the author, nine of the top 18 selling brands with websites present risk information via an ISI at the bottom of the webpage. An additional five brands supplement the ISI on the bottom of the webpage with the beginning of the ISI at the top of the webpage. So, 14 of the top 18 brands use some version of the persistent ISI at the bottom of the webpage to present risk information. At the time of the review, two of the top 20 selling brands did not have active websites, so they were excluded.
6. See page 3 to letter sent March 29, 2001, to Braintree Laboratories for MiraLax (polyethylene glycol 3350 NF Powder) MACMIS # 9769. Last accessed November 29, 2011 from http://www.fda.gov/Drugs/GuidanceComplianceRegulatoryInformation/EnforcementActivitiesbyFDA/WarningLettersandNoticeofViolationLetterstoPharmaceuticalCompanies/ucm164916.htm Note that MiraLax is now an OTC product, so the requirements for its promotion have changed.

7. Among the letters including this violation are MACMIS # 18378 sent to Slate Pharmaceuticals on March 24, 2010; MACMIS # 13850 sent to BioMarin Pharmaceutical on October 11, 2006; MACMIS # 13449 sent to Cytogen Corporation on July 18, 2005; MACMIS # 13490 sent to Dutch Ophthalmic USA on June 28, 2005; and MACMIS # 12413 sent to Bradley Pharmaceuticals on November 9, 2004. Letters last accessed on November 29, 2011, from http://www.fda.gov/Drugs/GuidanceComplianceRegulatory-Information/EnforcementActivitiesbyFDA/WarningLettersand-NoticeofViolationLetterstoPharmaceuticalCompanies/default.htm
8. It's also worth noting that this parallels an objection to offline promotional materials where FDA is sending letters indicating that materials are violative if they do not include risk information in all parts of the piece. See MACMIS # 17999 sent to Shire Development on November 5, 2009, and MACMIS # 17586 sent to Sirion Therapeutics on February 18, 2010. Letters last accessed on November 29, 2011, from http://www.fda.gov/Drugs/GuidanceComplianceRegulatoryInformation/EnforcementActivitiesbyFDA/WarningLettersandNoticeofViolationLetterstoPharmaceuticalCompanies/default.htm
9. MACMIS # 12413 sent to Bradley Pharmaceuticals on November 9, 2004, and MACMIS # 18219 sent to Lilly on January 27, 2010. Letters last accessed on November 29, 2011, from http://www.fda.gov/Drugs/GuidanceComplianceRegulatoryInformation/EnforcementActivitiesbyFDA/WarningLettersandNoticeofViolationLetterstoPharmaceuticalCompanies/default.htm
10. Presenting Risk, pages 7-8.
11. MACMIS # 18396 sent to Novartis on April 14, 2010, and MACMIS # 20151 sent to Cephalon on June 21, 2011. Letters last accessed on November 29, 2011, from http://www.fda.gov/Drugs/GuidanceComplianceRegulatoryInformation/EnforcementActivitiesbyFDA/WarningLettersandNoticeofViolationLetterstoPharmaceuticalCompanies/default.htm
12. Presenting Risk, page 15.
13. See again MACMIS # 18396 and MACMIS # 18378. Letters last accessed on November 29, 2011, from http://www.fda.gov/Drugs/GuidanceComplianceRegulatory Information/EnforcementActivitiesbyFDA/Warning LettersandNoticeofViolationLetterstoPharmaceuticalCompanies/default.htm
14. MA # 77 sent to Otsuka Pharmaceutical on October 17, 2011. Letter last accessed on November 29, 2011, from http://www.fda.gov/Drugs/GuidanceComplianceRegulatory Information/EnforcementActivitiesbyFDA/Warning LettersandNoticeofViolationLetterstoPharmaceutical Companies/default.htm
15. Presenting Risk, page 11.
16. MA # 77, pages 2-3.

Appendix B.
Reviewing Television Commercials

Direct-to-consumer television commercials are the highest profile marketing materials most pharmaceutical companies produce. Television commercials have always been treated as a separate category of promotional material necessitating a distinct review process. In this appendix, I discuss the review process that has traditionally been applied to television commercials. In addition, Congress authorized FDA to require that television commercials be submitted for review prior to airing the spots. FDA has released a draft guidance on how they intend to interpret that requirement. This appendix sets out how that draft guidance alters the traditional review and approval process for television advertisements. It must be emphasized that the draft guidance has NOT yet been implemented by FDA, and the guidance could undergo significant revision before implementation. The following is based on the draft as released in March 2012.

Traditional Review and Approval Process for Television Commercials

Because television commercials have such high profile and cost, pharmaceutical companies have always been exceedingly cautious about their development. That cautiousness was further enhanced by the Pharmaceutical Research and Manufacturers of America (PhRMA) establishing as one of its guiding principles for direct to consumer advertisements about Prescription Medicines that:

> Companies should submit all new DTC television advertisements to the FDA before releasing these advertisements for broadcast.

Technically, this principle is met by complying with the 2253 filing requirement to submit all promotional materials to the FDA at the time of initial dissemination. In practice, however, this principle has been interpreted as requiring a submission of a draft spot to the FDA for advisory comments. This is a voluntary submission that has not previously been required by law or regulation.

Companies have for the most part complied with this principle by adopting the following review and approval path:

1) MLR Committee Review of Script and Storyboard (with multiple re-reviews as needed)
2) Check Changes Review of Script and Storyboard after Approved with Changes Decision Reached by MLR Committee
3) Voluntary FDA Advisory Comments Submission of Script and Storyboard Fully Annotated and Referenced
4) MLR Committee Review of FDA Advisory Comments Received to Provide Direction on Revisions
5) MLR Committee Review of Rough Cut of Television Commercial
6) MLR Committee Review of Final Cut of Television Commercial
7) Check Changes Review of Final Cut of Television Commercial
8) 2253 Filing of Final Cut of Television Commercial

Revised Review and Approval Process Based on DRAFT Guidance

FDA's draft Guidance for Industry: Direct-to-Consumer Television Advertisements—FDAAA DTC Television Ad Pre-dissemination Review Program sets out the way FDA is proposing to implement new authority from

Congress to require that television spots be submitted to the FDA for pre-dissemination 45 days prior to airing the spots.

In the draft Guidance, FDA sets out the categories of drugs to which this requirement applies. Specifically, FDA identifies the following six categories:

> Category 1: The initial TV ad for any prescription drug or the initial TV ad for a new or expanded approved indication for any prescription drug
>
> Category 2: All TV ads for prescription drugs subject to a Risk Evaluation and Mitigation Strategy (REMS) with elements to assure safe use (see section 505-1(f) of the FD&C Act)
>
> Category 3: All TV ads for Schedule II controlled substances
>
> Category 4: The first TV ad for a prescription drug following a safety labeling update that affects the Boxed Warning, Contraindications, or Warnings & Precautions section of its labeling
>
> Category 5: The first TV ad for a prescription drug following the receipt by the sponsor of an enforcement letter (i.e. a Warning or untitled letter) for that product that either cites a TV ad or causes a TV ad to be discontinued because the TV ad contained violations similar to the ones cited in the enforcement letter
>
> Category 6: Any TV ad that is otherwise identified by FDA as subject to the pre-dissemination review provision

This requirement is in addition to the 2253 filing requirement for the final commercial. This also would not be a voluntary submission for the categories of ads set out in the guidance as falling under the requirement. In addition, this requirement would not be met by following the review path set out above because the spots would have to be "final" before they were submitted to the FDA for the 45-day pre-dissemination review. FDA explicitly discusses the current process followed by most companies of submitting a storyboard and script for voluntary comments and notes:

> FDA cannot provide final comments on the acceptability of a TV ad without viewing a final recorded version in its entirety. FDA understands that some sponsors may wish to receive comments from the Agency before producing a final recorded version of the ad. In such situations, sponsors can submit a pre-dissemination review package without a final recorded version of the ad, but once the final recorded version is produced, it will need to be submitted to the Agency for pre-dissemination review.

For affected products, there would be two options:

1) Submit television commercials only for the 45-day pre-dissemination review, but not for the earlier, voluntary advisory comments review.
2) Submit television commercials for both an advisory comments review of a draft spot and/or storyboard and for advisory comments on the final recorded spot.

If companies choose the former path (submitting materials only for the 45-day pre-dissemination review but not the earlier review), they risk receiving feedback from the FDA after all production has been completed that could result in significant costs including possibly completely redoing all of the production work including filming.

If companies submit television commercials for both reviews, then there has been significant time and cost entered into the development process. Companies generally allow six weeks for the voluntary advisory comments submissions, so this would effectively double the time spent under FDA review. In addition, there is no guarantee that having submitted a television ad for initial advisory comment alters the likelihood of getting substantial comment from the FDA when the 45-day pre-dissemination submission is provided. Comments received at that later stage still could result in the significant costs associated with changes at such a late stage, including potentially redoing the entire production.

FDA makes clear, however, that companies that choose to launch spots either without complying with the 45-day pre-dissemination requirement or without incorporating FDA feedback run significant risk, including "criminal penalties.... [and] monetary penalties."

The revised review and approval pathway for companies whose products fall within one of the six categories and who comply with the process set out in the draft guidance would most likely be the following:

1) MLR Committee Review of Script and Storyboard (with multiple re-reviews as needed)
2) Check Changes Review of Script and Storyboard after Approved with Changes Decision Reached by MLR Committee
3) Voluntary FDA Advisory Comments Submission of Script and Storyboard Fully Annotated and Referenced
4) MLR Committee Review of FDA Advisory Comments Received to Provide Direction on Revisions
5) MLR Committee Review of Rough Cut of Television Commercial
6) MLR Committee Review of Final Cut of Television Commercial
7) Check Changes Review of Final Cut of Television Commercial
8) FDA 45-day Pre-dissemination Review Submission
9) MLR Committee Review of FDA 45-day Pre-dissemination Comments Received to Provide Direction on Revisions
10) Check Changes Review of Final Cut of Television Commercial post-FDA Pre-dissemination Review
11) 2253 Filing of Final Cut of Television Commercial

Appendix C.
Where Things Stand on FDA Guidance about Social Media

Where Things Stand on FDA Guidance about Social Media

By Dale Cooke

Background

2009 was a landmark year for marketers of prescription medicine. In April of that year, the Food and Drug Administration's Division of Drug Marketing, Advertising, and Communications, which has since been reorganized into the Office of Prescription Drug Promotion, sent the infamous 14 letters for Google paid search promotion, making a clear statement to the industry that FDA was not providing an exemption to advertising and promotional labeling regulations for space-constrained contexts. At the time, the FDA was quoted in the Pink Sheet as saying, "While conducting our routine monitoring and surveillance activities, we noticed regulatory violations occurring in sponsored link promotion across multiple drug companies and therapeutic areas. In response, we developed and issued multiple letters on multiple drugs simultaneously to prompt the correction of the violations…and to maintain a level playing field for regulated industry."[1]

Dale Cooke is the President of PhillyCooke Consulting, which advises companies on the development of compliant promotional materials.

Then, in May, FDA released a 24-page guidance about presenting risk information.[2] That guidance included a section entitled "Considerations of Format," and many were shocked to learn that in 2009, just one month after the massive Google paid search enforcement action, that the FDA considered the only relevant formats to be print and non-print, lumping together such disparate media as television, radio, websites, live presentations, and other channels under the general category of non-print. In the entire 24-page guidance about presenting risk information correctly, which was one of the primary violations that the FDA found in ALL of the 14 letters issued a month earlier, the FDA made only three mentions of websites or the Internet in general as a promotional medium, and one of those three mentions was in a footnote in the section discussing print communications.[3]

There seemed to be a disconnect. Via its enforcement action, FDA seemed to be making clear that the industry did not understand the FDA's position on the presentation of risk information in space-limited contexts such as Google paid search advertising, yet via its guidance, FDA seemed to be saying that there was nothing worth discussing regarding such space-limited contexts and that the Internet and new communication channels did not present any importantly different considerations for the presentation of risk information.

It was no surprise then, when the FDA announced later that year, that there would be a two-day Part 15 hearing about appropriate use of the Internet and social media. The purpose of Part 15 hearings is for the FDA to hear from the public about a topic on which it is considering new regulation, rule making, or guidance. The "public" here is broadly construed to include everyone who is not part of the FDA, and the November 2009 Part 15 hearings included presentations from sponsors of prescription products, patient advocacy groups, industry coalitions, Internet companies, marketing agencies, and other concerned parties.

The Questions

Specifically, the FDA asked the public to provide information about five questions[4]. As presented in the Federal Register, those questions were:

1. For what online communications are manufacturers, packers, or distributors accountable?
2. How can manufacturers, packers, or distributors fulfill regulatory requirements (e.g., fair balance, disclosure of indication and risk information, postmarketing submission requirements) in their Internet and social media promotion, particularly when using tools that are associated with space limitations and tools that allow for real-time communications (e.g., microblogs, mobile technology)?
3. What parameters should apply to the posting of corrective information on Web sites controlled by third parties?
4. When is the use of links appropriate?
5. Questions specific to Internet adverse event reporting (including how sponsors are actually monitoring adverse event reporting, what challenges are they facing, and what uncertainties are there about reporting requirements).

Question 1: Accountability

In a series of guidances beginning in earnest in January of this year, FDA began addressing many of the topics raised in these five questions. In the first genuine social media guidance,[5] FDA addressed the question of accountability. It did so via a guidance dedicated to the issue of how marketers could meet their postmarketing submission requirements,[6] which was one aspect of the second question as well.

FDA's answer to the question of what communications a sponsor needs to file to meet its postmarketing requirement noted that "a firm generally is not responsible for UGC that is truly independent of the firm (i.e., is not produced by, or on behalf of, or prompted by the firm in any particular)"[7], and industry was pleased to see that common sense position adopted; however, its more detailed answer about what communications required a Form 2253 filing[8] took an expansive approach.

The FDA stated that a company was responsible for the 2253 filing of interactive promotional materials under three sets of circumstances:

1. Sites "owned, controlled, created, influenced, or operated by, or on behalf of the firm…. even if the influence is limited."[9]
2. Site pages if the firm "influenced the placement" of promotional materials.[10]
3. When agents or employees are "acting on behalf of the firm."[11]

The decision to address the question of accountability via this guidance was unfortunate for several reasons. First, medical device manufacturers do not have a requirement to file marketing communications with the FDA prior to use. Consequently, the Center for Devices and Radiological Health (CDRH) was not a signatory to the Postmarketing Guidance. That leaves medical device manufacturers unclear whether they should read the Postmarketing Guidance as providing guidance for their marketing efforts. Further complicating this issue is that CDRH is a signatory on the guidance regarding the correction of misinformation, which is discussed later in this article, and that guidance includes a footnote that directs readers to the Postmarketing Guidance. So, it seems as if CDRH is at some level endorsing much of the Postmarketing Guidance, even though it did not formally sign on to it.[12]

Second, FDA's view of the postmarketing filing requirement provided in this guidance seems to go far beyond the communications that a manufacturer genuinely controls or is able to take responsibility for. This concerns sponsors of prescription products because, as a rule, sponsors submit all and only those communications under cover of Form 2253 for which they are taking responsibility. Since FDA was expanding the responsibility to file materials via Form 2253 even when the firm "influenced" the material or the placement of its promotional material, that appears to many sponsors to imply that the FDA is expanding the accountability for those materials to the firm even when the firm did not have any control over those materials.

To make this concern vivid, consider the following situation. A sponsor of a men's health product considers placing a print ad in the *Sports Illustrated* issue dedicated to Major League Baseball's All-Star Game. Never has the FDA stated that the product's sponsor could be responsible for submitting the entire print magazine simply because the product's sponsor influenced the placement of the promotional material by virtue of specifying that specific issue. Yet, if the sponsor were to place an interactive banner ad promoting the product on the portion of SI.com that is dedicated to the MLB All-Star Game, then the sponsor would be responsible for submitting not just the banner ad, but also the pages on which the ad appears, according to the Postmarketing Guidance.

Even aside from the blatant disregard for establishing radically disparate requirements associated with print versus Internet promotion, that is problematic because the sponsor has no control over what content SI.com will run on those pages, there is no process in the 2253 Filing for indicating to the FDA that the sponsor has no control over that content, and (most importantly) that content will not exist when the banner ad is submitted to the FDA. The sponsor will develop the banner ad in ignorance of what news SI.com will cover in that section. So it is literally impossible for the sponsors to submit the pages on which their interactive promotional materials will appear because in many cases those pages will not exist until after the promotional materials have been submitted to the FDA under Form 2253.

Despite these problematic aspects of the Postmarketing Guidance, the industry generally welcomed the guidance, both because it was the first guidance to directly address the five questions from the 2009 hearings, and because many in industry saw the FDA as acknowledging some of the unique characteristics of social media and Internet communications and embracing a willingness to adapt regulatory requirements to meet these characteristics.[13] In particular, the FDA adopted a framework for the submission of information via Form 2253 that did not require every single interaction to be submitted via a separate submission, but instead to provide for monthly submissions that would enable real-time communication for sponsors of prescription drugs, biologics, and non-human animal drugs.[14]

Question 2: Space-limited Contexts

The 14 letters from 2009 cited Google paid search ads, and part of the challenge of providing those type of ads is that Google strictly constrains the character count that is available to provide a message. Consequently, the draft guidance on presenting risk information in space-limited contexts was certain to receive extensive discussion.[15]

FDA did provide a mechanism under certain circumstance to assure compliance of a message in such contexts with the provision of limited risk information, but at the same time, the FDA made clear that "some products" would not be able to meet the provisions of the guidance, and for those products, "the firm should reconsider using that platform" for promotional messages.[16] Industry saw this as a significant departure in the overall approach from that of the Postmarketing Guidance, which seemed to be enabling greater participation in these channels.

Another disappointing aspect of the guidance received from the FDA on this topic is its unwillingness to address the topic of mobile platforms.[17] While the initial five questions proposed by the FDA explicitly addressed the issue of mobile technology, FDA has disavowed any discussion of mobile technology in this guidance and has not announced any intention to provide guidance on that topic, despite the enormous growth of mobile technology.

In addition, FDA explicitly discusses in the Space-limited Guidance Google paid search ads. Unfortunately, its discussion demonstrates a misunderstanding of how Google's sitelinks work in paid search ads, and following FDA's proposal, would result in violative communications.[18]

Question 3: Correcting Misinformation

On the same day that FDA released the Space-limited Guidance, it also issued a guidance on correcting misinformation. The key questions for industry prior to this guidance's release were what obligation (if any) FDA believed industry had to engage in the correction of misinformation, whether FDA would hold industry accountable for the resulting information if it did attempt to correct information, and whether FDA would regard such activities as promotional labeling, subject to all of the labeling regulations.

In this guidance, FDA returned to the overarching approach of the Postmarketing Guidance, in that FDA put forth a position that encouraged industry to engage in such efforts[19] (though making clear that doing so was completely voluntary[20]), made clear that FDA would not regard such activities as promotional labeling (so long as the methodology set forth in the guidance was followed[21]), and that the FDA would not hold sponsors accountable for whether the misinformation was actually corrected.[22]

From an industry perspective, this seems to be the right answer to all of the questions that industry had prior to the guidance's release. This delight comes with a very large caveat that FDA has set up a process that some within industry might object to or find unduly burdensome. In particular, FDA has agreed that attempts to correct misinformation would not be regarded as promotional labeling, but the process it describes explicitly prohibits the use of promotional materials to correct misinformation, even if promotional materials would convey the appropriate correct information.[23]

In addition, some see a tension between FDA taking a widely expansive definition of influence when it comes to the 2253 filing requirement as set forth in the Postmarketing Guidance, and the much narrower definition of influence used in the Correcting Guidance. Indeed, in its efforts to provide a pathway to enable sponsors to engage in correcting misinformation, FDA is making clear that even if a company attempts to influence incorrect information, so long as it does so via non-promotional channels,[24] FDA will not consider the sponsor to be responsible for the resulting information. This is not a contradiction in FDA's reasoning, since it is applying the differing notions of influence to separate activities (promotion vs. non-promotional communications), but there definitely is a tension.

The Unanswered Questions

FDA has stated its intention to issue another social media guidance in 2014 via the Center for Drug Evaluation and Research (CDER) 2014 Guidance Agenda.[25] That guidance is intended to cover the topic of the appropriate use of hyperlinks. In its initial Federal Register notice, the FDA asked about whether the use of redirects[26] is OK to direct people to product websites and whether there needed to be any parameters established for the provision of links from a product website to information provided on non-company websites. Of course, FDA has already via the guidances presented made clear that it is comfortable with presenting much required information via links, but that other information cannot be presented solely via a link (such as risk information to meet the fair balance requirement).

Adverse Events

It is important to note that when FDA held its Part 15 hearings in 2009, there were so many people interested in discussing the issue of adverse events (AE), that FDA divided its agenda into two parts with the entire morning of day two dedicated solely to the topic of adverse event reporting. Clearly, this was an area where the public had a lot to say to the FDA, yet the FDA has not yet issued any further guidance about adverse event reporting in social media, and there is not any currently public statement about its intention to do so. For example, the current guidance agenda from CDER does not include any guidance in development about this topic.[27]

In the absence of any further guidance from FDA, there remains a schism within the industry. Some companies have taken the approach that so long as they do not actively monitor social media channels that they cannot be held accountable for submitting reports of adverse events in those channels, while other companies are actively mining social media channels to uncover potential adverse events and encouraging people to submit complete information to enable AE reporting.

Conclusion

Sponsors of prescription products subject to FDA promotional regulation have been by turns heartened and dismayed by the communications from the FDA about the use of social media. Regardless, the overarching situation remains the same. People, both consumers and health care professionals, are currently using social media and other new communications channels to access information about their products and to engage in discussion of those products. FDA has provided some preliminary guidance about these channels, and much remains unanswered. Most importantly, much will always remain unanswered, as it is not FDA's role to provide a road map to how to use social media correctly. Instead, FDA will set out some of the high-level regulatory requirements for communications within these channels, but given the ever-changing nature of these channels themselves, companies will always have to determine how to meet those requirements on a day-to-day basis. And they will either do so and participate in today's communication venues or they will choose to avoid them and gradually become irrelevant to the people who most need information about their products. ▲

1. The Pink Sheet Daily, April 6, 2009.
2. Draft Guidance for Industry: Presenting Risk Information in Prescription Drug and Medical Device Promotion ("Presenting Risk" hereinafter). Last accessed July 20, 2014, from http://www.fda.gov/downloads/Drugs/GuidanceComplianceRegulatoryInformation/Guidances/UCM155480.pdf

3. Presenting Risk Information, page 17n46.
4. Federal Register, 74 FR 48083 — Sep. 21, 2009, last accessed July 20, 2014 from http://www.gpo.gov/fdsys/pkg/FR-2009-09-21/pdf/E9-22618.pdf
5. I am here not discussing the 2011 guidance on addressing requests for off-label information, even though the FDA includes that guidance among its "social media guidances" on the web page dedicated to the topic. See http://www.fda.gov/AboutFDA/CentersOffices/OfficeofMedicalProductsandTobacco/CDER/ucm397791.htm Although that guidance discussed specific examples where social media was used, its primary purpose was to address a question that goes beyond the scope of the original five questions, and its guidance on the subject of using social media to address requests for off-label information could be fairly summarized as "Tell them to call or email you." For an overview of this guidance, see for example, http://www.scribd.com/doc/77257529/DH-Regulatory-Alert-Responding-to-Unsolicited-Requests
6. Draft Guidance to Industry: Fulfilling Regulatory Requirements for Postmarketing Submissions of Interactive Promotional Media for Prescription Human and Animal Drugs and Biologics. This guidance is herein referred to as "Postmarketing Guidance" and was last accessed on July 20, 2014 from the FDA website at http://www.fda.gov/downloads/Drugs/GuidanceComplianceRegulatoryInformation/Guidances/UCM381352.pdf
7. Postmarketing Guidance, page 5.
8. Note that Form 2253 is the form used by sponsors of prescription drugs and biologics for postmarketing submissions. The Postmarketing Guidance also applies to sponsors of drugs for non-human animals, who are required to use Form 2301. Otherwise, these requirements are the same, and I ignore this distinction in the following discussion and simply refer to these filings as "2253 filings" for simplicity.
9. Postmarketing Guidance, page 3.
10. Postmarketing Guidance, page 4.
11. Postmarketing Guidance, page 4.
12. Guidance for Industry: Internet/Social Media Platforms: Correcting Independent Third-Party Misinformation About Prescription Drugs and Medical Devices ("Correcting Guidance" hereinafter), page 4n6. Last accessed July 21, 2014, from http://www.fda.gov/downloads/Drugs/GuidanceComplianceRegulatoryInformation/Guidances/UCM401079.pdf
13. See, for example, the story by the Coalition for Healthcare Communications about the Postmarketing Guidance, published on January 14, 2014, http://www.cohealthcom.org/2014/01/14/fda-draft-guidance-addresses-postmarket-submission-of-online-promotional-material/
14. For further discussion of this guidance, see, for example, http://www.scribd.com/doc/199434412/DH-Regulatory-Alert-2253-Filing-Requirements-for-Social-Media
15. Draft Guidance for Industry: Internet/Social Media Platforms with Character Space Limitations— Presenting Risk and Benefit Information for Prescription Drugs and Medical Devices ("Space-limited Guidance" hereinafter). Last accessed July 20, 2014, from http://www.fda.gov/downloads/Drugs/GuidanceComplianceRegulatoryInformation/Guidances/UCM401087.pdf
16. Space-limited Guidance, page 5.
17. For more on this topic, see http://regulatoryrx.blogspot.com/2014/07/fda-still-not-ready-to-tackle-mobile.html and the FDA social media webinar Q&A from July 10, 2014, which was last accessed July 20, 2014 on the FDA website at http://www.fda.gov/AboutFDA/CentersOffices/OfficeofMedicalProductsandTobacco/CDER/ucm403810.htm
18. For a fuller discussion of why FDA's proposal on sitelinks would lead to non-compliant communications, see http://regulatoryrx.blogspot.com/2014/06/fda-was-wrong-about-google-functionality.html
19. Correcting Guidance, page 3, "FDA has determined it may benefit the public health for firms to correct misinformation about their products."
20. The guidance uses the word "voluntary" and its cognates six times throughout the draft guidance to refer to a company's attempt to correct misinformation.
21. Correcting Guidance, page 3, "If a firm voluntarily corrects misinformation in a truthful and non-misleading manner and as described in this draft guidance, FDA does not intend to object if the corrective information voluntarily provided by the firm does not satisfy otherwise applicable regulatory requirements regarding labeling or advertising, if any."
22. Correcting Guidance, page 8, "FDA will not hold a firm accountable for an independent third party's subsequent actions or lack thereof."
23. Correcting Guidance, page 6, "The information should not be provided by including a link to a promotional website even if the information is available on the promotional website."
24. And in accordance with the remaining procedure set forth in the Correcting Guidance.
25. The guidance agenda is released twice each year. The most recent version is available at http://www.fda.gov/downloads/Drugs/GuidanceComplianceRegulatoryInformation/Guidances/UCM314767.pdf
26. Redirects are URLs that take a user to a destination URL that is not identical to the URL that is displayed (e.g., the URL bit.ly/9skHKH takes users to http://www.scribd.com/dale_cooke).
27. See the CDER 2014 Guidance Agenda at http://www.fda.gov/downloads/Drugs/GuidanceComplianceRegulatoryInformation/Guidances/UCM314767.pdf

Relevant FDA Draft Guidances

The following guidances are included in this primer because they are relevant to the primer's focus. These guidances are the most current version as of the date of this primer's publication.
To ensure that you are working from the most current version of FDA's guidances, you should always refer to the FDA's website housing all of its guidances about prescription drugs:
https://www.fda.gov/Drugs/GuidanceComplianceRegulatoryInformation/Guidances/default.htm

Appendix D.

Draft Guidance on Presenting Risk Information

Guidance for Industry
Presenting Risk Information in Prescription Drug and Medical Device Promotion

DRAFT GUIDANCE

This guidance document is being distributed for comment purposes only.

Comments and suggestions regarding this draft document should be submitted within 90 days of publication in the *Federal Register* of the notice announcing the availability of the draft guidance. Submit comments to the Division of Dockets Management (HFA-305), Food and Drug Administration, 5630 Fishers Lane, rm. 1061, Rockville, MD 20852. All comments should be identified with the docket number listed in the notice of availability that publishes in the *Federal Register*.

For questions regarding this draft document contact (CDER) Kristin Davis at 301-796-1200, (CBER) Ele Ibarra-Pratt at 301-827-3028, (CVM) Martine Hartogensis at 240-453-6833, or (CDRH) Ann Simoneau at 240-276-0100.

U.S. Department of Health and Human Services
Food and Drug Administration
Center for Drug Evaluation and Research (CDER)
Center for Biologics Evaluation and Research (CBER)
Center for Veterinary Medicine (CVM)
Center for Devices and Radiological Health (CDRH)

May 2009

Guidance for Industry

Presenting Risk Information in Prescription Drug and Medical Device Promotion

Additional copies are available from:

Office of Communication, Training and Manufacturers Assistance, HFM-40
Center for Biologics Evaluation and Research
Food and Drug Administration
1401 Rockville Pike, Rockville, MD 20852-1448
http://www.fda.gov/cber/guidelines.htm.
(Tel) at 800-835-4709 or 301-827-1800

Office of Communication, Education and Radiological Programs
Division of Small Manufacturers, International and Consumer Assistance (HFZ-220)
Center for Devices and Radiological Health
Food and Drug Administration
1350 Piccard Drive
Rockville, MD 20850-4307 U.S.A.
http://www.fda.gov/cdrh/ggpmain.html
Email: dsmica@cdrh.fda.gov
Fax: 240.276.3151
(Tel) 800-638-2041 or 240-276-3150

Office of Training and Communication
Division of Drug Information, HFD-240
Center for Drug Evaluation and Research
Food and Drug Administration
5600 Fishers Lane
Rockville, MD 20857
(Tel) 301-827-4573
http://www.fda.gov/cder/guidance/index.htm

Communications Staff, HFV-12
Center for Veterinary Medicine
Food and Drug Administration
7500 Standish Place,
Rockville, MD 20855
(Tel) 301-594-1755
http://www.fda.gov/cvm/guidance/guidance.html

U.S. Department of Health and Human Services
Food and Drug Administration
Center for Drug Evaluation and Research (CDER)
Center for Biologics Evaluation and Research (CBER)
Center for Veterinary Medicine (CVM)
Center for Devices and Radiological Health (CDRH)
May 2009

TABLE OF CONTENTS

Guidance for Industry Presenting Risk Information in Prescription Drug and Medical Device Promotion

This draft guidance, when finalized, will represent the Food and Drug Administration's (FDA's) current thinking on this topic. It does not create or confer any rights for or on any person and does not operate to bind FDA or the public. You can use an alternative approach if the approach satisfies the requirements of the applicable statutes and regulations. If you want to discuss an alternative approach, contact the FDA staff responsible for implementing this guidance. If you cannot identify the appropriate FDA staff, call the appropriate number listed on the title page of this guidance.

I. INTRODUCTION

This draft guidance describes factors FDA considers when evaluating advertisements (ads) and promotional labeling for prescription drugs,[1] ads for restricted medical devices,[2] and promotional labeling for all medical devices for their compliance with the Federal Food, Drug, and Cosmetic Act (the FD&C Act or the Act) and relevant regulations.[3] The draft guidance discusses factors that are relevant to the disclosure of risk information and provides numerous examples to illustrate FDA's thinking on these factors. This guidance responds to stakeholder requests for specific guidance on how FDA evaluates prescription drug and medical device promotional pieces to determine whether they adequately present risk information. The recommendations contained in this draft guidance apply to promotional materials directed to both consumers and healthcare professionals.

---

[1] This draft guidance does not address over-the-counter (OTC) drug promotional labeling, which FDA also regulates. FDA encourages all manufacturers to ensure that their promotional labeling is truthful and non-misleading. FDA recognizes that the marketing status of animal drugs may vary, depending upon the intended species. For example, several anthelmintics on the market are available only by prescription for dogs and cats, yet very similar products are available OTC for horses and food animals. OTC drugs intended for food animals, in particular, may carry significant risks that may affect not only the intended food animal, but also other animal species and humans. OTC promotional labeling for animal drugs should convey the serious risks associated with use of the products, especially those affecting the public health.

[2] Devices may become restricted, either by regulation issued under section 520(e) of the Act (21 U.S.C. 360j(e), or by order approving an application for premarket approval (PMA), pursuant to section 515(d)(1)(B)(ii) (21 U.S.C. 360e(d)(1)(B)(ii)).

[3] This draft guidance also does not apply to those *reminder* promotions (labeling or advertising that calls attention to the name of a drug or device but does not include indications, dosage recommendations, or other information) that are exempted by regulation from the requirements under the FD&C Act for the disclosure of risk information. See 21 CFR 200.200, 201.100(f), 201.105(d)(2), 202.1(e)(2)(i), 801.109(d). But see 21 U.S.C. 352(r) (requiring certain risk information in all restricted device advertisements).

Although this draft guidance focuses on the presentation of risk information in prescription drug and medical device promotion, the factors relating to effective communication outlined below are also applicable to the presentation of benefit information in promotion. Indeed, when FDA evaluates promotional pieces for compliance with the Act and relevant regulations, it determines whether claims about both risk and benefit of the product are accurate and non-misleading, and it also looks at whether risks and benefits are presented in a comparably prominent manner. Thus, considerations involving the content and format of benefit information are an inherent part of FDA's evaluation of risk presentations in promotional pieces. FDA recommends that companies take the factors outlined in this document into account when developing both risk and benefit presentations in their promotional pieces, as the public health is best served when risk and effectiveness information about drug and device products is clearly and accurately communicated.

FDA's guidance documents, including this draft guidance, do not establish legally enforceable responsibilities. Instead, guidances describe FDA's current thinking on a topic and should be viewed only as recommendations, unless specific regulatory or statutory requirements are cited. The use of the word *should* in Agency guidances means that something is suggested or recommended, but not required.

II. BACKGROUND

The regulation of prescription drug and medical device promotion to healthcare professionals and consumers is a broad and complex topic.[4] This document addresses one key aspect of this topic – the presentation of risk information. FDA believes it is critically important to disclose risk information in prescription drug and medical device promotion appropriately and effectively to healthcare professionals and consumers.[5] This information helps consumers know whether drugs or devices may be appropriate for them as well as what they should tell their healthcare professionals about before taking or using or while taking or using a product. It also lets consumers know what risks they might experience and what steps they need to take for safety reasons (e.g., no driving) because of taking or using a product. Appropriate risk disclosures help healthcare professionals by giving them some of the information they need to know about the product that will enable them to safely use or prescribe it. Recently published industry guidelines encourage manufacturers to develop prescription medicine promotion that is

[4] Although beyond the scope of this document, the complexity of the topic can be demonstrated by past studies that have shown potential positive and negative effects of direct-to-consumer (DTC) advertising for prescription drugs. For example, FDA research suggests that DTC advertising seems to increase awareness of conditions and treatments, to motivate questions for the healthcare provider, and to help patients ask better questions. Yet this research also suggests that almost half of physicians feel some pressure to prescribe as a result of DTC advertising, and patients and physicians report a belief that these ads overstate the drug product's efficacy and do not present a fair balance of benefit and risk information. For the complete study results, see K. Aikin, J. Swasy & A. Braman, Patient and Physician Attitudes and Behaviors Associated With DTC Promotion of Prescription Drugs – Summary of FDA Survey Research Results, Final Report, November 19, 2004, available at: http://www.fda.gov/cder/ddmac/Final%20Report/FRfinal111904.pdf.

[5] Effectively disclosing risk information also requires a consideration of whether an advertisement or promotional material over warns. For example, a drug advertisement that includes a listing of side effects that are not included in the drug's approved labeling may lead to under-emphasis of the most important and serious risks. FDA takes care to ensure that important risk information is included in the drug's approved labeling, and sponsors have an obligation to update their labeling with appropriate new safety information. 21 CFR 201.57(c)(6); 201.80(e). Nothing in this guidance should be construed as recommending that the sponsor of a drug include in advertising or promotional materials risk information not in the product's approved labeling or appropriate for inclusion in the labeling. See 73 Fed. Reg. 2848, 2851 (January 16, 2008).

"designed to achieve a balanced presentation of both the benefits and the risks associated with the advertised" product.[6]

However, omission or minimization of risk information is the most frequent violation of the regulations cited in advertising and promotion enforcement letters sent to sponsors, and illustrative research in one of the areas this guidance covers, direct-to-consumer prescription drug advertising, has shown that 60 percent of patients believe ads directed at them do not provide enough information about risks, 60 percent of physicians believe that patients have little or no understanding from these ads about what the possible risks and negative effects of the products are, and 72 percent of physicians believe that patients have little or no understanding from these ads about who should not use the product.[7]

FDA is issuing this draft guidance to aid sponsors in effectively communicating risk information in their promotion to both healthcare professionals and consumers. This draft guidance describes how FDA reviews prescription drug and medical device promotional pieces to determine whether they adequately present risk information. The document begins with some background information, including a brief overview of legal requirements and a discussion of policy considerations related to drug and device promotional materials. The draft guidance then describes factors FDA considers when reviewing risk communication in promotional materials. Because the principles within this guidance are based on universal concepts of communication and understanding of risk information, the guidance will address promotion aimed at both lay consumer and healthcare professional audiences.

A. LEGAL OVERVIEW

Under the FD&C Act and FDA's implementing regulations, promotional pieces (such as promotional labeling for drugs and devices and advertisements for prescription drugs and restricted devices) making claims about a product are deemed misleading if they fail to disclose certain information about the product's risks.[8] Generally, to comply with the FD&C Act and FDA's implementing regulations, such promotional pieces:[9]

— Cannot be false or misleading in any particular[10]

— Must reveal material facts about the product being promoted, including facts about the consequences that can result from use of the product as suggested in the promotional piece[11]

---

[6] PhRMA, PhRMA Guiding Principles Direct to Consumer Advertisements About Prescription Medicines, Principle 11, November 2005, available at: http://www.phrma.org/files/DTCGuidingprinciples.pdf.

[7] K. Aikin, J. Swasy & A. Braman, Patient and Physician Attitudes and Behaviors Associated With DTC Promotion of Prescription Drugs – Summary of FDA Survey Research Results, Final Report, November 19, 2004, available at: http://www.fda.gov/cder/ddmac/Final%20Report/FRfinal111904.pdf.

[8] The relevant statutory provisions and regulations are discussed in more detail in the Attachment to this guidance.

[9] The terms *promotional piece*, *promotional materials*, and *promotional communications* are used in this guidance to refer generally to both advertising and promotional labeling, regardless of format. Promotional materials include, among others, television ads, brochures, booklets, detailing pieces, internet web sites, print ads, exhibits, and sound recordings or radio ads. As noted in the introduction, this guidance applies to all types of promotion for prescription drugs, advertisements for restricted devices and promotional labeling for all devices.

[10] Drugs and devices are misbranded under the Act if their labeling is false or misleading in any particular (21 U.S.C. 352(a)). Similarly, prescription drugs and restricted devices are misbranded if their advertising is false or misleading in any particular (21 U.S.C. 352(n) & (q)(1); 21 CFR 202.1(e)(5)(i)).

and

— Should present information about effectiveness and information about risk in a balanced manner[12]

This draft guidance document describes factors FDA considers when evaluating risk disclosure in prescription drug and medical device promotional materials to determine whether these materials comply with the statutory and regulatory requirements. The draft guidance also makes recommendations about how manufacturers can develop the content and format of promotional communications to comply with these requirements. The examples and recommendations provided are intended to provide guidance and illustrate possible approaches; manufacturers are free to use alternative approaches if these approaches satisfy the requirements of the statute and regulations. Unless otherwise specified in this draft guidance, the principles set forth below apply to all promotional pieces, regardless of the medium used or the target audience.

B. POLICY OVERVIEW

Section III of this guidance highlights several factors, including those related to content and format, that FDA uses to evaluate the risk communication in a promotional piece. We recommend that manufacturers consider these factors when trying to achieve effective risk communication. It is important to emphasize that when FDA evaluates the risk communication in a promotional piece, FDA looks not just at specific risk-related statements, but at the ***net impression*** – i.e., the message communicated by all elements of the piece as a whole. The purpose of the evaluation is to determine whether the piece ***as a whole*** conveys an accurate and non-misleading impression of the benefits and risks of the promoted product. Manufacturers should therefore focus not just on individual claims or presentations, but on the promotional piece as a whole.[13] A promotional communication that conveys a deceptive net impression of the product could be misleading, even if specific individual claims or presentations are not misleading.

FDA's consideration of the net impression of risk information is based on well-developed social science principles supported by decades of scientific research[14] and is consistent with the approach of other agencies and organizations. For example, the Federal Trade Commission (FTC) uses the interpretation of the net impression of the piece to determine whether a promotional piece is likely to mislead a consumer.[15] Pharmaceutical industry members have also conducted social science research showing that, when evaluating a promotional piece, the net impression conveyed by the piece as a whole is an important element to consider, independent of individual statements within the piece.

---

[11] 21 U.S.C. 321(n); 21 CFR 1.21 & 202.1(e)(5)(iii).

[12] See 21 CFR 202.1(e)(5)(ii).

[13] Manufacturers should note that, although this guidance focuses on risk disclosures in promotional pieces, any claims in a promotional piece that are misleading, whether risk-related or not, can cause the product being promoted to become misbranded (21 U.S.C. 352(a), (n) & (q)(1); 21 CFR 202.1(e)(5)(i)).

[14] For reviews of this field, see Kimble, G.A. (1985) The psychology of learning enters its second century. In Hammonds, B.L. (Ed.), *Psychology and learning.* Washington, DC: American Psychological Association (pp. 5-47) and Mayer, R.E. (2003) Memory and information processes. In Reynolds, W.M., & Miller, G.E. (Eds.), *Handbook of Psychology: Educational Psychology, 7.* New York: John Wiley & Sons, Inc. (pp. 47-57).

[15] See Federal Trade Commission, FTC Policy Statement on Deception, (Oct. 14, 1983), appended to *FTC v. Cliffdale Associates, Inc., et al.,* 103 F.T.C. 110, 170 (1984) (hereinafter "FTC Policy Statement on Deception" with page references to 103 F.T.C. 110).

Section III of the guidance contains examples of how various aspects of content and format can contribute to a misleading net impression in promotional pieces. The following two examples also illustrate this.

> *Example 1*: A broadcast television ad for a cholesterol-lowering drug contains a factually accurate audio risk statement that discloses the drug's major side effects and contraindications. This audio presentation is accompanied by quick scene changes showing comforting visual images of patients benefiting from the drug. It is also accompanied by loud, upbeat music. In this case, the audio disclosure may not adequately communicate risks because of the accompanying discordant visuals and distracting music.
>
> *Example 2*: A one-page prescription drug ad for an arthritis drug, run in a medical journal, prominently presents the following headline claims in large bolded font and with abundant surrounding white space:
>
> - ***Benefits!* DrugX is proven safe and effective for the relief of arthritis pain and stiffness**,
> - ***Difference!* DrugX's unique gel formulation is convenient and easy to use**, and
> - ***Reason to Believe!* Drug X is the most frequently prescribed arthritis drug in the United States**
>
> The bottom of the page contains an inconspicuous statement in small, non-bolded font and without surrounding white space: "Like all arthritis medications, Drug X has been associated with a risk of serious infection." The emphasis on benefit information in this piece – in terms of the way the information is formatted and framed – overwhelms the risk information and may cause readers to receive an erroneous impression that the drug is safer than it has proven to be, even though the statements themselves may be factually accurate.

Using the factors explained in Part III of this draft guidance, trained professionals at FDA with expertise in areas including communication, drug information, medicine and law, apply these factors and evaluate claims in promotional pieces from the perspective of a reasonable consumer. As FDA has stated,[16] the agency believes that the reasonable consumer standard is the appropriate standard to use in determining whether a claim in the labeling of a dietary supplement or conventional food is misleading. The agency confirms that the reasonable consumer standard will be used to evaluate communications covered by this guidance document. The *reasonable consumer standard* used by FDA in evaluating promotional materials is similar to the FTC standard:

> [W]e examine the practice from the perspective of a consumer acting reasonably in the circumstances. If the representation or practice affects or is directed primarily to a particular group, the Commission examines reasonableness from the perspective of that group.[17]

---

[16] Guidance for Industry: Qualified Health Claims in the Labeling of Conventional Foods and Dietary Supplements (Dec. 2002) (replaced by Guidance for Industry and FDA: Interim Procedures for Qualified Health Claims in the Labeling of Conventional Food and Human Dietary Supplements (July 2003)); see 70 Fed. Reg. 824 (Jan. 5, 2005) (noting that, although the Guidance for Industry on Qualified Health Claims in Labeling of Conventional Foods and Dietary Supplements (Dec. 2002) "has been 'replaced' by subsequent guidance, the agency has not abandoned the position in the 2002 guidance regarding reasonable consumer standard").

[17] See FTC Policy Statement on Deception at 170.

This standard does not preclude multiple interpretations of a claim, as long as they are reasonable. As the FTC's Policy Statement provides:

> To be considered reasonable, the interpretation or reaction does not have to be the only one. When a seller's representation conveys more than one meaning to reasonable consumers, one of which is false, the seller is liable for the misleading interpretation.[18]

In applying the reasonable consumer standard, FDA, like FTC, takes into account the different levels of expertise of lay consumers and healthcare professionals. Due to their training and experience, healthcare professionals develop a level of knowledge related to scientific concepts and medical conditions and products that lay consumers do not possess. FDA takes this difference in knowledge and experience into account when assessing promotional materials directed at healthcare professionals versus those directed at lay audiences. However, research has shown that experts (in this case, healthcare professionals) are subject to the same cognitive biases and processing limitations as non-experts.[19]

Cognitive science research has demonstrated that all people, regardless of expertise, are only able to think through and process a limited amount of information at one time.[20] However, our ability to process information can be greatly improved by considering and controlling for the factors that affect attention and comprehension. This guidance discusses those factors, how we apply them to our review of promotional materials, and what manufacturers can do to ensure that their materials comply with the regulations.

III. FACTORS CONSIDERED IN THE REVIEW OF RISK COMMUNICATION

FDA relies on a vast scientific body of knowledge regarding human cognition in assessing which factors to consider in evaluating promotional pieces and making regulatory decisions about the presentation of risk information. The following sections highlight factors that FDA considers when determining whether risk information is communicated in a fashion consistent with the regulations.

---

[18] *Id.* at 177.

[19] Although physicians generally do not believe that they are influenced by advertising, (Spiller & Wymer, 2001), research has shown that physicians are influenced by promotional activities (e.g., advertising: Avorn et al., 1982; sales representatives: Gonul et al., 2001). Avorn, J., Chen, M. & Hartley, R. (1982) Scientific versus commercial sources of influence on the prescribing behavior of physicians. *American Journal of Medicine, 73*, 4-8. Gonul, F.F., Carter, F., Petrova, E., & Srinivasan, K. (2001) Promotion of prescription drugs and its impact on physicians' choice behavior. *Journal of Marketing, 65*, 79-90. Spiller, L.D., & Wymer, W.W. (2001) Physicians' perceptions and uses of commercial drug information sources: An examination of pharmaceutical marketing to physicians. *Health Marketing Quarterly, 19*, 91-106.

[20] See, e.g., Lavie, N. (2001) Capacity limits in selective attention: Behavioral evidence and implications for neural activity. In Braun, J., Koch, C., et al. (Eds.), *Visual attention and cortical circuits.* Cambridge, MA: The MIT Press (pp. 49-68); Miller, G.A. (1994) The magical number seven, plus or minus two: Some limits on our capacity for processing information. Reprinted in Gutfreund, H., & Toulouse, G. (Eds.), Biology and computation: A physicist's choice. River Edge, NJ: World Scientific Publishing Co. (pp. 207-233); Shapiro, K. (Ed.) (2001) *The limits of attention: Temporal constraints in human information processing.* London: Oxford University Press.

A. GENERAL CONSIDERATIONS

This section explores some important factors that relate to both the content and the format of a promotional piece. FDA will consider the use of language and signals and how information is framed and ordered.

1. *Consistent Use of Language Appropriate for Target Audience*

Both language used to communicate benefits and language used to communicate risks should be comprehensible to the same audience for a piece to be considered accurate and non-misleading. Thus, promotional materials directed to professionals can reasonably describe benefits and risks in medical language, but promotional materials directed to consumers should convey benefits and risks in language understandable to consumers.[21]

> *Example 3:* A consumer-directed ad for a drug that presents benefit claims in consumer friendly language should mention a risk of "fainting," not "syncope."

With respect to consumer-directed materials, FDA encourages manufacturers to present both benefit and risk information in clear, understandable, and non-technical language for consumer audiences.[22]

2. *Use of Signals*

Signaling is an important component of information communication.[23] In written materials, *signaling* has been defined as the use of "writing devices designed to emphasize aspects of a text's structure or content without altering the information in the text."[24] Headlines and subheads are examples of commonly used signals.[25] Depending on the circumstance, "accurate information in the text may not remedy a false headline [or signal] because reasonable consumers may only glance at the headline" and skip the

---

[21] See Root, J., & Stableford, S. (1999) Easy-to-read consumer communications: A missing link in Medicaid managed care. *Journal of Health Politics, Policy, & Law, 24*, 1-26.

[22] Although not a true measure of "understandability," text reading level, often expressed as "grade level," is one way to assess text difficulty. Text that scores at a higher grade level (e.g., 12th grade) is considered more complex than text scoring at a lower grade level (e.g., 8th grade). Several validated reading level measures are available to provide an approximate measure of text complexity. See, e.g., Kincaid, J.P., Fishburne, R., Rogers, R.L., Chissom, B.S. (1975) *Derivation of New Readability Formulas (Automated Reliability Index, Fog Count, and Flesch Reading Ease Formula) for Navy Enlisted Personnel.* Research Branch Report 8-75. Memphis: Naval Air Station; McLaughlin, G.H. (1969) SMOG grading: A new readability formula. *Journal of Reading, 12*, 639-646; Mosenthal, P.B. (1998) A new measure of assessing document complexity: The PMOSE/IKIRSCH document readability formula. *Journal of Adolescent and Adult Literacy*, 41, 620-638. We encourage manufacturers to test text *comprehensibility* as well.

[23] Loman, N.L., & Mayer, R.E. (1983) Signaling techniques that increase the understandability of expository prose. *Journal of Educational Psychology, 75*, 402-412; Meyer, B.J.F. (2003) Text coherence and readability. *Topics in Language Disorders, 23*, 204-224; Spyridakis, J.H., & Standal, T.C. (1987) Signals in expository prose: Effects on reading comprehension. *Reading Research Quarterly, 22*, 285-298.

[24] Lorch, R.F., Lorch, E.P., & Inman, W.E. (1993) Effects of signaling structure on text recall. *Journal of Educational Psychology, 85*, 281-290, p. 281.

[25] Hyona, J., & Lorch, R.F. (2004) Effects of topic headings on text processing: Evidence from adult readers' eye fixation patterns. *Learning and Instruction, 14*, 131-152.

remainder of the text.[26] Signals are also used in broadcast situations, such as when an announcer draws attention to different items of information, when a word on the screen identifies a new topic, or when headlines emphasize some messages but not others.

When reviewing promotional materials, FDA looks to see if the use of signals is consistent across benefit and risk information, so that the materials provide accurate and non-misleading impressions of a drug or device.

> *Example 4:* If a piece contains headlines that signal benefit information, (e.g., "Drug X Provides Highly Effective Control"), some sort of headline should also signal risk information (e.g., "Side Effects for Drug X").

However, the mere presence of similar signals for both benefit and risk information is not necessarily sufficient to make a piece accurate and non-misleading. The content of the signals is also important. Certain headlines may *frame* (see next section) subsequent risk information in ways that emphasize or minimize its importance.

> *Example 5:* The headline "Important Risk Information about Device X" is preferable to "Important Information about Device X" because the former headline indicates what type of information follows. Similarly, "Common Side Effects Seen with Drug X," is preferable to "Other Information about Drug X." Specific and clear signals are preferable because they are more effective than vague or abstract terms.

Presenting risk information with no signal, or beginning the presentation of risk information with unrelated information (e.g. presenting risk information in a paragraph that begins with information on indication or dosing) can also minimize the risks of the product and mislead the audience. For example, the headlines in the following example convey additional benefit information, potentially misleading the audience about the overall risk-benefit profile of the product.

> *Example 6:* Placing risk information under headlines such as "Now Approved for Epilepsy" or "Safe Enough for Children Under 5" minimizes the risk information that follows, particularly if individuals only look at the headlines. Instead, headlines preceding risk presentations should signal that a risk presentation follows, for example, "Important Risk Information About Drug X."

In videos, broadcast ads, and other promotional pieces with audio components, a change of announcer or a statement in the audio portion of the piece to signal to the audience that risk information follows can aid effective communication. However, manufacturers should consider comparable voice characteristics, as discussed in Section III.C.2. Risk information may also be signaled graphically or visually. Similar to print pieces, specific and straightforward audio signals are most likely to adequately convey risk information.

3. Framing Risk Information

FDA evaluates how risk information is framed because framing can affect the presentation of risks and benefits in a promotional piece. Framing commonly refers to how a particular piece of information is stated or conveyed, such as by emphasizing either the positive or negative aspects of the information or by presenting the information in vague versus specific terms. Research consistently shows that framing

[26] FTC Policy Statement on Deception at 182.

the same information in different ways can change the way audience members respond to that information.[27] Thus, the way information is phrased can significantly influence the message the audience receives from a promotional piece.

Framing risk information in non-specific terms can undermine the effective communication of that information to the audience. Risk information should be presented in the same terms or with the same degree of specificity as benefit information. For example, if a promotional piece refers to the product by name in presenting efficacy information, it should refer to the product by name in presenting risk information, rather than by referring to the product's device or drug class.

> *Example 7:* If the benefit information refers to the brand name, "Drug X," then "Common side effects associated with Drug X" would be preferable to "Common side effects associated with [the generic name]."

Moreover, within the risk information presentation, phrases such as "*Like all medicines*, Drug X has some side effects," may have the effect of minimizing the risks that follow. Framing risk information in a way that minimizes the severity of a risk event may also cause a promotional piece to be considered false or misleading.

> *Example 8:* If a drug's package insert contains a boxed warning about the risk of life-threatening fevers associated with its use and reports that 55 percent of patients taking the drug experience dizziness, a statement such as "Adverse events associated with drug X include fevers. Some patients experienced dizziness" misleadingly describes the risk profile of the drug by failing to convey the seriousness of the fevers and the frequency of the dizziness. Statements like "Life-threatening fevers have been reported with the use of Drug X" and "More than half of patients taking Drug X experienced dizziness" would convey the seriousness and frequency of the two risks appropriately.

In addition, the risks conveyed in the piece should be framed in a way that accurately reflects their nature.

> *Example 9:* A statement such as "continuation of therapy may necessitate certain monitoring" is too vague for a product that requires monthly blood tests to check for liver damage. This statement fails to convey the risk of liver damage and also misleadingly suggests that routine monitoring may ***not*** be necessary for some patients. A statement like "Monthly blood tests should be performed to check for liver damage" would accurately convey the type of monitoring needed and the risk involved.

4. Hierarchy of Risk Information

FDA considers the ordering of risks within a presentation an important factor in determining the risk profile conveyed by a piece, regardless of whether it is directed toward healthcare professionals or

[27] See Armstrong, K., Schwartz, J.S., Fitzgerald, G., Putt, M., & Ubel, P.A. (2002) Effect of framing as gain versus loss on understanding and hypothetical treatment choices: survival and mortality curves. *Medical Decision Making, 22*, 76-83; Dunegan, K.J. (1993) Framing, cognitive modes, and imagery theory: Toward an understanding of a glass half full. *Journal of Applied Psychology, 78*, 491-503; Rothman, A.J., & Salovey, P. (1997) Shaping perceptions to motivate healthy behavior: The role of message framing. *Psychological Bulletin, 121*, 3-19; Smith, S.M., & Petty, R.E. (1996) Message framing and persuasion: A message processing analysis. *Personality and Social Psychology Bulletin, 22*, 257-268; Tversky, A., & Kahneman, D. (1981) The framing of decisions and the psychology of choice. *Science, 211*, 453-458.

consumers. As discussed in Section III.B.2 (below) and reflected in the format of the package insert for prescription drugs and medical devices, risks associated with a specific product are assigned a hierarchy of importance.

Memory research consistently shows that, in an experimental setting, when people process an entire list or text, they are better able to recall items at the beginning and the end than items in the middle.[28] Consequently, in a broadcast ad, where viewers do not have the opportunity to control the speed at which information is presented to help them to process it, the beginning or end, or both, should be reserved for the most important risk information. On the other hand, when reading a print promotional piece under normal circumstances, readers may lose interest toward the end of a lengthy paragraph, and it is not likely that the information at the end will be as well-comprehended as the information at the beginning. If a product's most important risks are located in the middle of a list of less important risks, the important risks may not be effectively communicated. FDA therefore recommends that the most important risk information, including relevant warnings and contraindications, be placed or stated first, especially in print materials. As discussed in Section III.C.1 (below), manufacturers should also note, however, that risk information should not just be presented in one location in a piece, but should, like benefit information, appear as an integral part of the piece.

FDA also considers the order in which risk information is presented to determine whether this ordering suggests that certain risks apply only to certain populations or only under certain conditions when this is not the case.

> *Example 10:* A statement in a broadcast ad that "Patients should not drink alcohol when taking Drug X. Common side effects are drowsiness and nausea" may suggest that these side effects occur only if alcohol is consumed when taking the drug. Instead, the sponsor should consider adding intervening information or changing the order of the presentation so that it is clear the side effects listed are not caused by drinking alcohol while taking the drug.

B. CONSIDERATIONS OF CONTENT

This section discusses how FDA evaluates the content of risk presentations in determining whether a promotional piece is accurate and non-misleading.

1. Quantity

One content factor FDA considers is the amount or quantity of information conveyed by a promotional piece. For example, a 30-second broadcast ad is likely to present less information than a 60-second broadcast ad. As the amount of benefit information conveyed increases, the amount of risk information conveyed should similarly increase.

The quantity of information presented can affect the net impression of the piece. The amount of information presented is one component that, together with choice of words, color, graphics, voiceover, and other aspects of the piece, can affect *cognitive load*, the mental effort required to understand the

---

[28] See Botvinik, M.M., & Plaut, D.C. (2006) Short-term memory for serial order: A recurrent neural network model. *Psychological Review, 113*, 201-233; Capitani, E.; della Sala, S.; Logie, R.H.; & Spinnier, H. (1992) Recency, primacy, and memory: Reappraising and standardizing the serial position curve. *Cortex, 28*, 315-342; Murdock, B.B. (1962) The serial position effect of free recall. *Journal of Experimental Psychology, 64*, 482-488.

various components of information in the piece.[29] If the benefit information is easily understood and maintained through repetition or other reinforcing techniques, and the risk information is not similarly reinforced, the net impression may not be appropriately balanced.

To ensure comparable benefit and risk presentations, manufacturers should consider the space or time devoted to benefits and risks, the comprehensibility of the language used, and the information provided on benefits and risks. FDA will look to see that promotional communications allot sufficient time and space to convey the important benefits and risks of the product being promoted to ensure that, ***as a whole***, the communication provides an accurate and non-misleading impression of the product.

A promotional piece with several paragraphs of information regarding benefits differs from a piece consisting mainly of one-line benefit claims. The treatment of risk information in each piece should be comparable to the treatment of benefit information, including how it is conveyed.

Promotional pieces do not have to convey an identical number of benefits and risks, and a given drug or device may have few or many risks.[30] FDA considers these factors when determining the comparability of benefits and risks in a piece:

— The number of statements about benefits and risks
— The completeness and depth of detail given about benefits and risks
— The amount of time (in both the audio and visual portions) devoted to benefits and risks in a video, audio, or broadcast communication
— The amount of space devoted to benefits and risks in a print communication
— The use of audio or visual components that enhance or distract from the presentation of risk or benefit information

As stated in the Background and discussed above, FDA evaluates the net impression created by promotional communications. This evaluation includes considering the above factors as well as the differences in the inherent risks associated with various drugs or devices. Simply satisfying one of the above factors (e.g., devoting the same amount of time or space to risk and benefit information) will not necessarily make a promotional piece accurate and non-misleading. Furthermore, certain important risk information should be in all promotional pieces regardless of their length (*see* Section III.B.2 below).

2. *Materiality and Comprehensiveness*

Generally speaking, *materiality* is determined by the degree to which information is objectively important, relevant, or substantial to the target audience. A promotional piece that omits material information about a product's risks could be considered misleading even if the piece devotes similar space or time to risk and effectiveness presentations.[31]

---

[29] See Mayer, R.E., & Moreno, R. (2003) Nine ways to reduce cognitive load in multimedia learning. *Educational Psychologist, 38*, 43-52; Pass, F., Renkl, A., & Sweller, J. (2004) Cognitive load theory: Instructional implications of the interaction between information structures and cognitive architecture. *Instructional Science, 32*, 1-8.

[30] If the drug or device being promoted is associated with a minimal number of risks, and *all* of these risks are conveyed in a format that is comparably prominent to the presentation of benefit information, then the risk presentation in such an ad or promotional labeling piece would be considered accurate, non-misleading and balanced even if the ad presented several more benefit than risk claims.

[31] 21 U.S.C. 321(n); see also 21 CFR 1.21 & 202.1(e)(5)(iii). Please see the Attachment to this document for a full description of the relevant requirements.

Material facts are those that would influence reasonable consumers (or healthcare professionals when they are the intended audience) about a product. Material facts include those that influence such people's understanding of the following:

- The relevant properties of a product
- Whether or not the product is appropriate for them or their patients
- Whether or not they are willing to accept the risks or burdens associated with using or prescribing a product

Some drug and device risks are material regardless of the amount or type of benefit claims in a piece. The most serious risks set forth in a product's labeling are generally material to ***any*** presentation of efficacy. A promotional piece that communicates a product's benefits should similarly communicate the most serious risks involved in using the product. Similarly, the most frequently occurring risks would usually be material to consumers and healthcare professionals in promotion, particularly if a product is only associated with a small number of more serious risks, because of the likelihood that they will affect patients taking the drug or using the device.

- Consideration of Target Audience

FDA considers the target audience of a promotional piece to be critical in determining what risk information is material. FDA evaluates the promotion from the perspective of a reasonable member of the targeted population (e.g., consumers, specific patient populations, healthcare professionals). As is explored in more detail below (e.g., Examples 11 and 13), different information can be material to different audiences. For example, in a piece promoting use of a product in a selected class of patients, risks especially applicable to that selected class of patients are material (see "The Nature of Benefit Claims," below).[32]

Generally speaking, communications directed to healthcare professionals should convey the most critical information they need to know about the product to help them decide whether it is appropriate for their patients and to help enable them to safely use the product or counsel patients on the safe use of the product. Consumer-directed communications should generally convey the following:

- What the drug or device is used for
- Who should or should not take a drug or use a device
- What can be expected from a drug or device
- What patients should ask their healthcare professionals about a drug or device
- What patients should tell their healthcare professionals about before or while taking a drug or using a device

Example 11: A drug's package insert includes a warning for healthcare professionals about dosing adjustments in patients with kidney disease. This information is material for healthcare professionals, both because of the seriousness indicated by its warning status and because of its relevance to safe prescribing. However, although this information is important to the safe use of the drug and should be considered by prescribers, it is not material to consumers, although the reasons for such care in dosing (e.g., the consequences of inappropriate dosing) could be.

[32] See 21 CFR 202.1(e)(7)(x).

- Importance of Package Insert

In determining the materiality of the risks associated with a drug or device, FDA refers to the product's package insert. FDA is more likely to consider as important or material a product's most serious or most frequently occurring risks than a product's less serious or less commonly occurring risks.[33] FDA characterizes the risks associated with a specific product along a hierarchy of importance reflected by placement in a risk-related section of the product's package insert – traditionally , the Contraindications, Warnings or Hazards, Precautions, Adverse Reactions or Side Effects sections, as well as the Overdosage, and Drug Abuse and Dependence sections in the case of prescription drugs – and in the use of various means to emphasize certain risks, such as boxed warnings and bolded statements. For labeling that complies with the new formatting requirements in the recently finalized Physician Labeling Rule for prescription drugs,[34] the risk-related sections include Boxed Warning, Contraindications, Warnings and Precautions, Adverse Reactions, Drug Interactions, Use in Specific Populations, Drug Abuse & Dependence, and Overdosage.

For prescription drug physician labeling that follows the new requirements, the risks included in the *Highlights* section of labeling are the most important risks associated with the drug. For other labeling, contraindications and warnings or hazards are considered to contain the most serious and material risk information associated with a drug or device and convey information that must be understood before the product is prescribed or used. Contraindications and boxed warnings are generally considered the most important. Precautions also convey important risk information that can help healthcare professionals and patients use a drug or device more safely. These include ways to avoid adverse effects and information about important differences in individual response and, for drugs, about interactions with other drugs or food. Risks conveyed only in the adverse events or side effects section are generally less serious or less well-documented than those in the preceding three categories. They are often the most commonly experienced risks associated with a product, however, and they therefore may constitute important information for both healthcare professionals and consumers.

- The Nature of Benefit Claims

Promotional pieces should reveal risk information that is material in light of the specific benefit claims made in the piece.

> *Example 12:* If a piece claims convenience because the promoted drug is dosed once-weekly, information about risks directly related to the regimen's convenience is material. Such risk information might include, for example, that inflammatory reactions such as swelling have been reported at the application site for a topical product, or that patients must restrict their activities for some time after taking an oral medication because of a risk of fainting.

[33] As indicated above, the most serious risks set forth in a product's labeling are generally material to any presentation of efficacy. Frequently occurring, less serious risks (e.g., those reflected in Adverse Reactions) can be material, particularly for a product that is not associated with serious risks, but these less serious risks may not be material for a product that has many serious risks that need to be disclosed in promotion, or whose most frequently occurring risks occur at a very low rate. In general, FDA believes that exhaustive lists of minor risks distract from and make it difficult to comprehend and retain information on the more important risks. To this end, we have issued a draft guidance for prescription drugs entitled *Brief Summary Disclosing Risk Information in Consumer-Directed Print Advertisements*, which suggests approaches to communicating less, but better, information in consumer brief summaries. Once finalized, this guidance will represent the Agency's thinking on this topic.

[34] See 71 Fed. Reg. 3922 (Jan. 24, 2006). The rule became effective June 30, 2006.

Similarly, as stated above, for promotional pieces that promote a product's benefits in a selected class of patients, the significant risks applicable to that class of patients are material.[35]

> *Example 13:* If a Web site for a product approved to treat high blood pressure presents information about a product's benefits in postmenopausal women, any risks specific to postmenopausal women are particularly material.

- Accuracy and Comprehensiveness of Risk Information

When it evaluates the content of a promotional piece's risk information, FDA assesses the quality as well as the quantity of the information. Both consumer and professional audiences expect that certain information will be present in promotions for prescription drugs and medical devices. This expectation results from schemas,[36] or mental frameworks, about these promotional pieces that have developed from previous exposures (i.e., preconceived expectations based on past experience). Consumers have preconceived ideas about the amount of scrutiny these ads undergo. Many believe FDA exercises tight regulatory control over the content of these ads and to some extent, believe that all ads have been pre-reviewed prior to airing.[37] As a result, consumers are likely to expect that the most relevant risks have been included in the ad. Because people expect to see risk information, there is no reason for them to imagine that the product has important risks that have been omitted. Instead, the audience is likely to believe that all significant risks are included, especially if some risks are included. This missing risk information can have serious effects; it may cause consumers to fail to inform their healthcare professionals of important considerations, and healthcare professionals to prescribe inappropriately or even dangerously.

> *Example 14:* A product is associated with the rare but serious risk of a heart attack. FDA is likely to consider an ad misleading if it devotes a certain amount of time or space to the presentation of claims about the product's efficacy in treating migraines and then devotes a similar amount of time or space to describing only the frequently occurring, least serious adverse events, or only one of several significant risks.

Even though a similar *quantity* of risk and benefit information may be conveyed, a promotional piece that presents information on the benefits of the product but then communicates only its least serious risks, or an inadequate set of its serious risks, will not have conveyed an accurate understanding of the product's relevant properties.

C. CONSIDERATIONS OF FORMAT

FDA also considers formatting factors when assessing whether a piece is false or misleading. *Format* includes the shape, size, and general layout of all portions of a print promotional piece, as well as the

---

[35] See 21 CFR 202.1(e)(7)(x).

[36] See Kardash, C.A.M., Royer, J.M., & Greene, B.A. (1988) Effects of schemata on both encoding and retrieval of information from prose. *Journal of Educational Psychology, 80*, 324-329; Smith, E.E., & Swinney, D.A. (1992) The role of schemas in reading text: A real-time examination. *Discourse Processes, 15*, 303-316.

[37] See, e.g., K. Aikin, J. Swasy & A. Braman, Patient and Physician Attitudes and Behaviors Associated With DTC Promotion of Prescription Drugs – Summary of FDA Survey Research Results, Final Report, November 19, 2004, available at: http://www.fda.gov/cder/ddmac/Final%20Report/FRfinal111904.pdf; Prevention Magazine (2004) *5th Annual Survey: Consumer Reaction to DTC Advertising of Prescription Medicines*. Emmaus, PA: Rodale.

general plan of organization, arrangement, and theme in non-print promotional pieces such as videos and broadcast ads.

To process information, a person must first pay attention to it. Several factors contribute to whether people will pay attention to information. These factors also may help or hinder people's understanding of information once it has drawn their attention. When evaluating whether a promotional piece appropriately communicates risk information, FDA considers several formatting factors.[38] Because these factors apply to information processing in general, prescription drug and medical device manufacturers should keep them in mind when developing promotional pieces.

As a general matter, risk and benefit information should be comparably noticeable or conspicuous in promotional pieces, and audiences should be able to read both risk and benefit information with similar ease (e.g., comparably legible and understandable; *see* Section III.A.1 above).[39] Manufacturers should note that any one of the following formatting factors could make a piece false or misleading and that each factor could interact with others to increase this problem or to create a false or misleading impression when there might not be one if a factor were considered in isolation.

1. Print Promotion

The layout of a print promotional piece (generally, its plan, design, or arrangement) influences readers' ability to pay attention to and process specific features of the piece.[40] FDA considers the following selected aspects of the layout of a print promotional piece when assessing the comparable prominence and readability of risk and efficacy information. This is not an exhaustive list; other issues, such as language comprehension and the risk hierarchy, are covered in other sections.

- Overall Location of Risk Information

For a piece to be accurate and non-misleading, risk information should be included in the main part of a piece. If the omission of risk information in any part of a piece makes that part of the piece false or misleading, the problem cannot be corrected simply by including the risk information in a separate part of the piece.[41] To be comparably prominent to benefit information, risk information should generally appear in the same parts of the piece as the benefits.

---

[38] See, e.g., 21 CFR 202.1(e)(7)(viii) for a list of implementing factors FDA takes into consideration when evaluating the balance between benefit and risk information in an ad. *See generally* 21 CFR 202.1(e)(6)-(7).

[39] See 21 U.S.C. § 352(c).

[40] See Adams, A.S., & Edworthy, J. (1995) Quantifying and predicting the effects of basic text display variables on the perceived urgency of warning labels: Tradeoffs involving font size, border weight, and color. *Ergonomics, 38*, 2221-2237; Brundage, M., Feldman-Stewart, D., Leis, A., Bezjak, A., Degner, L., Velji, K., et al. (2005) Communicating quality of life information to cancer patients: A study of six presentation formats. *Journal of Clinical Oncology*, 23, 6949-6956; Frantz, J.P. (1993) Effect of location and presentation format on attention to and compliance with product warnings and instructions. *Journal of Safety Research, 24*, 131-154; Morrow, D., Leirer, V., Altieri, P. (1995) List formats improve medication instructions for older adults. *Educational Gerontology, 21*, 151-166; Niemela, M., & Saariluoma, P. (2003) Layout attributes and recall. *Behaviour and Information Technology, 22*, 353-363; Wogalter, M.S., & Vigilante, W.J., Jr. (2003) Effects of label format on knowledge acquisition and perceived readability by younger and older adults. *Ergonomics, 46*, 327-344.

[41] See 21 CFR 202.1(e)(3)(i). The prescription drug regulations allow the presentation of risk information in a particular part of a promotional piece to be concise if it is supplemented by a prominent reference on each page to the presence and location of a more complete discussion of such information elsewhere in the piece. *Id.* However,

Complete separation of benefit and risk information (e.g., presenting several pages of benefits before any risks) is one example of a lack of appropriate prominence.[42] FDA will also look to see that risk information is not placed in such a way as to interfere with readers' perceptions of the relative importance or utility of the information.

- Location of Risk Information within a Part of the Promotional Piece

In addition to appearing with or near benefit presentations, risk information should appear as an integral part of the piece, just as benefit information does. For example, a prescription drug ad should not present risks only on a brief summary page.

> *Example 15:* A product's logo and a tagline are often used to signal the end of a piece. Readers may assume that any risk information placed below the logo and tagline is there only for liability purposes or to fulfill a regulatory requirement and is unrelated to the main message, especially if the information is presented in small type or otherwise lacking in emphasis.

> *Example 16:* A seven-page sales aid devotes the first six pages to effectiveness claims, which are prominently presented with colorful graphics, abundant white space, and large, colorful headers. Three of these pages also include a footnote referring readers to "Important Information on page 7." The seventh page summarizes some risk information from the PI in single-spaced paragraph format without headers or other presentation elements to emphasize to the reader that it is important risk information. Such a presentation creates problems regarding the adequate presentation of risk. The important risk information about the drug should instead be integrated into the piece and presented with similar prominence to the effectiveness claims.

Similarly, problems can arise when parts of a print promotional piece appear so unrelated that the risks do not look to be part of the piece.

> *Example 17:* Risk information is placed in a thin column along the side of an ad in a different font and color scheme, so that the visuals and benefit information form a complete whole, separate from the risk information. This is not likely to be considered an adequate presentation of risk information.

- Font Size and Style

Font size and type style are format factors that can affect the prominence and readability of information.[43] FDA does not object to a presentation on the basis of minor differences in font size alone, depending on

---

although the regulations allow for the "concise" presentation of such information, the nature and importance of this information should be accurately conveyed. For example, if a drug contains a boxed warning with information on the risk of elevations in potassium levels that can lead to life-threatening complications in some patients, a statement in a part of a promotional piece that "Drug X may increase your potassium levels; see Prescribing Information (PI) for more information" is not likely to convey to consumers or healthcare professionals the magnitude (i.e., life-threatening nature) of the risk.

[42] 21 CFR 202.1(e)(3)(i); see also 21 U.S.C. 321(n), 21 CFR 202.1(e)(5)(iii).

[43] Adams, A.S., & Edworthy, J. (1995) Quantifying and predicting the effects of basic text display variables on the perceived urgency of warning labels: Tradeoffs involving font size, border weight, and color. *Ergonomics, 38*, 2221-2237; Arditi, A., & Cho, J. (2005) Serifs and font legibility. *Vision Research, 45*, 2926-2933; Baker, S.

other factors used to achieve emphasis (e.g., bolded lettering, bullets). However, FDA may object to substantial differences in font size or the presentation of risk information in a difficult to read font size, irrespective of the font size of benefit information, because this may seriously reduce the ability to see or comprehend the risk information.

Even with identical risk and benefit font sizes, differences in type styles can render some information easier to read than other information.[44] To be comparably prominent and readable, FDA recommends that risk and benefit information be presented in type styles that are similar in the use of capitalization, serifs, the weight of the type-face, the angle of the letters, the degree of flourishes and scripting, and other typographical factors such as spacing (e.g., leading and kerning).[45]

- Contrast

Contrast between text and background should not highlight the benefit information more than the risk information.

> *Example 18:* If benefit information in a piece is presented in white letters on a black background, risk information should be presented with similar contrast. If the piece presents risk information in a way that would make it difficult to discern (e.g., using white letters on a light gray background or gray letters on a black background), the presentation may be considered false or misleading.

Even if the background is a color designed to attract attention, the contrast influences the prominence of the words once attention has been gained. In fact, printing words in some attention-grabbing colors (e.g., red) may make the words difficult to read.[46] Similarly, the placement of risk information over pictures or

---

(2006). Provision of effective information. *British Dental Journal, 201*, 100; Sheedy, J.E., Subbaram, M.V., Zimmerman, A.B., & Hayes, J.R. (2005) Text legibility and the letter superiority effect. *Human Factors, 47*, 797-815; Tantillo, J., Di Lorenzo-Aiss, J., & Mathisen, R.E. (1995) Quantifying perceived differences in type styles: An exploratory study. *Psychology and Marketing, 12*, 447-457; Wogalter, M.S., & Vigilante, W.J. (2003) Effects of label format on knowledge acquisition and perceived readability by younger and older adults. *Ergonomics, 46*, 327-344.

[44] English, E. (1944) A study of the readability of four newspaper headline types. *Journalism Quarterly, 21*, 217-229; Mansfield, J.S., Legge, G.E., & Bane, M.C. (1996) Psychophysics of reading. XV: Font effects in normal and low vision. *Investigative Opthamology and Visual Science, 37*, 1492-1501; Sheedy, J.E., Subbaram, M.V., Zimmerman, A.B., & Hayes, J.R. (2005) Text legibility and the letter superiority effect. *Human Factors, 47*, 797-815; Tantillo, J., Di Lorenzo-Aiss, J., & Mathisen, R.E. (1995) Quantifying perceived differences in type styles: An exploratory study. *Psychology and Marketing, 12*, 447-457.

[45] See Arditi, A., & Cho, J. (2005) Serifs and font legibility. *Vision Research,* 45, 2926-2933; Baker, S. (2006) Provision of effective information. *British Dental Journal,* 201, 100; Moriarty, S.E., & Scheiner, E.C. (1984) A study of close-set text type. *Journal of Applied Psychology, 69*, 700-702; Paterson, D.G., & Tinker, M.A. (1947) Influence of leading upon readability of newspaper type. *Journal of Applied Psychology, 31*, 160-163; Smither, J.A., & Braun, C.C. (1994) Readability of prescription drug labels by older and younger adults. *Journal of Clinical Psychology in Medical Settings, 1*, 149-159; Tinker, M.A., & Paterson, D.G. (1946) Effect of line width and leading on readability of newspaper type. *Journalism Quarterly, 23*, 307-309.

[46] See Pearson, R., & van Schaik, P. (2003) The effect of spatial layout and link colour in web pages on performance in a visual search task and an interactive search task. *International Journal of Human-Computer Studies, 59*, 327-353; but see Adams, A.S., & Edworthy, J. (1995) Quantifying and predicting the effects of basic text display variables on the perceived urgency of warning labels: Tradeoffs involving font size, border weight, and color. *Ergonomics, 38*, 2221-2237.

other visual elements with multiple colors can cause this information or portions of this information to lack prominence and be difficult to read.[47] Furthermore, a print piece that superimposes risk information over a visual image could compromise the accuracy of the piece as a whole by drawing attention away from the risk information.[48]

- White Space

Background space (often called *white space*) between and around letters can influence the prominence and readability of text.[49] Presenting benefit information in multiple paragraphs with double spaces between each paragraph, while presenting risk information in one block paragraph without spacing or indentation could reduce the comparability of the risk and benefit presentations. Moreover, if a promotional piece uses headings, bullets, and other attention-getting symbols to emphasize product benefits, FDA recommends that it use similar techniques to present product risks.[50]

2. Non-Print Promotion

Some print formatting issues also apply to non-print promotion such as videos, broadcast ads, and similar audio and visual pieces. However, the unique features of non-print media add complexity. As with print, FDA considers factors such as location, proximity, type size, type style, and contrast when evaluating these materials. These factors are especially important with regard to text that is superimposed on other images in videos or broadcast ads (SUPERs) and other visual components, such as graphics, within the scene. In non-print pieces, FDA also evaluates other formatting factors in addition to those described above to determine whether a particular piece is considered false or misleading (e.g., audio components, motion within the visual component, the juxtaposition of visual and audio components, and duration of exposure).

- Textual Elements

Prescription drug broadcast ads must present major product risks in the audio or audio and visual parts of the ad.[51] Thus, broadcast ads and videos often use SUPERs and other text to present risk-related qualifying information. When used to disclose risk, SUPERs can pose particular problems of readability, comprehensibility, and proximity to benefit information. For example, the FTC, which requires that

---

[47] See, e.g., Hillstrom, A.P., & Chai, Y. (2006) Factors that guide or disrupt attentive visual processing. *Computers in Human Behavior, 22*, 648-656; Petty, R.E., Wells, G.L., & Brock, T.C. (1976) Distraction can enhance or reduce yielding to propaganda: Thought disruption versus effort justification. *Journal of Personality and Social Psychology, 34*, 874-884; Zimbardo, P.G., Snyder, M., Thomas, J., Gold, A., & Gurwitz, S. (1970) Modifying the impact of persuasive communications with external distraction. *Journal of Personality and Social Psychology, 16*, 669-680.

[48] See Shiffrin, R.M., & Schneider, W. (1977) Controlled and automatic human information processing II: Perceptual learning, automatic attending, and a general theory. *Psychological Review, 84*, 127-190.

[49] Adams, A.S., & Edworthy, J. (1995) Quantifying and predicting the effects of basic text display variables on the perceived urgency of warning labels: Tradeoffs involving font size, border weight, and color. *Ergonomics, 38*, 2221-2237; Pracejus, J.W., Olsen, G.D., & O'Guinn, T.C. (2006) How nothing became something: White space, rhetoric, history, and meaning. *Journal of Consumer Research, 33*, 82-90.

[50] See Luckiesh, M., & Moss, F.K. (1940) Boldness as a factor in type-design and typography. *Journal of Applied Psychology, 24*, 170-183.

[51] 21 CFR 202.1(e)(1).

"[q]ualifying disclosures…be legible and understandable," recognizes that, "in many circumstances reasonable consumers do not read the entirety of an ad or are directed away from the importance of the qualifying phrase by acts or statements of the seller."[52] FDA has similar concerns.

FDA assesses the temporal location of SUPERs within a broadcast ad or video when evaluating whether it is false or misleading. If claims must be qualified to avoid misleading the audience, we recommend that the qualifier be vocalized, presented through visual images, or placed in a prominent SUPER that runs ***concurrently*** with the claim.[53] If SUPERs do not appear close enough to the claim or risk information requiring qualification, a misleading impression of the product may result.[54] In addition, if qualifying information is complex and requires more than one line of text, we recommend that manufacturers use other means to convey this information.

Other issues FDA considers important that manufacturers should keep in mind include the following:

— SUPERs, if used, should be reasonably visible to a person under typical viewing conditions.
— All SUPERs should be on screen long enough to allow the audience to read and understand their full content.
— Graphics that distract from the presentation of risk information, including from risk-related SUPERs (e.g., busy scenes, frequent scene changes, vivid and compelling visuals[55] and moving camera angles) can misleadingly minimize the risks of the product being promoted by detracting from the audience's comprehension of the risk presentation.
— Competition from other SUPERs (e.g., presenting a SUPER related to a particular risk while unrelated SUPERs are on the screen) hampers the audience's ability to read and understand the SUPERs and could compromise the communication of risk information and make a piece misleading.[56]
— Factors such as font size, type style, and capitalization can also affect the readability of SUPERs.[57] Words presented in all upper case letters are more difficult to read than words presented in upper and lower case letters.[58]

[52] FTC Policy Statement on Deception at 183.

[53] See 21 CFR 202.1(e)(3)(i).

[54] Manrai, L.A., Manrai, A.K., & Murray, N. (1994) Comprehension of info-aid supers in television advertising for social ideas: Implications for public policy. *Journal of Business Research, 30*, 75-84.

[55] Vivid visual images are those images, pictures or other visual stimuli that are emotionally or cognitively interesting, attention-getting, compelling, provoking, or personal in a sensory, temporal or spatial manger (after Nisbett, R., and Ross, L. (1980) *Human Inference: Strategies and Shortcomings of Social Judgment*. Englewood Cliffs, NJ: Prentice-Hall). Background music can also be distracting (Furnham, A., & Strbac, L. (2002). Music is as distracting as noise: The differential distraction of background music and noise on the cognitive test performance of introverts and extraverts. *Ergonomics, 45*, 203-217).

[56] See, e.g., Mackie, D.M., & Worth, L.T. (1989) Processing deficits and the mediation of positive affect in persuasion. *Journal of Personality and Social Psychology, 57*, 27-40; Manrai, L.A., Manrai, A.K., & Murray, N. (1994) Comprehension of info-aid supers in television advertising for social ideas: Implications for public policy. *Journal of Business Research, 30*, 75-84.

[57] Baker, S. (2006) Provision of effective information. *British Dental Journal,* 201, 100; Manrai, L.A., Manrai, A.K., & Murray, N. (1994) Comprehension of info-aid supers in television advertising for social ideas: Implications for public policy. *Journal of Business Research, 30*, 75-84.

[58] Paterson, D.G., & Tinker, M.A. (1941) Caps vs. lower-case in headlines. *Editor & Publisher, 74*, 51.

- Contrast

Contrast is an important visual factor[59] that FDA considers when evaluating television ads and videos.[60] As in print pieces, risk disclosures presented in SUPERs should be in a font color that reasonably contrasts with the background visuals. Because important non-benefit information is often conveyed by SUPERs, any obstacle to the prominence and readability of this information, and thus to the audience's understanding of SUPERs, may result in a misleading risk presentation.

- Dual Mode Considerations

The interplay of visual and audio components in pieces such as television ads and videos introduces unique factors FDA must consider when evaluating the adequacy of risk disclosure. The issues raised above in Textual Elements about distracting visuals apply not only to the SUPER presentation but also to the audio presentation of risks.[61] If visuals in a broadcast ad distract the audience from the statement of a product's risks, the ad will not, as a whole, convey an accurate impression of the risks of the advertised product. This distraction could be caused by factors including busy scenes, frequent scene changes, moving camera angles, and even inherently compelling, vivid visuals. In addition, the overall tone of the ad or of specific background visuals can affect the comparable prominence of the risks, particularly if the tone is contrary to the risk message.

> *Example 20:* A video or broadcast ad depicts a joyous or exhilarating moment, contains images of people enjoying the benefits of the product, or includes otherwise compelling or distracting non-risk related images while major risks are communicated in a voiceover. The inconsistent tone or images may be too distracting for the audience to listen to or process the risks, causing the video or broadcast ad to communicate a false or misleading net impression of the product.

- Audio Considerations

FDA considers several audio-related factors when evaluating pieces such as sound recordings, videos, or broadcast ads, including television, radio, and telephone communications.

- — The qualities of speech should be similar across benefit and risk information for these components to be considered comparably prominent.
- — A critical speech consideration is *pacing*. If risk information is considerably more difficult to hear and process than benefit information because it is presented at a much faster pace, the piece will not convey an accurate impression of the product.
- — Markedly reducing volume or being less articulate when discussing risks compared to benefits may hinder the audience's comprehension of the risks.
- — Background music should be comparable in volume and distraction potential during both benefit and risk presentations.

---

[59] Mitzner, T.L., & Rogers, W.A. (2006) Reading in the dark: Effects of age and contrast on reading speed and comprehension. *Human Factors,* 48, 229-240.

[60] Seibert, W.F., Kasten, D.F., & Potter, J.R. (1959) A study of factors influencing the legibility of televised characters. *Journal of the Society of Motion Picture & Television Engineers, 68*, 467-472.

[61] See, e.g, Regan, D.T., & Cheng, J.B. (1973) Distraction and attitude change: A resolution. *Journal of Experimental Social Psychology, 9*, 138-147.

IV. CONCLUSION

The FDA's regulation of prescription drug and medical device promotion to healthcare professionals and consumers is a broad and complex topic. A vast scientific body of knowledge is available regarding human cognition, and FDA relies on this knowledge when evaluating promotional pieces and making regulatory decisions about the presentation of benefit and risk information. The Agency hopes that by discussing the most relevant factors and by providing specific examples, manufacturers will gain a better understanding of what they should consider as they develop the content and format of their promotional communications.

It is important to re-emphasize that, in addition to specific risk-related claims, FDA also considers the net impression conveyed by all the elements of a piece. For this reason, manufacturers should focus not just on individual claims or presentations, but on the messages conveyed by the promotional piece as a whole.

ATTACHMENT: STATUTORY AND REGULATORY REQUIREMENTS FOR LABELING AND ADVERTISING

FDA regulates the manufacture, sale, and distribution of drugs and devices in the United States under the authority of the Federal Food, Drug, and Cosmetic Act (the Act). This authority includes oversight of labeling for all drugs and devices and of advertising for prescription drugs and restricted devices. 21 U.S.C. 352(a), (n), (q), & (r). In regulating the labeling and advertising of drugs and devices, FDA attends to the First Amendment.

The Act defines label to mean "a display of written, printed, or graphic matter upon the immediate container of any article . . . ." 21 U.S.C. 321(k). According to FDA regulations (21 CFR 1.3(b)): "Label means any display of written, printed, or graphic matter on the immediate container of any article, or any such matter affixed to any consumer commodity or affixed to or appearing upon a package containing any consumer commodity." The Act defines labeling to mean "all labels and other written, printed, or graphic matter (1) upon any article or any of its containers or wrappers, or (2) accompanying such article." 21 U.S.C. 321(m). Similarly, FDA regulations (21 CFR 1.3(a)) provide that labeling includes "all written, printed, or graphic matter accompanying an article at any time while such article is in interstate commerce or held for sale after shipment or delivery in interstate commerce."

According to *Kordel v. United States*, 335 U.S. 345, 350 (1948), the language "accompanying such article" in the "labeling" definition includes materials that supplement or explain an article, "in the manner that a committee report of the Congress accompanies a bill. No physical attachment one to the other is necessary. It is the textual relationship that is significant." FDA's prescription drug advertising regulations (21 CFR 202.1(l)(2)) thus provide as examples of labeling a wide variety of written, printed, or graphic matter that bears a textual relationship with a product.

FDA generally recognizes two types of labeling for drugs and devices: FDA-required labeling and promotional labeling. Much FDA-required labeling is subject to FDA review and approval. For example, after drafting by the manufacturer, required labeling is reviewed and approved by FDA as part of the new drug application (NDA), new animal drug application (NADA), biologics license application (BLA) or premarket approval application (PMA) review (21 CFR 314.50(c)(2), 514.1(b)(3), 601.2(a), and 814.20(b)(10)).

For devices that are not subject to premarket approval, but instead are subject to premarket notification requirements or are exempt from premarket review, there is no agency review or approval of labeling, but such devices remain subject to all of the requirements of applicable labeling regulations, including those for adequate directions for use. For a prescription drug or prescription device to be exempted from the Act's requirement of adequate directions for use (21 U.S.C. 352(f)(1)), its FDA-required labeling must contain, among other information, information addressing product hazards and other risk information, as specified in FDA regulations.[62]

Promotional labeling is generally any labeling other than the FDA-required labeling that is devised for promotion of the product. Promotional labeling may include items such as "brochures, booklets, mailing pieces, detailing pieces, file cards, bulletins, calendars, price lists, catalogs, house organs, letters, motion picture films, film strips, lantern slides, sound recordings, exhibits, literature, and reprints and similar

[62] 21 CFR 201.100(d)(1), (3), 201.105(c)(1), & 801.109(d).

pieces of printed, audio, or visual matter . . . ."[63] The Act specifies that a drug or device shall be deemed to be misbranded if its labeling is false or misleading in any particular. 21 U.S.C. 352(a). The Act further specifies that labeling or advertising may be considered misleading if it fails to reveal material facts about the product being promoted, including facts about the consequences that can result from use of the product as suggested in a promotional piece. 21 U.S.C. 321(n). In addition, the Act specifies that a drug or device will be deemed to be misbranded if any word, statement, or other information required under the Act to appear on the label or labeling is not "prominently placed thereon with such conspicuousness (as compared with other words, statements, designs, or devices, in the labeling) and in such terms as to render it likely to be read and understood by the ordinary individual under customary conditions of purchase and use." 21 U.S.C. 352(c).

Advertising[64] for prescription drugs and restricted devices is also subject to requirements under the Act for the disclosure of risk and other information. Under section 502(n) of the Act (21 U.S.C. 352(n)) and FDA's implementing regulations (21 CFR Part 202), an ad for a prescription drug must include, in addition to the product's established name and quantitative composition, a "true statement" of information in brief summary "relating to side effects, contraindications and effectiveness" of the product with respect to the use or uses that the message promotes.[65] Advertisements for restricted devices must include "a brief statement of the intended uses of the device and relevant warnings, precautions, side effects, and contraindications . . . ." 21 U.S.C. 352(r)(2). For prescription drug advertisements, FDA's implementing regulations specify that, among other things, the statutory requirement of a "true statement" is not satisfied if an ad for a prescription drug product is false or misleading with respect to side effects, contraindications or effectiveness or if it fails to reveal material facts about "consequences that may result from the use of the drug as recommended or suggested in the advertisement." 21 CFR 202.1(e)(5). Similarly, the Act also specifies that restricted device advertisements must not be false or misleading (21 U.S.C. 352(q)(1)) and must reveal facts that are material about the product being advertised, including facts about the consequences that can result from use of the product as suggested in an ad. 21 U.S.C. 321(n).

The prescription drug regulations also specify that ads must present a fair balance between information relating to risks and benefits, which is achieved when the treatment of risk and benefit information in a promotional piece is comparably thorough and complete throughout the piece. 21 CFR 202.1(e)(5)(ii). These regulations also provide illustrations of the factors FDA considers in determining whether promotional pieces comply with the above requirements relating to risk disclosure. Specifically, these regulations identify twenty types of advertising communications that FDA considers "false, lacking in fair balance, or otherwise misleading." 21 CFR 202.1(e)(6). These include, for example, representations or suggestions that a drug is more effective or safer than has been demonstrated by substantial evidence or substantial clinical experience, the use of pictures or graphics in a way that is misleading, and the presentation of risk information "by means of a general term for a group" rather than disclosing specific

---

[63] See, e.g., 21 CFR 202.1(l)(2).

[64] The act does not define "advertising" or "advertisement." According to FDA regulations (21 CFR 202.1(l)(1)), "Advertisements subject to section 502(n) of the act include advertisements in published journals, magazines, other periodicals, and newspapers, and advertisements broadcast through media such as radio, television, and telephone communication systems."

[65] According to 21 CFR 202.1(e)(3)(iii), the information in brief summary relating to side effects and contraindications must disclose "*each specific side effect and contraindication* (which include side effects, warnings, precautions, and contraindications and include any such information under such headings as cautions, special considerations, important notes, etc. . . .) contained in required, approved, or permitted labeling for the advertised drug dosage form(s)" (emphasis added).

risks. 21 CFR 202.1(e)(6)(i), (xviii), & (xx). Representing or suggesting that a drug product is "safer than has been demonstrated by substantial evidence or substantial clinical experience" means obscuring or failing to include the most serious risk information set forth in the drug's FDA-approved labeling, and does not refer to a failure to include risk information that is not set forth in the drug's FDA-approved labeling.

In addition, these regulations identify thirteen additional types of advertising communications that "may be false, lacking in fair balance, or otherwise misleading." 21 CFR 202.1(e)(7). These include, for example, advertising communications that fail to "present information relating to side effects and contraindications with a prominence and readability reasonably comparable with the presentation of information relating to effectiveness of the drug." 21 CFR 202.1(e)(7)(viii).

Although the regulations discussed above were promulgated in the context of prescription drug advertising, the guidance they provide on what FDA considers false or misleading in promotion has broader applicability. For example, promotional pieces that fail to present a balanced view of the risks and benefits of a product are generally considered to be false or misleading and also generally fail to reveal material facts about the product being promoted. Because both labeling pieces for drugs and devices, and advertising pieces for prescription drugs and restricted devices, are considered to misbrand a product if they are false or misleading or fail to reveal material facts,[66] drug and device manufacturers should take into account the guidance provided by these regulations when developing promotional labeling and advertising pieces for their products.

[66] 21 U.S.C. 352(a), (n), (q)(1) & 321(n); 21 CFR 202.1(e)(5).

Appendix E.

Draft Guidance on Post-marketing Submissions of Interactive Promotional Materials

Guidance for Industry

Fulfilling Regulatory Requirements for Postmarketing Submissions of Interactive Promotional Media for Prescription Human and Animal Drugs and Biologics

DRAFT GUIDANCE

This guidance document is being distributed for comment purposes only.

Comments and suggestions regarding this draft document should be submitted within 90 days of publication in the *Federal Register* of the notice announcing the availability of the draft guidance. Submit electronic comments to http://www.regulations.gov. Submit written comments to the Division of Dockets Management (HFA-305), Food and Drug Administration, 5630 Fishers Lane, rm. 1061, Rockville, MD 20852. All comments should be identified with the docket number listed in the notice of availability that publishes in the *Federal Register*.

For questions regarding this draft document contact (CDER) Barbara Chong at (301) 796-1200; (CBER) Office of Communication, Outreach and Development at 800-835-4709 or 301-827-1800; or (CVM) Dorothy McAdams at (240) 276-9300.

U.S. Department of Health and Human Services
Food and Drug Administration
Center for Drug Evaluation and Research (CDER)
Center for Biologics Evaluation and Research (CBER)
Center for Veterinary Medicine (CVM)

January 2014
Advertising

Guidance for Industry

Fulfilling Regulatory Requirements for Postmarketing Submissions of Interactive Promotional Media for Prescription Human and Animal Drugs and Biologics

Additional copies are available from:

Office of Communications, Division of Drug Information
Center for Drug Evaluation and Research
Food and Drug Administration
10903 New Hampshire Ave., Bldg. 51, rm. 2201
Silver Spring, MD 20993-0002
Tel: 301-796-3400; Fax: 301-847-8714; E-mail: druginfo@fda.hhs.gov
http://www.fda.gov/Drugs/GuidanceComplianceRegulatoryInformation/Guidances/default.htm

Office of Communication, Outreach and Development (HFM-40)
Center for Biologics Evaluation and Research
Food and Drug Administration
1401 Rockville Pike, Suite 200N
Rockville, MD 20852-1448
Tel: 800-835-4709 or 301-827-1800; E-mail: ocod@fda.hhs.gov
http://www.fda.gov/BiologicsBloodVaccines/GuidanceComplianceRegulatoryInformation/default.htm

Communications Staff (CVM)
Center for Veterinary Medicine
Food and Drug Administration
7519 Standish Place, HFV-12
Rockville, MD 20855
Tel: 240-276-9300; E-mail: AskCVM@fda.hhs.gov
http://www.fda.gov/AnimalVeterinary/GuidanceComplianceEnforcement/GuidanceforIndustry/default.htm

U.S. Department of Health and Human Services
Food and Drug Administration
Center for Drug Evaluation and Research (CDER)
Center for Biologics Evaluation and Research (CBER)
Center for Veterinary Medicine (CVM)

January 2014
Advertising

TABLE OF CONTENTS

Fulfilling Regulatory Requirements for Postmarketing Submissions of Interactive Promotional Media for Prescription Human and Animal Drugs and Biologics

This draft guidance, when finalized, will represent the Food and Drug Administration's (FDA's or Agency's) current thinking on this topic. It does not create or confer any rights for or on any person and does not operate to bind FDA or the public. You can use an alternative approach if the approach satisfies the requirements of the applicable statutes and regulations. If you want to discuss an alternative approach, contact the FDA staff responsible for implementing this guidance. If you cannot identify the appropriate FDA staff, call the appropriate number listed on the title page of this guidance.

I. INTRODUCTION

This draft guidance is intended to describe FDA's current thinking about how manufacturers, packers, and distributors (firms), that may either be the applicant or acting on behalf of the applicant, of prescription human and animal drug and biological products (drugs) can fulfill regulatory requirements for postmarketing submissions[1] of interactive promotional media for their FDA-approved products.[2,3] For the purposes of this guidance, the phrase *interactive promotional media* includes modern tools and technologies that often allow for real-time communications and interactions (e.g., blogs, microblogs, social networking sites, online communities, and live podcasts) that firms use to promote their drugs. Although some interactive promotional media are substantially similar in presentation and content to certain traditional promotional media, such as print media, FDA recognizes that in other cases they possess certain unique technological features and offer novel presentation and content features. This draft guidance describes FDA's current thinking on what the Agency considers to be interactive promotional media and outlines the considerations taken into account in determining if product communications using interactive technologies are subject to FDA's postmarketing submission requirements. Furthermore, this draft guidance provides FDA's recommendations for how firms can fulfill the regulatory requirement to submit postmarketing promotional materials to the FDA in a practical manner to address the potential

[1] 21 CFR 314.81(b)(3)(i); 21 CFR 601.12(f)(4); and 21 CFR 514.80(b)(5)(ii). See Section III for a detailed description of these postmarketing submission requirements.

[2] This draft guidance has been prepared by the Office of Prescription Drug Promotion (OPDP) in the Center for Drug Evaluation and Research (CDER) in consultation with the Center for Biologics Evaluation and Research (CBER) and the Center for Veterinary Medicine (CVM).

[3] The recommendations in this draft guidance also apply to biological products that are approved for marketing under section 351 of the Public Health Service Act (PHS Act). Because each biological product also meets the definition of "drug" or "device" under the Federal Food, Drug, and Cosmetic Act (FD&C Act), it is also subject to provisions of the FD&C Act applicable to drugs or devices, as well as the regulations implementing these provisions, except that a biological product licensed under section 351 of the PHS Act is not required to have an approved new drug application under section 505 of the FD&C Act (21 U.S.C. 355). See PHS Act section 351(j), (42 U.S.C. 262(j)). The recommendations in this draft guidance do not apply to veterinary biological products regulated under the Virus-Serum-Toxin Act (21 U.S.C. 151, et seq.) by the U.S. Department of Agriculture.

volume of real-time information that is continuously posted and shared through various interactive promotional media platforms.

The organization of the draft guidance is as follows: after some background information regarding postmarketing submission requirements (Section II), a brief legal overview of statutory and regulatory requirements for labeling and advertising is presented, including postmarketing submission requirements (III). Then, considerations related to submission of interactive promotional media are discussed with some illustrative examples (IV), and, finally, FDA's recommendations for submitting such promotional materials are provided (V).

FDA's guidance documents, including this draft guidance, do not establish legally enforceable rights or responsibilities. Instead, guidances describe the Agency's current thinking on a topic and should be viewed only as recommendations, unless specific regulatory or statutory requirements are cited. The use of the word *should* in Agency guidances means that something is suggested or recommended, but not required.

II. BACKGROUND

FDA's regulation of prescription drug product promotion extends both to promotional activities that are carried out by the firm itself, and to promotion conducted on the firm's behalf. In determining whether the firm is accountable for a communication about its product(s), the Agency considers whether the firm or anyone acting on its behalf is influencing or controlling the product promotional activity or communication in whole or part. Firms may have a variety of options for how much control they exert over activities that utilize interactive promotional media, regardless of whether the promotional activity occurs on firm-sponsored or third-party venues. For example, a firm may promote its products through product websites, discussion boards, chat rooms, or other public electronic forums that it maintains and over which it has full control. In addition, third-party sites (i.e., websites and other venues that are either entirely independent of a firm's control and influence, or not fully controlled by a firm) may promote a firm's products.

As part of the postmarketing reporting requirements under the Federal Food, Drug, and Cosmetic Act (FD&C Act), application holders are required to submit all promotional labeling and advertising pieces at the time of initial dissemination of the labeling and at the time of initial publication of the advertisement for a drug. However, for some interactive promotional media, submission "at the time of initial dissemination" may pose a challenge for firms, particularly when these media communicate information that is displayed in real time. While "at the time of initial dissemination" does not refer to submissions on a weekly, monthly, or other routine schedule, FDA intends to exercise its enforcement discretion under certain circumstances due to the high volume of information that may be posted within short periods of time using interactive promotional media that allow for real-time communications. If a firm submits interactive promotional media in the manner described in this draft guidance, FDA intends to exercise enforcement discretion regarding the regulatory requirements for postmarketing submissions related to promotional labeling and advertising.

III. LEGAL OVERVIEW OF STATUTORY AND REGULATORY REQUIREMENTS FOR LABELING AND ADVERTISING

Under the FD&C Act, the Agency has responsibility for regulating the manufacture, sale, and distribution of drugs in the United States. This authority includes oversight of the labeling and advertising of prescription drugs and biologics (21 U.S.C. 352 (a) & (n)).

Section 201(m) of the FD&C Act defines *labeling* as "all labels and other written, printed, or graphic matter (1) upon any article or any of its containers or wrappers, or (2) accompanying such article" (21 U.S.C. 321(m)).[4] The U.S. Supreme Court has explained that the language "accompanying such article" in the "labeling" definition is interpreted broadly, to include materials that supplement or explain an article. No physical attachment between the materials and the article is necessary; rather, it is the textual relationship between the items that is significant. *Kordel v. United States*, 335 U.S. 345, 350 (1948). FDA generally recognizes two types of labeling for drugs: FDA-required labeling and promotional labeling. Promotional labeling is generally any labeling, other than the FDA-required labeling, that is devised for promotion of the product. Examples of promotional labeling pieces are described at 21 CFR 202.1(l)(2).

Also, under the FD&C Act and FDA's implementing regulations, the applicant shall submit specimens of mailing pieces and any other labeling or advertising devised for promotion of the drug product at the time of initial dissemination of the labeling and at the time of initial publication of the advertisement for a prescription drug product. Each submission is required to be accompanied by a completed Form FDA 2253 (Transmittal of Advertisements and Promotional Labeling for Drugs for Human Use) (21 CFR 314.81(b)(3)(i) and 21 CFR 601.12(f)(4)).

For prescription and over-the-counter new animal drugs, the applicant must submit at the time of initial dissemination one set of specimens of mailing pieces and other labeling. For prescription new animal drugs, the applicant must also submit one set of specimens of any advertisement at the time of initial publication or broadcast. Each submission of promotional labeling or advertisements must be accompanied by a completed Form FDA 2301 (21 CFR 514.80(b)(5)(ii)).

IV. FACTORS CONSIDERED IN DETERMINING POSTMARKETING SUBMISSION REQUIREMENTS FOR INTERACTIVE PROMOTIONAL MEDIA

FDA considers the following in determining a firm's responsibility for submitting interactive promotional media to FDA as required by postmarketing submission requirements:

1. A firm is responsible for product promotional communications on sites that are owned, controlled, created, influenced, or operated by, or on behalf of, the firm.

Such product promotional communications may include firm-sponsored microblogs (e.g., Twitter), social networking sites (e.g., Facebook), firm blogs, and other sites that are under the control or influence of the firm. In determining whether a firm must submit promotional material about its product(s) to FDA, the Agency considers whether the firm, or anyone acting on its behalf, is influencing or controlling the promotional activity or communication in whole or part. Thus, a firm is responsible if it exerts influence over a site in any particular, even if the influence is limited in scope. For example, if the firm collaborates on or has editorial, preview, or review privilege over the content provided, then it is responsible for that content.

Example 1: A firm provides on its product website an online forum that gives users the opportunity to post comments about the use of its product. In this case, the firm is responsible for submitting to FDA the product website to meet the postmarketing submission requirements because the firm created, owns, or

[4] See also 21 CFR 1.3(a).

operates the website. (See the discussion regarding user generated content (UGC) on firm-owned or firm-controlled venues at the end of this section.)

2. Under certain circumstances, a firm is responsible for promotion on third-party sites.

A firm is responsible for promotion on a third-party site if the firm has any control or influence on the third-party site, even if that influence is limited in scope. For example, if a firm collaborates, or has editorial, preview, or review privilege, then it is responsible for its promotion on the site and, as such, that site is subject to submission to FDA to meet postmarketing submission requirements. However, if a firm provides only financial support (e.g., through an unrestricted educational grant) and has no other control or influence on that site, then the firm is *not* responsible for information on a third-party site, and has no obligation to submit the content to FDA. Furthermore, if a firm is merely providing promotional materials to a third-party site but does not direct the placement of the promotion within the site and has no other control or influence on that site, the firm is responsible only for the content it places there and, thus, is responsible only for submitting to FDA promotional content that was disseminated on that site.

Example 2: A firm does not have any control of, or influence on, information on an independent third-party site but chooses to promote its product on this site (e.g., by providing specific promotional content such as firm-initiated UGC). In this situation, to meet postmarketing submission requirements, the firm is responsible for submitting to FDA the promotional content it provided to the site. (See Section V for FDA's recommendations for how to submit.)

Example 3: A firm makes suggestions on the placement of its promotional messages on an independent third-party site. Because the firm influenced the placement of its promotion within the third-party site, the firm is responsible for submitting to FDA the promotion, along with the surrounding pages, to adequately provide context to facilitate the review of the third-party site, in order to fulfill the postmarketing submission requirements.

In summary, regardless of financial support, if a firm has any control of, or influence on, the third-party site, even if limited in scope, it is responsible for submission to FDA to meet the postmarketing submission requirements.

3. A firm is responsible for the content generated by an employee or agent who is acting on behalf of the firm to promote the firm's product.

FDA's regulation of prescription drug product promotion extends both to promotional activities that are carried out by the firm itself, and to promotion conducted on the firm's behalf. Therefore, a firm is responsible for the content generated by its employees or any agents acting on behalf of the firm who promote the firm's product. For example, if an employee or agent of a firm, such as a medical science liaison or paid speaker (e.g., a key opinion leader) acting on the firm's behalf, comments on a third-party site about the firm's product, the firm is responsible for the content its employee or agent provides. A firm is also responsible for the content on a blogger's site if the blogger is acting on behalf of the firm. Therefore, a firm is responsible for UGC and communications of its employees or anyone acting on behalf of the firm and, as such, those materials are subject to submission to FDA to meet the postmarketing submission requirements.

All UGC meeting these parameters for interactive promotional media should be submitted to the FDA as recommended below in Section V.

Example 4: A sales representative acting on behalf of a firm posts comments about the innovative release mechanism of the firm's product on an independent third-party site. Because the sales representative is acting on behalf of the firm, the firm is responsible for submitting the comments to FDA to meet the postmarketing submission requirements.

Example 5: A representative of a firm, such as a blogger paid by the firm, maintains a blog about the firm's product. The firm is responsible for submitting the blog to FDA to meet the postmarketing submission requirements.

FDA recommends that a firm be transparent in disclosing its involvement on a site by clearly identifying the UGC and communications of its employees or third parties acting on behalf of the firm. This could be achieved by inclusion of the firm's identifier (e.g., name or logo) as part of the communication. However, a firm generally is not responsible for UGC that is truly independent of the firm (i.e., is not produced by, or on behalf of, or prompted by the firm in any particular).[5] FDA will not ordinarily view UGC on firm-owned or firm-controlled venues such as blogs, message boards, and chat rooms as promotional content on behalf of the firm as long as the user has no affiliation with the firm and the firm had no influence on the UGC.

FDA recommends that a firm submit to the Agency on Form FDA 2253 or Form FDA 2301 specimens of the interactive promotional media being used on the firm-owned or firm-controlled venue (e.g., blog, message board, or chat room), as described below in Section V. FDA recognizes that firms may be submitting both firm-generated and independent UGC on Form FDA 2253 or Form FDA 2301 as both firm-generated and independent UGC may be dispersed throughout the interactive promotional venue.

V. RECOMMENDATIONS FOR SUBMITTING INTERACTIVE PROMOTIONAL MEDIA

FDA recognizes the challenges of submitting promotional materials that display real-time information and, in this section, recommendations for submitting interactive promotional media are provided. If a firm submits interactive promotional media in the manner described in this draft guidance, FDA intends to exercise enforcement discretion regarding the regulatory requirements for postmarketing submissions related to promotional labeling and advertising. However, the Agency's expectations for submitting static promotional materials (e.g., sites that do not allow real-time communications and emails with predetermined content) that are substantially similar to traditional promotional materials in presentation and content remain unchanged.[6]

Unless otherwise specified in this guidance, the principles set forth below apply to the submission of interactive promotional media that display real-time communications, regardless of the target audience.

[5] Cf. 47 U.S.C. 230(c)(1) ("no provider or user of an interactive computer service shall be treated as the publisher or speaker of any information provided by another information content provider"). The Communications Decency Act further defines "information content provider" as someone "responsible, in whole or in part, for the creation or development of information provided through the Internet or any other interactive computer service." 47 U.S.C. 230(f)(3).

[6] Please note that the Agency expects that submissions of static promotional materials should remain unchanged. For example, a firm should submit its entire static product website at the time of first use. If the firm then updates one page or section of this static product website, the firm can submit only the updated page or section with a cross-reference to the original submission of the website noted on Form FDA 2253 or Form FDA 2301, including the date of the original submission. If the website is substantially revised, the firm should submit the revised website in its entirety.

The examples and recommendations provided are intended to provide guidance and illustrate possible approaches. Firms are free to use alternative approaches if these approaches satisfy the requirements of the statute and regulations.

1. At the time of initial display, a firm should submit in its entirety all sites for which it is responsible on Form FDA 2253 or Form FDA 2301. For example, the firm should submit the comprehensive static product website with the addition of the interactive or real-time components.[7]

The firm should include annotations to describe the parts that are interactive and allow for real-time communications. Any subsequent changes should be annotated and resubmitted to the Agency on Form FDA 2253 or Form FDA 2301 at the time of initial display (i.e., resubmission). The firm should also provide a cross-reference by noting the submission date of the most recent version of the site in the comments section of the form. However, after the initial submission or resubmission, if the site is publically accessible without restrictions such as a password or subscription ("non-restricted") and remains unchanged other than displaying real-time information, FDA does not intend to object if the firm submits to the Agency on Form FDA 2253 or Form FDA 2301 an updated listing of the site that does not include screenshots or other visual representations of the actual interactive or real-time communication, as described in number 3 below. If access to the site is restricted (e.g., is password protected or a subscription is required), see number 4 below.

2. For third-party sites on which a firm's participation is limited to interactive or real-time communications, a firm should submit the home page of the third-party site, along with the interactive page within the third-party site and the firm's first communication, on Form FDA 2253 or Form FDA 2301 at the time of initial display.

The firm may include any annotations that describe its communications within the third-party site. After the initial submission, if the firm remains an active participant on the third-party site, and that site is non-restricted, FDA does not intend to object if the firm submits to the Agency on Form FDA 2253 or Form FDA 2301 an updated listing of the site that does not include screenshots or other visual representations of the actual interactive or real-time communication, as described in number 3 below. If access to the site is restricted, see number 4 below.

3. Once every month, a firm should submit an updated listing of all non-restricted sites for which it is responsible or in which it remains an active participant and that include interactive or real-time communications. Firms need not submit screenshots or other visual representations of the actual interactive or real-time communications with the monthly updates.

Once every month, the firm should submit a Form FDA 2253 or Form FDA 2301 for the non-restricted sites for which the firm is responsible or in which it remains an active participant and that include interactive or real-time communications. Multiple sites and the corresponding documents can be submitted with a single Form FDA 2253 or Form FDA 2301. Firms should include a separate document for each site which includes the site name, URL, and date range, as well as a cross-reference to the date of the most recent submission of the site. Screenshots or other visual representations of the actual interactive or real-time communications need not be submitted with the monthly updates if the site is non-

[7] It is preferable for the firm to submit the interactive or real-time communications in an archivable format that allows FDA to view and interact with the submission in the same way as the end user (e.g., working links). Alternatively, firms should submit screen shots or other visual representations.

restricted. The appropriate FDA center (CDER, CBER, or CVM) should be informed via general correspondence on the first day the firm ceases to be active on a site.

4. However, if a site has restricted access and, as such, FDA may not have access to the site, a firm should submit all content related to the discussion (e.g., all UGC about the topic), which may or may not include independent UGC, to adequately provide context to facilitate the review. Screenshots or other visual representations of the actual site, including the interactive or real-time communications, should be submitted monthly on Form FDA 2253 or Form FDA 2301.

5. When submitting the site, FDA recommends that a firm take formatting factors (e.g., appearance, layout, visual impression) into consideration to enable the Agency to view the communications as a whole.

Appendix F.

Draft Guidance on Character-space Limited Promotions

Guidance for Industry

Internet/Social Media Platforms with Character Space Limitations— Presenting Risk and Benefit Information for Prescription Drugs and Medical Devices

DRAFT GUIDANCE

This guidance document is being distributed for comment purposes only.

Comments and suggestions regarding this draft document should be submitted within 90 days of publication in the *Federal Register* of the notice announcing the availability of the draft guidance. Submit electronic comments to http://www.regulations.gov. Submit written comments to the Division of Dockets Management (HFA-305), Food and Drug Administration, 5630 Fishers Lane, Rm. 1061, Rockville, MD, 20852. All comments should be identified with the docket number listed in the notice of availability that publishes in the *Federal Register*.

For questions regarding this draft document, contact (CDER) Jean-Ah Kang at 301-796-1200; (CBER) Office of Communication, Outreach and Development at 800-835-4709 or 240-402-7800; (CVM) Dorothy McAdams at 240-453-6802; or (CDRH) Deborah Wolf at 301-796-5732.

U.S. Department of Health and Human Services
Food and Drug Administration
Center for Drug Evaluation and Research (CDER)
Center for Biologics Evaluation and Research (CBER)
Center for Veterinary Medicine (CVM)
Center for Devices and Radiological Health (CDRH)

June 2014
Advertising

Guidance for Industry
Internet/Social Media Platforms with Character Space Limitations—Presenting Risk and Benefit Information for Prescription Drugs and Medical Devices

Additional copies are available from:

Office of Communications, Division of Drug Information
Center for Drug Evaluation and Research
Food and Drug Administration
10903 New Hampshire Ave., Bldg. 51, rm. 2201
Silver Spring, MD 20993-0002
Tel: 301-796-3400; Fax: 301-847-8714;
E-mail: druginfo@fda.hhs.gov
http://www.fda.gov/Drugs/GuidanceComplianceRegulatoryInformation/Guidances/default.htm

Communications Staff (CVM)
Center for Veterinary Medicine
Food and Drug Administration
7519 Standish Place, HFV-12
Rockville, MD 20855
Tel: 240-276-9300;
E-mail: AskCVM@fda.hhs.gov
http://www.fda.gov/AnimalVeterinary/GuidanceComplianceEnforcement/GuidanceforIndustry/default.htm

Office of Communication, Outreach and Development
Center for Biologics Evaluation and Research
Food and Drug Administration
10903 New Hampshire Ave., WO71, Room 3128
Silver Spring, MD 20993
Tel: 800-835-4709 or 240-402-7800;
E-mail: ocod@fda.hhs.gov
http://www.fda.gov/BiologicsBloodVaccines/GuidanceComplianceRegulatoryInformation/default.htm

Office of the Center Director
Guidance and Policy Development
Center for Devices and Radiological Health
Food and Drug Administration
10903 New Hampshire Ave., Bldg. 66, rm. 5431
Silver Spring, MD 20993-0002
Tel: 301-796-5900;
E-mail: CDRH-Guidance@fda.hhs.gov
http://www.fda.gov/MedicalDevices/DeviceRegulationandGuidance/GuidanceDocuments/default.htm

U.S. Department of Health and Human Services
Food and Drug Administration
Center for Drug Evaluation and Research (CDER)
Center for Biologics Evaluation and Research (CBER)
Center for Veterinary Medicine (CVM)
Center for Devices and Radiological Health (CDRH)

June 2014
Advertising

TABLE OF CONTENTS

Guidance for Industry[1]

Internet/Social Media Platforms with Character Space Limitations—Presenting Risk and Benefit Information for Prescription Drugs and Medical Devices

This draft guidance, when finalized, will represent the Food and Drug Administration's (FDA's or Agency's) current thinking on this topic. It does not create or confer any rights for or on any person and does not operate to bind FDA or the public. You may use an alternative approach if the approach satisfies the requirements of the applicable statutes and regulations. If you want to discuss an alternative approach, contact the FDA staff responsible for implementing this guidance. If you cannot identify the appropriate FDA staff, call the appropriate number listed on the title pages of this guidance.

I. INTRODUCTION

This draft guidance is intended to describe FDA's current thinking about how manufacturers, packers, and distributors (firms) of prescription human and animal drugs (drugs) and medical devices for human use (devices)[2] that choose to present benefit information should present both benefit and risk information within advertising and promotional labeling (sometimes collectively referred to in this guidance document as "promotion") of their FDA-regulated medical products on electronic/digital platforms that are associated with character space limitations—specifically on the Internet and through social media or other technological venues (Internet/social media). Examples of Internet/social media platforms with character space limitations include online microblog messaging (e.g., messages on Twitter or "tweets," which are currently limited to 140 character spaces per tweet) and online paid search (e.g., "sponsored links" on search engines such as Google and Yahoo, which have limited character spaces as well as other platform-imposed

[1] This draft guidance has been prepared by the Office of Prescription Drug Promotion (OPDP) in the Center for Drug Evaluation and Research (CDER) in consultation with the Center for Biologics Evaluation and Research (CBER), the Center for Veterinary Medicine (CVM), and the Center for Devices and Radiological Health (CDRH).

[2] The recommendations in this draft guidance also apply to biological products that are approved for marketing under section 351 of the Public Health Service Act (PHS Act). Because each biological product also meets the definition of "drug" or "device" under the Federal Food, Drug, and Cosmetic Act (FD&C Act), it is also subject to regulation under provisions of the FD&C Act applicable to drugs or devices, as well as the regulations implementing these provisions, except that a biological product licensed under section 351 of the PHS Act is not required to have an approved new drug application under section 505 of the FD&C Act (21 U.S.C. 355). See PHS Act section 351(j) (42 U.S.C. 262(j)). References to "drugs" and "devices" in this guidance therefore also include biological products that fall within each of those definitions. The recommendations in this draft guidance do not apply to veterinary biological products regulated under the Virus-Serum-Toxin Act (21 U.S.C. 151, et seq.) by the U.S. Department of Agriculture. This draft guidance does not address devices solely intended for use in animals.

considerations).[3] This draft guidance presents considerations to illustrate FDA's thinking on factors that are relevant to the communication of benefit and risk information on Internet/social media platforms with character space limitations.[4]

Please note that this draft guidance does not address promotion via product websites, webpages on social media networking platforms (e.g., individual product pages on websites such as Facebook, Twitter, YouTube), and online web banners, as the Agency believes that these specific types of Internet/social media platforms do not impose the same character space constraints as online microblog messaging and online paid search. This draft guidance also does not address responsive web design or other technology-specific layout features that may result in product promotion presentations that differ depending on the technology used to view them (e.g., desktop computer monitors, mobile devices, tablets).

FDA's guidance documents, including this draft guidance, do not establish legally enforceable rights or responsibilities. Instead, guidances describe the Agency's current thinking on a topic and should be viewed only as recommendations, unless specific regulatory or statutory requirements are cited. The use of the word *should* in Agency guidances means that something is suggested or recommended, but not required.

II. BACKGROUND

Under the Federal Food, Drug, and Cosmetic Act (FD&C Act), the Agency has responsibility for regulating the manufacture, sale, and distribution of drugs and medical devices in the United States. This authority includes oversight of the labeling of drugs and medical devices (21 U.S.C. 352(a)) and the advertising of prescription drugs and restricted medical devices (21 U.S.C. 352(n), (q), and (r)).[5]

Section 201(m) of the FD&C Act defines *labeling* as "all labels and other written, printed, or graphic matter (1) upon any article or any of its containers or wrappers, or (2) accompanying such article" (21 U.S.C. 321(m)).[6] The U.S. Supreme Court has explained that the language "accompanying such article" in the "labeling" definition is interpreted broadly, to include materials that supplement or explain an article. No physical attachment between the materials and the article is necessary; rather, it is the textual relationship between the items that is significant (*Kordel v.*

---

[3] While online microblog messaging and online paid search examples are specifically illustrated within this draft guidance, FDA's recommendations may also apply to advertising and promotional labeling on other types of Internet/social media platforms with character space limitations.

[4] This guidance document focuses on use of character-space-limited platforms by firms to make claims about their legally marketed drugs and devices that are consistent with their approved or required labeling. Representations by a firm in character-space-limited platforms may also provide evidence of the intended use of the product, but that issue is not the focus of this draft guidance.

[5] Devices may become restricted by regulation issued under section 520(e) of the FD&C Act (21 U.S.C. 360j(e)), by performance standard issued pursuant to section 514(a)(2)(B)(v) (21 U.S.C. 360d(a)(2)(B)(v)), or by order approving an application for premarket approval (i.e., a PMA) pursuant to section 515(d)(1)(B)(ii) (21 U.S.C. 360e(d)(1)(B)(ii)).

[6] See also 21 CFR 1.3(a).

United States, 335 U.S. 345, 350 (1948)). FDA generally recognizes two types of labeling: (1) FDA-required labeling[7] and (2) promotional labeling. Promotional labeling is generally any labeling, other than the FDA-required labeling, that is devised for promotion of the product. Examples of materials that may be considered promotional labeling pieces for prescription drugs are described in 21 CFR 202.1(l)(2). The scope of labeling for prescription medical devices is described in 21 CFR 801.109.

The FD&C Act does not define what constitutes an "advertisement," but FDA regulations provide several examples, including "advertisements in published journals, magazines, other periodicals, and newspapers, and advertisements broadcast through media such as radio, television, and telephone communication systems" (21 CFR 202.1(l)(1)).

Under the FD&C Act and FDA's implementing regulations, promotional labeling for drugs and devices and advertisements for prescription drugs and restricted devices misbrand the product if they make representations about the use of a firm's product without disclosing certain information about the product's risk (FD&C Act sections 502(a)(n)(q)(r), 201(n); 21 CFR 1.21(a); 21 CFR 201.1). When using Internet/social media platforms with character space limitations for product promotion, firms should consider the following provisions[8]:

- Any promotional labeling for a drug or device must be truthful and non-misleading (FD&C Act sections 502(a), 201(n)).

- Any promotional labeling that makes claims about a firm's prescription drug or prescription device must include certain information, such as the indicated use of the product and the risks associated with use of the product (21 CFR 201.100(d), 201.105(d) and 801.109(d)).

- Pursuant to section 502(c) for drugs and devices, information required to appear on the label or labeling must be placed prominently thereon with such conspicuousness and in such terms as to render it likely to be read and understood by the ordinary individual under customary conditions of purchase and use.

---

[7] Much FDA-required labeling is subject to FDA review and approval. For example, after drafting by the manufacturer, labeling is reviewed and approved by FDA as part of the new drug application (NDA), new animal drug application (NADA), biologics license application (BLA) or premarket approval application (PMA) review (see 21 CFR 314.50(c)(2), 514.1(b)(3), 601.2(a), 814.20(b)(10) and 814.44(d)). For devices that are subject to premarket notification (510(k)) requirements, the 510(k) must contain the proposed labeling sufficient to describe the device, its intended use, and the directions for its use (21 CFR 807.87(e)). All devices, including those exempt from premarket review, are subject to the requirements of applicable labeling regulations, including requirements for adequate directions for use (see 21 CFR Part 801). For a prescription drug or prescription device to be exempted from the FD&C Act's requirement of adequate directions for use (21 U.S.C. 352(f)(1)), its FDA-required labeling must contain, among other information, information addressing product hazards and other risk information, as specified in FDA regulations (21 CFR 201.100(d)(1), (3), 201.105(c)(1), and 801.109).

[8] This is not an exhaustive list.

- Any advertising that makes representations about the use of a firm's prescription drug must include certain risk information (FD&C Act section 502(n); 21 CFR 202.1).[9] Similarly, section 502(r) of the FD&C Act requires a "brief statement of intended uses" and relevant risk information in restricted-device advertising. Section 502(q) of the FD&C Act provides that restricted-device advertising that "is false or misleading in any particular" misbrands the device. Note that "reminder" promotion, which calls attention to the name of a product but does not make any representations or suggestions about the product, is exempt from many of these labeling and advertising disclosure requirements (21 CFR 200.200, 201.100(f), 201.105(d)(2), 202.1(e)(2)(i), 801.109(d)).[10]

- Prescription drug advertisements must present a fair balance between information relating to risk and information relating to benefit (21 CFR 202.1(e)(5)(ii)). In addition, risk information must be presented with a prominence and readability reasonably comparable to claims about drug benefits (21 CFR 202.1(e)(7)(viii)).

- Furthermore, for prescription drug advertisements to be truthful and non-misleading, they must contain risk information in each part, as necessary, to qualify any representations and/or suggestions made in that part about the drug. The risk information may be concise if supplemented by a prominent reference to the presence and location elsewhere in the advertisement of a more complete discussion (21 CFR 202.1(e)(3)(i)).

- In addition, section 201(n) of the FD&C Act provides that in determining whether a drug or device is misbranded because its labeling or advertising is misleading, it must be considered whether the labeling or advertising fails to reveal facts that are material with respect to possible consequences of the use of the product as represented in the labeling or advertising or under conditions of use that are customary or usual.

Risk information should be comparable in content and prominence to benefit claims within the product promotion (i.e., a balanced presentation). Achieving a balanced presentation requires firms to carefully consider the desired benefit claims and risk profiles for their products when choosing a promotional platform. FDA acknowledges that Internet/social media platforms associated with character space limitations may pose challenges for firms in providing a balanced presentation of both risks and benefits of medical products, as discussed above.

---

[9] As set forth above, with regard to devices, the Agency's authority over promotional labeling extends to all devices, whereas its authority over advertising extends to restricted devices. Regardless of the type of device, FDA encourages firms to use the practices outlined in this guidance to benefit the public health.

[10] This draft guidance does not apply to those *reminder* promotions (labeling or advertising that calls attention to the name of a drug or device but does not include indications, dosage recommendations, or other information) that are exempted by regulation from the requirements under the FD&C Act for the disclosure of risk information. See 21 CFR 200.200, 201.100(f), 201.105(d)(2), 202.1(e)(2)(i), 801.109(d). But see 21 U.S.C. 352(r) (requiring certain risk information in all restricted-device advertisements).

FDA is issuing this draft guidance to aid firms in effectively communicating benefit and risk information in product promotion using character-space-limited platforms such as online microblog messaging and online paid search.[11] However, regardless of the platform, truthful, accurate, non-misleading, and balanced product promotion best serves the public health. For some products, particularly those with complex indications or extensive serious risks, character space limitations imposed by platform providers may not enable meaningful presentations of both benefit and risk (although they may be sufficient for "reminder" promotions—see footnote 10). If an accurate and balanced presentation of both risks and benefits of a specific product is not possible within the constraints of the platform, then the firm should reconsider using that platform for the intended promotional message (other than for permitted reminder promotion).

III. OVERVIEW OF FDA'S POLICY ON PRESENTING RISK AND BENEFIT INFORMATION ON INTERNET/SOCIAL MEDIA PLATFORMS WITH CHARACTER SPACE LIMITATIONS

Regardless of character space constraints that may be present on certain Internet/social media platforms, if a firm chooses to make a product benefit claim, the firm should also incorporate risk information within the same character-space-limited communication. The firm should also provide a mechanism to allow direct access to a more complete discussion of the risks associated with its product.

Section IV discusses general factors that firms should consider in the communication of benefit information on Internet/social media platforms with character space limitations, which directly impacts the communication of risk information. Section V explains in detail the factors that FDA considers in the disclosure of risk information on Internet/social media platforms with character space limitations. Section VI provides firms with additional recommendations for the inclusion of other product information (including certain required product information other than risk/benefit information, as applicable) on Internet/social media platforms with character space limitations.

Please note that sections IV, V, and VI provide hypothetical examples[12] that, when taken in totality, illustrate FDA's recommendations for how firms may disseminate product promotion on Internet/social media platforms with character space limitations. The examples build on the considerations set forth from the previous section and are numbered accordingly to identify related examples (e.g., examples 1A, 1B, and 1C are related to the same hypothetical product—example 1A incorporates benefit information, example 1B adds risk information to example 1A, and example 1C provides additional recommendations for examples 1A and 1B to illustrate, in totality,

---

[11] CDER's OPDP, formerly known as the Division of Drug Marketing, Advertising, and Communications (DDMAC), issued 14 enforcement letters involving sponsored link promotion on Apr 2, 2009 (see FDA's enforcement website available at http://www.fda.gov/Drugs/GuidanceComplianceRegulatoryInformation/EnforcementActivitiesbyFDA/WarningLettersandNoticeofViolationLetterstoPharmaceuticalCompanies/ucm055773.htm).

[12] The hypothetical examples involve fictitious products and are not an endorsement of the fictitious product names.

a final example of promotion on an Internet/social media platform with character space limitations to which the Agency would not intend to object).

FDA recommends that firms first carefully consider the complexity of the indication and risk profiles for each of their products to determine whether a character-space-limited platform is a viable promotional tool for a particular product, and then take the factors, recommendations, and hypothetical examples outlined in this guidance document into account when developing benefit and risk presentations. The public health is best served when risk and effectiveness information about drug and device products is clearly and accurately communicated.

IV. GENERAL FACTORS CONSIDERED IN THE COMMUNICATION OF BENEFIT INFORMATION ON INTERNET/SOCIAL MEDIA PLATFORMS WITH CHARACTER SPACE LIMITATIONS

When the Agency evaluates advertising and promotional labeling for compliance with the FD&C Act and FDA's implementing regulations, it determines whether claims about both the benefits and risks of the product are accurate and non-misleading. The Agency also looks at whether benefits and risks are presented in a comparably prominent manner (as outlined above in section II). Thus, considerations involving the content and format of benefit information are an inherent part of FDA's evaluation of risk presentations on Internet/social media platforms.

In communicating benefit information on Internet/social media platforms with character space limitations, firms should consider the following points:

1. Benefit information should be accurate and non-misleading and reveal material facts within each individual character-space-limited communication (e.g., each individual message or tweet).

When communicating benefit information about its product, a firm should ensure that benefit information is accurate and non-misleading. In doing so, the firm should also reveal material facts about the use of its product, such as limitations to an indication or the relevant patient population. For example, a firm should refer to the "Indications and Usage" portion of the Highlights of Prescribing Information that is available for many human prescription drugs to help determine what information to convey, although the firm is generally not required to use the precise wording found there. Labeling for an approved premarket approval application (PMA) for class III medical devices or use information consistent with a cleared intended use for 510(k) medical devices provides the basis for the benefit information related to devices. Such information would include material facts that the firm should present within the individual character-space-limited communication because, without doing so, the benefit information in totality may be misleading.

2. Benefit information should be accompanied by risk information within each individual character-space-limited communication.

A firm should also consider whether, once benefit information is conveyed in an accurate and non-misleading manner, enough capacity will remain in the character-space-limited communication to adequately convey required risk information. Please refer to section V for factors firms should consider in the disclosure of risk information. In addition, a firm should consider whether enough capacity will remain in the character-space-limited communication to adequately convey certain other required information, as applicable. Please refer to section VI for additional recommendations firms should consider for the inclusion of other product information.

3. If a firm concludes that adequate benefit and risk information, as well as other required information, cannot all be communicated within the same character-space-limited communication, then the firm should reconsider using that platform for the intended promotional message.

Example 1A: A firm is considering promotion of its prescription drug *NoFocus* on Twitter, which is limited to 140 character spaces per message or tweet. *NoFocus* is indicated for mild to moderate memory loss. Any benefit information that the firm communicates about *NoFocus* should be accurate and non-misleading and include material facts about the use of *NoFocus*, i.e., that it is indicated for **mild to moderate** memory loss.

The firm considers including the following benefit information within the tweet [the information in brackets denotes character spaces used/140 available character spaces in a tweet]:

> NoFocus for mild to moderate memory loss [*40/140*]

The benefit information for *NoFocus* that is communicated within the first 40 character spaces of this tweet is accurate and non-misleading and includes material facts about the indication and limitations to the use of *NoFocus*. The firm should consider whether the remaining 100 character spaces are enough to include risk information and certain other required information, as applicable, about *NoFocus*. See examples 1B and 1C in sections V and VI in this draft guidance, respectively, for further considerations on the disclosure of risk and other information for *NoFocus* within this tweet. If the firm concludes that adequate benefit and risk information, as well as other required information, cannot all be communicated within the same tweet, then the firm should reconsider using Twitter for the intended promotional message for *NoFocus*.

Example 2A: A firm is considering promotion of its prescription drug *Headhurtz* using Google's Sitelink extensions (sponsored link promotion that contains character space limitations and specific formatting requirements, sometimes referred to in this guidance document as "Sitelinks").[13] *Headhurtz* is indicated for severe headache associated with traumatic brain injury. Any benefit information that the firm communicates about *Headhurtz* should be accurate and non-misleading

[13] The example featured in this guidance relies on one specific Google formatting option (current as of Jan 22, 2014); however, it may be possible to follow the concepts outlined in this draft guidance for other types of sponsored link promotion or Internet/social media platforms with character space limitations.

and include material facts about the use of *Headhurtz*, i.e., that it is indicated for **severe** headache **associated with traumatic brain injury**.

The firm considers including the following benefit information within the sponsored link promotion [the information in brackets denotes character spaces used/available character spaces per line of the sponsored link promotion]:

> Headhurtz [*9/25*]
> www.headhurtz.com [*17/35*]
> For severe headache from traumatic brain injury [*47/70*]

The benefit information for *Headhurtz* that is communicated within the character spaces for this specific sponsored link format is accurate and non-misleading and includes material facts about the indication and limitations to the use of, and the specific patient population for, *Headhurtz*. The firm should consider whether risk information and certain other required information, as applicable, about *Headhurtz* can also be included within the remaining character spaces for this specific sponsored link format. See examples 2B and 2C in sections V and VI in this draft guidance, respectively, for further considerations on the disclosure of risk and other information for *Headhurtz* within this sponsored link format. If the firm concludes that adequate benefit and risk information, as well as other required information, cannot all be communicated within this same sponsored link format, then the firm should reconsider using Google's Sitelinks for the intended promotional message for *Headhurtz*.

V. FACTORS CONSIDERED IN THE DISCLOSURE OF RISK INFORMATION ON INTERNET/SOCIAL MEDIA PLATFORMS WITH CHARACTER SPACE LIMITATIONS

This section of the draft guidance outlines factors considered in the disclosure of risk information on Internet/social media platforms with character space limitations. As previously stated, regardless of character space constraints that may be present on certain Internet/social media platforms, if a firm chooses to make a product benefit claim, the firm should also incorporate risk information within the same character-space-limited communication. The firm should also provide a mechanism to allow direct access to a more complete discussion of the risks associated with its product.

In general, the Agency considers two primary factors to determine whether risk information is comparable in scope to benefit information within promotional materials: (1) whether the risk information qualifies any representations made about the product (i.e., content of the risk information compared to content of the benefit information) and (2) whether the risk information is presented with a prominence and readability comparable to the benefit claims about the product.[14]

[14] FDA has developed separate draft guidance that, when final, will represent the Agency's current thinking on how firms should, in general, present risk information in other types of promotional materials. See the draft guidance for

However, the Agency is aware of the challenges in balancing benefit and risk information within the character space constraints of certain Internet/social media platforms—particularly in terms of content—because of the sheer volume of information. The Agency believes that a concise disclosure of specific risk information may be presented together with benefit information within the confines of character-space-limited Internet/social media platforms if supplemented by a prominent reference to the presence and location elsewhere of a more complete discussion of the risks associated with the product (or for restricted-device advertising, a "brief statement" of intended use and relevant risk information) and that this is consistent with requirements of the FD&C Act and FDA's implementing regulations (see section II). These concepts are further elucidated below in this section of the guidance document.

In communicating risk information on Internet/social media platforms with character space limitations, firms should consider the following points:

1. Risk information should be presented together with benefit information within each individual character-space-limited communication (e.g., each individual message or tweet).

2. The content of risk information presented within each individual character-space-limited communication should, at a minimum, include the most serious risks associated with the product.

At a minimum, a firm should communicate the most serious risks associated with the product together with the benefit information within the individual character-space-limited communication. For a prescription human drug, the most serious risks would generally include all risk concepts from a boxed warning, all risks that are known to be fatal or life-threatening, and all contraindications[15] from the approved product labeling (the PI). If a prescription human drug does not have a boxed warning, fatal or life-threatening risks, or any contraindications, the most significant warnings or precautions about the product should be communicated. For animal drugs, the most serious risks would include potential injury to human handlers/animal patients and risk of drug residues entering the human food chain. For devices, if a particular risk is associated with a particular identifiable use or population, then each of those should be included. The Agency believes that communication of the most serious risks as outlined above would provide a concise statement of risk information about the product for promotion on Internet/social media platforms with character space limitations.

industry entitled *Presenting Risk Information in Prescription Drug and Medical Device Promotion* available at http://www.fda.gov/downloads/Drugs/GuidanceComplianceRegulatoryInformation/Guidances/UCM155480.pdf.

[15] For prescription human drugs, if the only contraindication listed in the PI is hypersensitivity, the Agency would not expect that contraindication to be included as part of the risk disclosure within the character-space-limited communication unless there were documented cases of hypersensitivity occurring in patients who took the product.

3. A mechanism, such as a hyperlink, should also be provided within each individual character-space-limited communication to allow direct access to a more complete discussion of risk information about the product.

In addition to presenting the most serious risks within the individual character-space limited communication, FDA recommends that a firm also include in that communication a ***direct*** hyperlink to a destination (e.g., landing page) that is devoted exclusively to the communication of risk information about the product. Examples of such landing pages providing direct and exclusive access to risk information could include a website devoted to providing comprehensive risk information about the product, a particular webpage within a website that is devoted to providing comprehensive risk information about the product, or a portable document format (PDF) file that is devoted to providing comprehensive risk information about the product. An example that the Agency would not consider to provide direct and exclusive access to risk information would include a hyperlink only to a product's home page that also includes benefit information and other claims or graphics. Firms may include *supplemental* hyperlinks (e.g., to a product home page, to a PI, or to a brief summary) either within the character-space-limited communication itself or on the landing page of risk information, but the Agency recommends that a direct hyperlink to a landing page that is devoted exclusively to comprehensive risk information about the product be initially included within the original character-space-limited communication.[16]

Many Internet/social media platforms allow the use of uniform resource locator (URL) shortening services, which are likely to result in a URL or web address with fewer character spaces. The Agency does not intend to object to the use of such URL shortening services; however, when possible, the Agency recommends that the URL or web address itself denote to the user that the landing page consists of risk information (e.g., www.product.com/risk). Please note that if the URL or web address itself is promotional in content or tone, FDA may take into consideration whether any resulting claims are false or misleading or provide evidence in support of other violations under the FD&C Act and FDA's implementing regulations (e.g., a URL such as www.bestcancercuredrug.com may be misleading).

4. The prominence of risk information should be comparable to the benefit information within each individual character-space-limited communication, taking into consideration any formatting capabilities available on the specific Internet/social media platform.

If a firm uses techniques to emphasize benefit information within the character-space-limited communication, the firm should consider similar techniques to achieve comparable emphasis of

[16] A firm should consider how to fulfill other regulatory requirements for advertising or promotional labeling as applicable, such as providing an accompanying brief summary or PI with promotion for a drug (see 202.1(e)(1) and 201.100(d)). Where such requirements apply, the Agency expects that a firm would provide access to a brief summary or PI to accompany the communication in the character-space-limited Internet/social media platform, for example, by providing a direct hyperlink to those materials either within the character-space-limited communication itself or on the landing page of risk information. However, note that a link to a brief summary or PI should not be used **in place of** disclosing risk information within the original character-space-limited communication.

risk information for its product.[17] Additionally, FDA recommends that, where the platform enables the use of different formatting, a firm utilize those formatting capabilities to highlight significant risk information, such as a boxed warning (e.g., a firm should present the boxed warning in bolded text to convey the seriousness of that particular risk for its product).

***Example 1B** (continued from example 1A)*: A firm is considering promotion of its prescription drug *NoFocus* on Twitter, which is limited to 140 character spaces per message or tweet. *NoFocus* is indicated for mild to moderate memory loss. There are no boxed or other warnings and no known fatal or life-threatening risks included in the PI for *NoFocus*. The most serious precaution associated with *NoFocus* is that it may cause seizures in patients with a seizure disorder. Since benefit information was provided within the tweet (example 1A), the firm should communicate, at a minimum, the most serious risks associated with *NoFocus* within the same tweet. The firm should also include within the same tweet a direct hyperlink to a more complete discussion of risk information about *NoFocus*. Additionally, the prominence of risk information should be comparable to the benefit information contained within the tweet, taking into consideration any formatting capabilities that may be available.

The firm considers including the following benefit and risk information within the tweet:

> NoFocus for mild to moderate memory loss; may cause seizures in patients with a seizure disorder www.nofocus.com/risk [*117/140*]

In the above example, benefit information for *NoFocus* is accurate and non-misleading, and the most serious risks associated with *NoFocus* are communicated together with the benefit information within the tweet. The firm includes a direct hyperlink to the "Important Safety Information" webpage (within the product website) that is devoted to providing comprehensive risk information about *NoFocus*. In addition, the URL www.nofocus.com/**risk** (emphasis added) denotes that the landing page is comprised of risk information, and the URL is not promotional in tone. The firm conveys risk information within the tweet in a comparable manner to the benefit information. See example 1C in section VI in this draft guidance for further considerations on the inclusion of other product information for *NoFocus* within this tweet.

***Example 2B** (continued from example 2A)*: A firm is considering promotion of its prescription drug *Headhurtz* using Google's Sitelinks.[18] *Headhurtz* is indicated for severe headache associated

---

[17] FDA acknowledges that providers of character-space-limited platforms frequently dictate aspects controlling the presentation of text that affect prominence and readability (e.g., font size and style). Where the platform provider only permits one type of text, issues affecting comparability are less likely to arise.

[18] Google's "Sitelink extensions" format allows up to six additional links (Sitelinks) to be shown in addition to the display URL (www.headhurtz.com in this example). Under parameters set by Google, the link text for each of the Sitelinks must be 25 characters or fewer. The link text must directly relate to the content on the landing page for that link and point to different content, i.e., no Sitelinks may lead to the same landing page or to the same content. In addition, Sitelinks may not direct to the same landing page as the destination URL (the landing page for www.headhurtz.com in this example). Furthermore, up to two optional description lines (35 characters or fewer per line) may be created for display underneath each of the Sitelinks. This information is current as of Jan 22, 2014;

with traumatic brain injury. The PI for *Headhurtz* includes a boxed warning about the potential for brain swelling and warnings about a potentially fatal drug reaction and a drop in heart rate that may be life-threatening. Since benefit information was provided within the sponsored link format (example 2A), the firm should communicate, at a minimum, the most serious risks associated with *Headhurtz* within the same sponsored link format. The firm should also include within the same sponsored link format a direct hyperlink to a more complete discussion of risk information about *Headhurtz*. Additionally, the prominence of the risk information should be comparable to the benefit information contained within the sponsored link format, taking into consideration any formatting capabilities that may be available.

The firm considers including the following benefit and risk information within the sponsored link promotion:

Headhurtz [*9/25*]
www.headhurtz.com [*17/ 35*]
For severe headache from traumatic brain injury [*47/ 70*]

Boxed warning [*13/25*]	Warning [*7/25*]
Potential for brain swelling [*28/35*]	Potentially fatal drug reaction [*31/35*]
Warning [*7/25*]	Risk information [*16/25*]
Life-threatening drop in heart rate [*35/35*]	Important safety information [*28/35*]

In the above example, benefit information for *Headhurtz* is accurate and non-misleading. Consistent with the Google-imposed formatting requirements outlined in footnote 18, the firm chooses to utilize three of the six Sitelinks to convey the most serious risks associated with *Headhurtz*, including the boxed warning and additional warnings about fatal and life-threatening risks. Therefore, the most serious risks associated with *Headhurtz* are communicated together with the benefit information within the sponsored link format. The firm also includes a fourth Sitelink that provides direct access to a more complete discussion of risk information about *Headhurtz*. Furthermore, consistent with the Google-imposed link requirements outlined in footnote 18, the firm creates four different landing pages, each with different content. The first Sitelink is a direct hyperlink to a webpage that is devoted to providing detailed information about the boxed warning on the potential for brain swelling. The second and third Sitelinks are direct hyperlinks to webpages that are each devoted to a discussion of the specific warning conveyed within the descriptions under these Sitelinks (i.e., a potentially fatal drug reaction and a life-threatening drop in heart rate). The fourth Sitelink is a direct hyperlink to the "Important Safety Information" webpage (within the product website) that is devoted to providing comprehensive risk information about *Headhurtz*. The firm conveys risk information within the sponsored link format in a comparable manner to the benefit information. See example 2C in section VI in this draft guidance for further considerations on the inclusion of other product information for *Headhurtz* within this sponsored link format.

---

please refer to Google's website for more specific information on its advertising policies. See *Sitelink extensions* available at https://support.google.com/adwordspolicy/answer/1054210 and *Show additional links below your ad text* available at https://support.google.com/adwords/answer/2375416.

VI. RECOMMENDATIONS FOR THE INCLUSION OF OTHER PRODUCT INFORMATION ON INTERNET/SOCIAL MEDIA PLATFORMS WITH CHARACTER SPACE LIMITATIONS

This section of the draft guidance provides additional recommendations regarding the inclusion of other product information (including certain required product information other than risk/benefit information, as applicable) on Internet/social media platforms with character space limitations. In addition to including both benefit and risk information within a character-space-limited communication, there may be other applicable legal requirements to consider.

In communicating product information on Internet/social media platforms associated with character space limitations, firms should consider the following:

- Sections 502(e), (n), and (r) of the FD&C Act (21 USC 352(e), (n), and (r)) require that the established name accompany the trade or brand name in labeling and in prescription drug and restricted-device advertising. Drug regulations specifically require that the established name be in direct conjunction with the proprietary name or designation (21 CFR 201.10(g)(1) and 202.1(b)(1)).[19]

- The drug regulations also stipulate that advertisements shall prominently display the name of at least one specific dosage form and have the quantitative ingredient information required by section 502(n) of the FD&C Act in direct conjunction with such display. If other dosage forms are listed in the advertisement, the quantitative ingredient information for such dosage forms shall appear in direct conjunction and in equal prominence with the most prominent listing of the names of such dosage forms (21 CFR 202.1(d)(2)).

With regard to the above regulatory provisions when using Internet/social media platforms with character space limitations, the Agency does not intend to object where the following approaches are used:

- Firms should communicate both the proprietary (trade or brand) name and established name (for drugs, often referred to as the generic name) within the character-space-limited communication. The generic name of the product should be listed directly to the right of, or directly below, the brand name.

- On the landing page associated with each hyperlink provided in the character-space-limited communication, firms should again communicate both the brand and established names as recommended in the preceding bullet. In addition, for prescription drugs, firms should

[19] FDA has developed separate guidance that addresses product name placement and size in promotion. See the draft guidance *Product Name Placement, Size, and Prominence in Advertising and Promotional Labeling* available at http://www.fda.gov/downloads/Drugs/GuidanceComplianceRegulatoryInformation/Guidances/ucm070076.pdf.

prominently display at least one dosage form and quantitative ingredient information in direct conjunction with the brand and established names.

In addition, the Agency believes that common abbreviations (including scientific and medical abbreviations), punctuations marks, and other symbols may, in many cases, reasonably be used to help address character space constraints. The following examples illustrate instances where the Agency does not intend to object to such usage:

- Commonly recognized linguistic symbols may be substituted for words. For example, the ampersand symbol (&) may be used in place of the word *and.*

- Punctuation marks may be used to help with the presentation of information. For example, dashes may be used to help separate benefit and risk information.

- A scientific abbreviation may be used to denote a chemical ingredient name (e.g., "HCl" for hydrochloride; "HBr" for hydrobromide).

***Example 1C** (continued from example 1B)*: A firm is considering promotion of its prescription drug *NoFocus* on Twitter, which is limited to 140 character spaces per message or tweet. *NoFocus* is indicated for mild to moderate memory loss. There are no boxed or other warnings and no known fatal or life-threatening risks included in the PI for *NoFocus*. The most serious precaution associated with *NoFocus* is that it may cause seizures in patients with a seizure disorder. The FDA-approved name is *NoFocus (rememberine hydrochloride) Capsules*, and *NoFocus* is available as 200mg capsules. In addition to taking into consideration factors for communicating benefit and risk information within the character-space-limited communication as described in sections IV and V, the firm should also communicate the brand and established names within the tweet.

The firm considers including the following product information, together with benefit and risk information about *NoFocus*, within the tweet:

> NoFocus (rememberine HCl) for mild to moderate memory loss-May cause seizures in patients with a seizure disorder www.nofocus.com/risk [*134/140*]

In the above example, the brand and established names are communicated together within the tweet. Note that the firm uses the abbreviation *HCl* in place of *hydrochloride* within the established name presentation. The firm uses a dash with no additional spaces to separate the benefit and risk information. As specified in example 1B, the firm includes a direct hyperlink to the "Important Safety Information" webpage (within the product website) that is devoted to providing comprehensive risk information about *NoFocus*. At the top of the landing page, the firm again communicates the brand and established names together with the dosage form and quantitative information in direct conjunction as follows: NoFocus (rememberine hydrochloride)

200mg Capsules. FDA would not intend to object to this tweet for *NoFocus*, as described in totality in examples 1A, 1B, and 1C.

Example 2C *(continued from example 2B)*: A firm is considering promotion of its prescription drug *Headhurtz* using Google's Sitelinks. *Headhurtz* is indicated for severe headache associated with traumatic brain injury. The PI for *Headhurtz* includes a boxed warning about the potential for brain swelling and warnings about a potentially fatal drug reaction and a drop in heart rate that may be life-threatening. The FDA-approved name is *Headhurtz (ouchafol) Tablets*, and *Headhurtz* is available as 200mg tablets. In addition to taking into consideration factors for communicating benefit and risk information within the character-space-limited communication as described in sections IV and V, the firm should also communicate the brand and established names within the sponsored link format.

The firm considers including the following product information, together with benefit and risk information about *Headhurtz*, within the sponsored link format:

Headhurtz (ouchafol) [*20/25*]
www.headhurtz.com [*17/ 35*]
For severe headache from traumatic brain injury [*47/ 70*]

Boxed warning [*13/25*]	Warning [*7/25*]
Potential for brain swelling [*28/35*]	Potentially fatal drug reaction [*31/35*]
Warning [*7/25*]	Risk information [*16/25*]
Life-threatening drop in heart rate [*35/35*]	Important safety information [*28/35*]

In the above example, the brand and established names are communicated together within the sponsored link format. As specified in example 2B, consistent with the Google-imposed link requirements outlined in footnote 18, the firm creates four different landing pages, each with different content, to convey risk information for *Headhurtz*. At the top of each of these landing pages, the firm again communicates the brand and established names together with the dosage form and quantitative information in direct conjunction as follows: Headhurtz (ouchafol) 200mg Tablets. FDA would not intend to object to this sponsored link format for *Headhurtz*, as described in totality in examples 2A, 2B, and 2C.

Appendix G.

Draft Guidance on Correcting Misinformation on Third-party Sites

Guidance for Industry

Internet/Social Media Platforms: Correcting Independent Third-Party Misinformation About Prescription Drugs and Medical Devices

DRAFT GUIDANCE

This guidance document is being distributed for comment purposes only.

Comments and suggestions regarding this draft document should be submitted within 90 days of publication in the *Federal Register* of the notice announcing the availability of the draft guidance. Submit electronic comments to http://www.regulations.gov. Submit written comments to the Division of Dockets Management (HFA-305), Food and Drug Administration, 5630 Fishers Lane, rm. 1061, Rockville, MD 20852. All comments should be identified with the docket number listed in the notice of availability that publishes in the *Federal Register*.

For questions regarding this draft document, contact (CDER) Julie Chronis at 301-796-1200; (CBER) Office of Communication, Outreach and Development at 800-835-4709 or 240-402-7800; (CVM) Thomas Moskal at 240-276-9300; or (CDRH) Deborah Wolf at 301-796-5732.

U.S. Department of Health and Human Services
Food and Drug Administration
Center for Drug Evaluation and Research (CDER)
Center for Biologics Evaluation and Research (CBER)
Center for Veterinary Medicine (CVM)
Center for Devices and Radiological Health (CDRH)

June 2014
Advertising

Guidance for Industry

Internet/Social Media Platforms: Correcting Independent Third-Party Misinformation About Prescription Drugs and Medical Devices

Additional copies are available from:

Office of Communications, Division of Drug Information
Center for Drug Evaluation and Research
Food and Drug Administration
10903 New Hampshire Ave., Bldg. 51, rm. 2201
Silver Spring, MD 20993-0002
Tel: 301-796-3400; Fax: 301-847-8714;
E-mail: druginfo@fda.hhs.gov
http://www.fda.gov/Drugs/GuidanceComplianceRegulatoryInformation/Guidances/default.htm

Communications Staff (CVM)
Center for Veterinary Medicine
Food and Drug Administration
7519 Standish Place, HFV-12
Rockville, MD 20855
Tel: 240-276-9300;
E-mail: AskCVM@fda.hhs.gov
http://www.fda.gov/AnimalVeterinary/GuidanceComplianceEnforcement/GuidanceforIndustry/default.htm

Office of Communication, Outreach and Development
Center for Biologics Evaluation and Research
Food and Drug Administration
10903 New Hampshire Ave., WO71, Room 3128
Silver Spring, MD 20993
Tel: 800-835-4709 or 240-402-7800;
E-mail: ocod@fda.hhs.gov
http://www.fda.gov/BiologicsBloodVaccines/GuidanceComplianceRegulatoryInformation/default.htm

Office of the Center Director
Guidance and Policy Development
Center for Devices and Radiological Health
Food and Drug Administration
10903 New Hampshire Ave., Bldg. 66, rm. 5431
Silver Spring, MD 20993-0002
Tel: 301-796-5900;
E-mail: CDRH-Guidance@fda.hhs.gov
http://www.fda.gov/MedicalDevices/DeviceRegulationandGuidance/GuidanceDocuments/default.htm

U.S. Department of Health and Human Services
Food and Drug Administration
Center for Drug Evaluation and Research (CDER)
Center for Biologics Evaluation and Research (CBER)
Center for Veterinary Medicine (CVM)
Center for Devices and Radiological Health (CDRH)

June 2014
Advertising

TABLE OF CONTENTS

Guidance for Industry[1]

Internet/Social Media Platforms: Correcting Independent Third-Party Misinformation About Prescription Drugs and Medical Devices

This draft guidance, when finalized, will represent the Food and Drug Administration's (FDA's or Agency's) current thinking on this topic. It does not create or confer any rights for or on any person and does not operate to bind FDA or the public. You can use an alternative approach if the approach satisfies the requirements of the applicable statutes and regulations. If you want to discuss an alternative approach, contact the FDA staff responsible for implementing this guidance. If you cannot identify the appropriate FDA staff, call the appropriate number listed on the title page of this guidance.

I. INTRODUCTION

This draft guidance is intended to describe FDA's current thinking about how manufacturers, packers, and distributors (firms) of prescription human and animal drugs (drugs) and medical devices for human use (devices)[2] should respond, if they choose to respond, to misinformation related to a firm's own FDA-approved or -cleared products when that information is created or disseminated by independent third parties on the Internet or through social media or other technological venues (Internet/social media), regardless of whether that misinformation appears on a firm's own forum or an independent third-party forum or website. This draft guidance responds to (among other things) stakeholder requests for specific guidance regarding a firm's voluntary correction of misinformation when that misinformation is created or disseminated by an independent third party.

---

[1] This draft guidance has been prepared by the Office of Prescription Drug Promotion (OPDP) in the Center for Drug Evaluation and Research (CDER) in consultation with the Center for Biologics Evaluation and Research (CBER), the Center for Veterinary Medicine (CVM), and the Center for Devices and Radiological Health (CDRH).

[2] The recommendations in this draft guidance also apply to biological products that are approved for marketing under section 351 of the Public Health Service Act (PHS Act). Because each biological product also meets the definition of "drug" or "device" under the Federal Food, Drug, and Cosmetic Act (FD&C Act), it is also subject to regulation under provisions of the FD&C Act applicable to drugs or devices, as well as the regulations implementing these provisions, except that a biological product licensed under section 351 of the PHS Act is not required to have an approved new drug application under section 505 of the FD&C Act (21 U.S.C. 355). See PHS Act section 351(j) (42 U.S.C. 262(j)). References to "drugs" and "devices" in this guidance therefore also include biological products that fall within each of those definitions. The recommendations in this draft guidance do not apply to veterinary biological products regulated under the Virus-Serum-Toxin Act (21 U.S.C. 151, et seq.) by the U.S. Department of Agriculture. This draft guidance does not address devices solely intended for use in animals.

FDA's guidance documents, including this draft guidance, do not establish legally enforceable rights or responsibilities. Instead, guidances describe the Agency's current thinking on a topic and should be viewed only as recommendations, unless specific regulatory or statutory requirements are cited. The use of the word *should* in Agency guidances means that something is suggested or recommended, but not required.

II. BACKGROUND

Under the Federal Food, Drug, and Cosmetic Act (FD&C Act), the Agency has responsibility for regulating the manufacture, sale, and distribution of drugs and medical devices in the United States. This authority includes oversight of the labeling of drugs and medical devices (21 U.S.C. 352(a)) and the advertising of prescription drugs and restricted medical devices (21 U.S.C. 352(n), (q), and (r)). [3]

Section 201(m) of the FD&C Act defines *labeling* as "all labels and other written, printed, or graphic matter (1) upon any article or any of its containers or wrappers, or (2) accompanying such article" (21 U.S.C. 321(m)).[4] The U.S. Supreme Court has explained that the language "accompanying such article" in the "labeling" definition is interpreted broadly, to include materials that supplement or explain an article. No physical attachment between the materials and the article is necessary; rather, it is the textual relationship between the items that is significant (*Kordel v. United States*, 335 U.S. 345, 350 (1948)). FDA generally recognizes two types of labeling: (1) FDA-required labeling[5] and (2) promotional labeling. Promotional labeling is generally any labeling, other than the FDA-required labeling, that is devised for promotion of the product. Examples of materials that may be considered promotional labeling pieces for prescription drugs are described in 21 CFR 202.1(l)(2). The scope of labeling requirements for prescription medical devices is described in 21 CFR 801.109.

The FD&C Act does not define what constitutes an "advertisement," but FDA regulations provide several examples, including "advertisements in published journals, magazines, other

---

[3] Devices may become restricted by regulation issued under section 520(e) of the FD&C Act (21 U.S.C. 360j(e)), by performance standard issued pursuant to section 514(a)(2)(B)(v) (21 U.S.C. 360d(a)(2)(B)(v)), or by order approving an application for premarket approval (i.e., a PMA) pursuant to section 515(d)(1)(B)(ii) (21 U.S.C. 360e(d)(1)(B)(ii)).

[4] See also 21 CFR 1.3(a).

[5] Much FDA-required labeling is subject to FDA review and approval. For example, after drafting by the manufacturer, labeling is reviewed and approved by FDA as part of the new drug application (NDA), new animal drug application (NADA), biologics license application (BLA) or premarket approval application (PMA) review (see 21 CFR 314.50(c)(2), 514.1(b)(3), 601.2(a), 814.20(b)(10), and 814.44(d)). For devices that are subject to premarket notification (510(k)) requirements, the 510(k) must contain the proposed labeling sufficient to describe the device, its intended use, and the directions for its use (21 CFR 807.87(e)). All devices, including those exempt from premarket review, are subject to the requirements of applicable labeling regulations, including requirements for adequate directions for use (see 21 CFR Part 801). For a prescription drug or prescription device to be exempted from the FD&C Act's requirement of adequate directions for use (21 U.S.C. 352(f)(1)), its FDA-required labeling must contain, among other information, information addressing product hazards and other risk information, as specified in FDA regulations (21 CFR 201.100(d)(1), (3), 201.105(c)(1), and 801.109).

periodicals, and newspapers, and advertisements broadcast through media such as radio, television, and telephone communication systems" (21 CFR 202.1(l)(1)).

The Internet and Internet-based technologies have made it easier for third parties who are independent of firms to disseminate information about drugs and devices. Information created by third parties (which for purposes of this guidance is *user-generated content* (UGC)) might appear on an interactive portion of a firm-controlled website or other interactive Internet/social media platform, or information might appear on a website or other Internet/social media platform that is independent of, or not under the control or influence of, a firm. Many Internet/social media platforms allow for real-time and continuous communications and interactions (e.g., blogs, microblogs, social networks, online communities, and live podcasts) while other platforms do not provide a means for interactive content to be posted. Whether a forum is interactive may affect the means by which a firm is able to respond to information.

Although the Internet has facilitated the transmission of information, allowing patients and other interested parties the opportunity to share experiences as well as to communicate with others about drugs and devices, UGC might not always be accurate and may be dangerous or harmful to the public health. For the purposes of this draft guidance, *misinformation* is defined as positive or negative incorrect representations or implications about a firm's product created or disseminated by independent third parties who are not under the firm's control or influence and that is not produced by, or on behalf of, or prompted by the firm in any particular. FDA has determined it may benefit the public health for firms to correct misinformation about their products (including, for example, situations in which a firm is aware of misinformation that may be dangerous or harmful to the public health).

If a firm voluntarily corrects misinformation in a truthful and non-misleading manner and as described in this draft guidance, FDA does not intend to object if the corrective information voluntarily provided by the firm does not satisfy otherwise applicable regulatory requirements regarding labeling or advertising, if any. If a firm chooses to respond to misinformation about its products using non-truthful or misleading information or in a manner other than that recommended in this draft guidance, however, FDA may object if the information provided by the firm does not comply with applicable regulatory requirements related to labeling or advertising, if any.

III. DETERMINING WHETHER THIS DRAFT GUIDANCE APPLIES

This draft guidance does not apply when a firm *is* responsible for the product communication that contains misinformation. A firm is responsible for communications that are owned, controlled, created, or influenced, or affirmatively adopted or endorsed, by, or on behalf of, the firm. A firm is thus responsible for communications on the Internet and Internet-based platforms, such as social media, made by its employees or any agents acting on behalf of the firm to promote the firm's product, and these communications must comply with any applicable regulatory requirements.[6] Firms should not use this guidance in these situations.

> ***Example 1*:** As part of a marketing campaign, a member of a firm's marketing department posts incorrect statements about a product's safety or efficacy compared to the efficacy of a competitor's product on a discussion board hosted by an independent third party. The firm is responsible for the content of the communication because the member of the firm's marketing department is acting on behalf of the firm. Thus, this draft guidance would not apply.

Additionally, if a firm writes, collaborates on, or exerts control or influence on product-specific content provided by a third party, to the extent that responsibility for the development of the content is imputable to the firm, the recommendations set forth in this guidance do not apply. Accordingly, as a general matter, the firm must comply with all applicable regulatory requirements related to labeling or advertising for that content.

> ***Example 2*:** A firm hosts a discussion group on its own website, monitors the discussion for content that does not speak positively about its product, then removes or edits postings that portray its product in a negative light, and adds positive postings about the product. This firm is exerting control over the UGC and is responsible for the resulting content. Thus, the firm's actions would not fall under the scope of this guidance.

In contrast, this draft guidance applies when a firm is *not* responsible for a product-related communication that appears on the firm's own forum, an independent third-party website, or through social media, and the firm chooses to correct misinformation about its own product contained in that communication. In such cases, we recommend that the firm do so as described in this draft guidance.

Firms are generally not responsible for third-party UGC about their products when the UGC is truly independent of the firm (e.g., is not produced by, or on behalf of, or prompted by the firm in any particular) regardless of whether the firm owns or operates the platform on which the communication appears.[7] If the firm owns or operates the platform or created or initiated the

---

[6] For example, with respect to prescription drugs and biologics, firms should consult the draft guidance for industry *Fulfilling Regulatory Requirements for Postmarketing Submissions of Interactive Promotional Media for Prescription Human and Animal Drugs and Biologics* for recommendations regarding how firms can fulfill regulatory requirements for postmarketing submissions of interactive promotional media (e.g., blog, message board, or chat room) for their FDA-approved products. When final, this guidance will represent the FDA's current thinking on this topic. For the most recent version of a guidance, check the FDA Drugs guidance webpage at http://www.fda.gov/Drugs/GuidanceComplianceRegulatoryInformation/Guidances/default.htm.

[7] *Cf.* 47 U.S.C. 230(c)(1) ("no provider or user of an interactive computer service shall be treated as the publisher or speaker of any information provided by another information content provider"). The Communications Decency Act further defines "information content provider" as someone "responsible, in whole or in part, for the creation or development of information provided through the Internet or any other interactive computer service" (47 U.S.C. 230(f)(3)).

forum on which such UGC appears, the firm should include an overarching clear and conspicuous statement that the firm did not create or control the UGC.

> ***Example 3:*** A firm becomes aware of a blogger who is posting inaccurate information about the firm's product. The blogger does not have a relationship with the firm and the firm does not compensate the blogger for the blog or for any other activity. The firm is not responsible for the content of the blog. The firm may decide to attempt to correct the misinformation, but it is not obligated to attempt to correct it.

> ***Example 4*:** A firm hosts a discussion forum about its drug's or device's FDA-approved use on its corporate website and does not participate in the discussion, but it does monitor the forum for profanity and obscenity. The forum includes an overarching clear and conspicuous statement that the firm did not create the content of the forum. The firm is not responsible for the information that is posted by independent third parties and can, if it so chooses, correct misinformation according to this guidance.

However, a firm's control over, involvement with, or influence over a product-related communication, even when generated by a third party, may result in the firm being responsible for the information as a promotional communication. Thus, firms might be responsible for UGC that they solicit or influence, regardless of the forum.

IV. RECOMMENDATIONS FOR THE CORRECTION OF MISINFORMATION ABOUT PRESCRIPTION DRUGS AND MEDICAL DEVICES

A. Appropriate Corrective Information

This draft guidance sets forth approaches a firm may use once it decides to voluntarily correct misinformation about its own product that is created or disseminated by an independent third party who is not under the firm's control or influence. In accordance with the approaches discussed below, a firm may choose to provide appropriate truthful and non-misleading corrective information or, alternatively, it may provide a reputable source from which to obtain the correct information, such as the firm's contact information.[8] For purposes of this draft guidance, to be considered "appropriate corrective information," a firm's communication should:

- Be relevant and responsive to the misinformation;

- Be limited and tailored to the misinformation;

- Be non-promotional in nature, tone, and presentation;

- Be accurate;

[8] For example, a firm may choose to provide contact information for the firm's Medical Affairs Department.

- Be consistent with the FDA-required labeling for the product;

- Be supported by sufficient evidence, including substantial evidence, when appropriate, for prescription drugs;

- Either be posted in conjunction with the misinformation in the same area or forum (if posted directly to the forum by the firm), or should reference the misinformation and be intended to be posted in conjunction with the misinformation (if provided to the forum operator or author) (see section IV.B); and

- Disclose that the person providing the corrective information is affiliated with the firm that manufactures, packs, or distributes the product.

Because risk and other information about the product are not necessarily part of corrective information, the FDA-required labeling should be included or provided in a readily accessible format. As two examples, a firm may provide a link that goes directly to the FDA-required labeling or may provide a link that opens a new window to a portable document format (PDF) file. The information should not be provided by including a link to a promotional website even if the information is available on the promotional website. Please note that if the uniform resource locator (URL), web address, or link where viewers are directed to obtain the respective FDA-required labeling is promotional in content or tone, FDA would not consider the corrective information to fall within the scope of this draft guidance.

> ***Example 5*:** A firm discovers a chat room where participants are discussing the firm's product for one of its approved indications—diabetes. The firm finds misinformation posted by an independent third party about the diabetes indication that the firm would like to correct according to this draft guidance. Although the product has multiple approved indications, the firm should limit its corrective information to the relevant diabetes indication being discussed.

> ***Example 6*:** An independent third party writes an online post stating that one reason he likes taking a prescription drug (or using a device) is that it has no food restrictions, which is inconsistent with information from the required labeling regarding the need to avoid taking the drug with fatty foods (or to avoid using the device in a certain way). The firm decides to correct the misinformation according to this draft guidance. The firm's representative identifies herself as being affiliated with the firm and posts the corrective information from the required labeling. She also includes a direct link to the FDA-required labeling.

B. Correcting a Clearly Defined Portion of a Forum

FDA recognizes that the Internet, social media, and other technological venues contain a vast amount of information and even one particular forum might have a large quantity of information. It may be difficult for a firm to correct all misinformation about its products in one forum depending on the nature of the forum, the quantity of information, and the length of time the forum encompasses. Furthermore, technologies or platforms that may be used to view the forum affect what information will simultaneously be displayed to users. In light of these considerations, if a firm corrects one or more occurrences of misinformation, it is *not* expected to correct each piece of misinformation in an entire forum. However, a firm should clearly identify the misinformation it is correcting, define the portion of the forum it is correcting, and should correct all the misinformation that appears in that clearly defined portion. A firm should describe the location or the nature of the misinformation that was corrected and should provide a date the correction is made to ensure that parties reading the information do not assume the firm has responded to the entire forum.

> ***Example 7*:** A firm decides to correct misinformation posted by an independent third party on one page of an interactive website. The misinformation consists of three consecutive sentences about the firm's product. The firm should correct all three sentences. It should provide a statement that the firm is responding only to the specified information on that one page and provide the date the change was made. The firm is not expected to correct misinformation that appears on other webpages of the website.

> ***Example 8*:** A firm decides to correct misinformation posted by an independent third party who has commented on a blog that allows comments. The firm should correct each piece of misinformation in the particular comment to which it is responding. The firm should provide a statement that it is responding only to one particular comment along with the date the correction is provided. The firm is not expected to correct misinformation that appears in other comments.

A firm should correct all misinformation in the clearly defined portion of the forum it identifies. For example, if a firm chooses to correct only misinformation that portrays its product in a negative light in a third-party communication but does not address misinformation that overstates the benefits of its product in that same clearly defined portion of the communication, the firm's actions do not meet the recommendations in this draft guidance. Additionally, if a firm chooses to correct more than one piece of misinformation in a forum, the portion of the forum that the firm is expected to correct may be defined, in part, by the locations of the pieces of misinformation the firm corrects and the location of additional pieces of misinformation.

> ***Example 9*:** A firm decides to correct misinformation posted on a blog that allows comments. The firm corrects misinformation in several blog postings that provide incorrect risk information associated with the product and makes clear it is only correcting those pieces of misinformation, but the firm does not address exaggerated efficacy claims in favor of the firm's product in other postings that appear to readers between the postings it is correcting. Even if the firm corrects the misinformation in the limited posts it chose, the firm's actions are not in accord with this guidance because it has intentionally selected only negative information about its product to correct while readily accessible and visible positive misinformation was not corrected.

C. Approaches to Correcting Misinformation

If a firm chooses to correct misinformation, it may do so by correcting misinformation directly on the forum. Alternatively, the firm may provide the corrective information to the independent author for the author to incorporate; the firm may request that the author remove the misinformation or allow comments to be posted; or the firm may request that the site administrator remove the misinformation or allow comments to be posted. The following are examples of approaches that FDA considers to be within the scope of this draft guidance and that firms may take to correct misinformation.

> ***Example 10***: A firm encounters misinformation posted by an independent third party about its product on a website sponsored by a patient group. The website allows comments to be posted by viewers. The firm may post corrective information directly on the website.

> ***Example 11***: A firm finds a webpage about its product that was written by an independent third party on an Internet-based, interactive, collaboratively edited encyclopedia. The firm may choose to contact the author of the webpage and provide corrective information to the author.

> ***Example 12***: An independent third party posts a video on a video hosting website about a firm's product. It is not possible for viewers, such as a firm, to post comments about the video. The firm may contact the entity that administers the website and ask that entity to allow comments about the video to be posted so that the firm may post corrective information.

FDA recognizes that a firm cannot control whether an independent third party refuses to correct the misinformation, or corrects only a portion of the misinformation even though the firm provided complete corrective information, or declines to include the respective required labeling, or declines to remove misinformation, or does not correct all the misinformation in one clearly defined part (if the firm sought to correct more than one piece of misinformation). Accordingly, FDA will not hold a firm accountable for an independent third party's subsequent actions or lack thereof.

> ***Example 13***: A firm finds a webpage about its product that was written by an independent third party on an interactive reference website. The firm contacts the author of the webpage and provides corrective information to the author. The firm is not accountable for the author's subsequent actions or lack thereof.

D. Communications That Fall Outside the Scope of This Guidance

Once a firm undertakes the correction of misinformation, FDA does not expect the firm to continue to monitor the website or communication that previously included UGC containing misinformation. However, when a communication by or on behalf of the firm to the UGC author, site administrator, or the forum goes beyond the correction of misinformation, the communication falls outside the scope of this draft guidance.

> ***Example 14***: A firm decides to correct misinformation found in a blog entry where the blogger is not affiliated with the firm. The firm is not obligated to continue to monitor the blog although it may choose to do so. The blogger responds to the firm's correction,

disputes the corrective information, and also brings up another facet of the product's adverse event profile. The firm replies with additional corrective information that is consistent with the original corrective information and that corrects the new misinformation about the product's adverse event profile. The blogger replies again and now disputes the effectiveness of the product. The firm responds again with slogans and examples of patient profiles from its marketing campaign. The slogans and patient profiles go beyond providing corrective information. The firm's communications now must comply with any applicable regulatory requirements related to labeling or advertising.

***Example 15*:** An independent third party downplays a labeled contraindication on an email distribution list. A firm provides, to the distribution list recipients, the corrective information regarding the contraindication, and additionally provides information unrelated to the contraindication comparing the safety profile of its product to a competitor's product. The firm's communication goes beyond providing corrective information with respect to the third party's statements about the product's contraindication and, therefore, is not considered to be a correction of misinformation within the scope of this draft guidance.

E. The Consequences of Correcting Misinformation

When a firm voluntarily undertakes the correction of misinformation in a truthful and non-misleading manner pursuant to the recommendations in this draft guidance, FDA does not intend to object if these voluntary corrections do not satisfy otherwise applicable regulatory requirements, if any. If a firm chooses to provide information outside the scope of this draft guidance, the firm should ensure the information it provides complies with any applicable requirements related to labeling or advertising. Information considered to be outside the scope of this guidance includes information that does not meet criteria listed above.

FDA does not expect firms to submit corrections to the Agency when correcting misinformation pursuant to this draft guidance; however, FDA recommends that firms keep records to assist in responding to questions that may come from the Agency. The records should include, for example, the content of the misinformation, where it appeared, the date it appeared or was located, the corrective information that was provided, and the date the corrective information was provided.

Appendix H.

Draft Guidance on Submitting Promotional Materials in Electronic and Non-Electronic Format

Providing Regulatory Submissions in Electronic and Non-Electronic Format—Promotional Labeling and Advertising Materials for Human Prescription Drugs

Guidance for Industry

DRAFT GUIDANCE

This guidance document is being distributed for comment purposes only.

Comments and suggestions regarding this draft document should be submitted within 90 days of publication in the *Federal Register* of the notice announcing the availability of the draft guidance. Submit electronic comments to http://www.regulations.gov. Submit written comments to the Division of Dockets Management (HFA-305), Food and Drug Administration, 5630 Fishers Lane, rm. 1061, Rockville, MD 20852. All comments should be identified with the docket number listed in the notice of availability that publishes in the *Federal Register*.

For questions regarding this draft document contact (CDER) Marci Kiester at (301) 796-1200; or (CBER) Office of Communication, Outreach, and Development at 800-835-4709 or 240-402-7800.

U.S. Department of Health and Human Services
Food and Drug Administration
Center for Drug Evaluation and Research (CDER)
Center for Biologics Evaluation and Research (CBER)

April 2015
Electronic Submissions

Providing Regulatory Submissions in Electronic and Non-Electronic Format—Promotional Labeling and Advertising Materials for Human Prescription Drugs

Guidance for Industry

Additional copies are available from:

Office of Communications,
Division of Drug Information
Center for Drug Evaluation and Research
Food and Drug Administration
10001 New Hampshire Ave., Hillandale Bldg., 4th Floor
Silver Spring, MD 20993-0002
Phone: 855-543-3784 or 301-796-3400; Fax: 301-431-6353
Email: druginfo@fda.hhs.gov
http://www.fda.gov/Drugs/GuidanceComplianceRegulatoryInformation/Guidances/default.htm

and/or

Office of Communication, Outreach, and Development
Center for Biologics Evaluation and Research
Food and Drug Administration
10903 New Hampshire Ave., Bldg. 71, Room 3128
Silver Spring, MD 20993-0002
Phone: 800-835-4709 or 240-402-7800;
E-mail: ocod@fda.hhs.gov
http://www.fda.gov/BiologicsBloodVaccines/GuidanceComplianceRegulatoryInformation/default.htm

U.S. Department of Health and Human Services
Food and Drug Administration
Center for Drug Evaluation and Research (CDER)
Center for Biologics Evaluation and Research (CBER)

April 2015
Electronic Submissions

TABLE OF CONTENTS

Providing Regulatory Submissions in Electronic and Non-Electronic Format—Promotional Labeling and Advertising Materials for Human Prescription Drugs Guidance for Industry[1]

I. INTRODUCTION

This draft guidance pertains to submissions of promotional materials for human prescription drugs (drugs)[2] to the Food and Drug Administration (FDA or the Agency) made by manufacturers, packers, and distributors (firms), whether the applicant or an entity acting on behalf of the applicant. Specifically, this draft guidance pertains to submissions made to the Office of Prescription Drug Promotion (OPDP) in the Center for Drug Evaluation and Research (CDER) and the Advertising and Promotional Labeling Branch (APLB) in the Center for Biologics Evaluation and Research (CBER), and explains certain aspects of electronic submission of promotional materials in module 1 of the electronic Common Technical Document (eCTD) using version 3.3 or higher of the *us-regional-backbone* file.

For the purpose of this draft guidance, the terms *promotional materials* and *promotional pieces* collectively refer to advertising (ads) and promotional labeling materials, regardless of the format, manner, or medium by which they are presented. Promotional materials may include, but are not limited to, television ads, brochures, booklets, detailing pieces, Internet websites, print ads, exhibits, sound recordings, and radio ads.

II. BACKGROUND

A. Electronic Submissions to FDA Under Section 745A(a) of the Federal Food, Drug, and Cosmetic Act

Section 745A(a) of the Federal Food, Drug, and Cosmetic Act (FD&C Act), added by section 1136 of the Food and Drug Administration Safety and Innovation Act (FDASIA) (Pub. L. 112-

---

[1] This guidance has been prepared by the Office of Prescription Drug Promotion (OPDP) in the Center for Drug Evaluation and Research (CDER) in cooperation with the Advertising and Promotional Labeling Branch (APLB) in the Center for Biologics Evaluation and Research (CBER) at the Food and Drug Administration.

[2] The recommendations in this draft guidance apply to biological products that are approved for marketing under section 351 of the Public Health Service Act (PHS Act) and that also meet the definition of "drug" under section 201(g) of the Federal Food, Drug, and Cosmetic Act (FD&C Act). For such products, the provisions of the FD&C Act applicable to drugs also apply, as well as the regulations implementing these provisions, except that a biological product licensed under section 351 of the PHS Act is not required to have an approved new drug application under section 505 of the FD&C Act (21 U.S.C. 355). See PHS Act section 351(j) (42 U.S.C. 262(j)). Therefore, references to "drugs" in this guidance also include human biological products that fall within the definition. However, this draft guidance does not apply to those devices that CBER regulates as biological products under section 351 of the PHS Act. These submissions are subject to the requirements under section 745A(b) of the FD&C Act. See the final guidance entitled *eCopy Program for Medical Devices Submissions* that implements the electronic copy provisions of section 745A(b) for medical device submissions to FDA. We update guidances periodically. To make sure you have the most recent version of a guidance, check the FDA webpage at http://www.fda.gov/RegulatoryInformation/Guidances/default.htm.

144), requires that submissions under section 505(b), (i), or (j) of the FD&C Act, and submissions under section 351(a) or (k) of the Public Health Service Act (PHS Act), be submitted in electronic format specified by FDA, beginning no earlier than 24 months after FDA issues a final guidance specifying such electronic submission format. Certain types of promotional material-related submissions discussed in this guidance are "submissions under subsection (b), (i), or (j) of section 505 of this Act or subsection (a) or (k) of section 351 of the Public Health Service Act," and are, therefore, subject to the requirements of section 745A(a). Specifically, (1) postmarketing submissions of promotional materials using Form FDA 2253 (required by 21 CFR 314.81(b)(3)(i) and 21 CFR 601.12(f)(4)), and (2) submissions of promotional materials for accelerated approval products (required by FD&C Act section 506(c)(2)(B), 21 CFR 314.550 and 21 CFR 601.45) and other products where such submissions are required for approval[3], fall within section 745A(a).

The draft guidance entitled *Providing Regulatory Submissions in Electronic Format—Submissions under Section 745A(a) of the Federal Food, Drug, and Cosmetic Act* (745A(a) Implementation Draft Guidance),[4] published in February 2014, sets forth general information on how FDA interprets and intends to implement the electronic submission requirements of section 745A(a) of the FD&C Act. The 745A(a) Implementation Draft Guidance states that it is not feasible to describe and implement the electronic format(s) that would apply to all the submissions covered by section 745A(a) in one guidance document. Instead, FDA will periodically issue guidances specifying the electronic format for certain types of submissions. The revised draft guidance entitled *Providing Regulatory Submissions in Electronic Format—Certain Human Pharmaceutical Product Applications and Related Submissions Using the eCTD Specifications* (eCTD Revised Draft Guidance) specifies the general format for certain types of electronic submissions using eCTD, including the specifications for module 1.[5]

In addition to the more general information and implementation timeline found in those guidances, this draft guidance provides additional information regarding the format to be used for electronic submission of promotional labeling and advertising materials using eCTD. Accordingly, 24 months after the issuance of this guidance in final form, firms will be required to submit all promotional submissions that fall within the ambit of section 745A(a) electronically as specified in the final guidance. As of that date, paper hard copies will no longer be accepted

---

[3] In the Federal Register of May 31, 2002 (67 FR 37988), FDA published final regulations (21 CFR 314.640 (Subpart I) and 21 CFR 601.94 (Subpart H)) under which the Agency would allow appropriate studies in animals, in certain cases, to provide substantial evidence of the effectiveness of new drug and biological products used to reduce or prevent the toxicity of chemical, biological, radiological, or nuclear substances. This rule applies when adequate and well-controlled clinical studies in humans cannot be ethically conducted and field efficacy studies are not feasible. Sponsors with products approved under these provisions are subject to similar presubmission requirements as accelerated approval products and can use the same procedures outlined in this draft guidance for submitting promotional materials to FDA.

[4] When final, this guidance will represent the FDA's current thinking on this topic.

[5] When final, this guidance will represent the FDA's current thinking on this topic. The current version of the associated technical specification entitled *The eCTD Backbone Files Specification for Module 1* provides additional information. See http://www.fda.gov/downloads/Drugs/DevelopmentApprovalProcess/FormsSubmissionRequirements/ElectronicSubmissions/UCM163552.pdf.

for such submissions. Note that while only the promotional submissions that fall within the purview of section 745A(a) will be *required* to be submitted electronically in the format specified in this guidance, firms *may* voluntarily choose to submit electronically other types of promotional material submissions discussed in this guidance. If firms voluntarily opt to submit other types of promotional-related materials electronically, the Agency is currently able to process, review, and archive electronic formats in eCTD and firms are strongly encouraged to make such submissions electronically.

In section 745A(a) of the FD&C Act, Congress granted explicit statutory authorization to FDA to specify in guidance the format for the electronic submissions required under that section. Accordingly, to the extent that this document provides such requirements under section 745A(a), indicated by the use of the words *must* or *required*, this document is not subject to the usual restrictions in FDA's good guidance practice (GGP) regulations, such as the requirement that guidances not establish legally enforceable responsibilities. See 21 CFR 10.115(d).

FDA guidances ordinarily contain standard language explaining that guidances should be viewed only as recommendations unless specific regulatory or statutory requirements are cited. FDA is not including this standard language in this guidance because it is not an accurate description of all of the effects of this guidance. This guidance contains both binding and nonbinding provisions. Insofar as this guidance specifies the format for electronic submissions pursuant to section 745A(a) of the FD&C Act, it will have binding effect.

At the same time, this document also discusses types of promotional materials that are ***not*** subject to the mandatory electronic submission requirement in section 745A, because they are not submissions under section 505(b), (i), or (j) of the FD&C Act or section 351(a) or (k) of the PHS Act (i.e., all promotional materials discussed in this document other than postmarketing submissions of promotional materials using Form FDA 2253 and submissions of promotional materials for accelerated approval products). To the extent that this document includes provisions that do not pertain to the requirements under section 745A(a), this document does not create or confer any rights for or on any person and does not operate to bind FDA or the public, but does represent the Agency's current thinking on this topic. The use of the word *should* in such parts of this guidance means that something is suggested or recommended, but not required. You can use an alternative approach if the approach satisfies the requirements of the applicable statutes and regulations. If you want to discuss an alternative approach, contact the FDA staff responsible for implementing this guidance. If you cannot identify the appropriate FDA staff, call the appropriate number listed on the title page of this guidance.

B. Promotional Labeling and Advertising

Section 201(m) of the FD&C Act defines *labeling* as "all labels and other written, printed, or graphic matter (1) upon any article or any of its containers or wrappers, or (2) accompanying such article" (21 U.S.C. 321(m)).[6] The U.S. Supreme Court has explained that the language "accompanying such article" in the "labeling" definition is interpreted broadly, to include materials that supplement or explain an article. No physical attachment between the materials

[6] See also 21 CFR 1.3(a).

and the article is necessary; rather, it is the textual relationship between the items that is significant (*Kordel v. United States*, 335 U.S. 345, 350 (1948)).

FDA generally recognizes two types of labeling for drugs: (1) FDA-required labeling and (2) promotional labeling. FDA-required labeling is labeling that is necessary to fulfill the minimum requirements of the FD&C Act and its implementing regulations. For prescription drugs, the required labeling is the labeling, drafted by the manufacturer, that is reviewed and approved by FDA as part of a new drug application (NDA), abbreviated new drug application (ANDA), or biologics license application (BLA) (21 CFR 314.50(c)(2), 314.94(a)(8), and 601.2(a)). Promotional labeling is generally any labeling, other than the FDA-required labeling, that is devised for promotion of the product. Examples of materials that may be considered promotional labeling pieces for prescription drugs are described in 21 CFR 202.1(l)(2).

The FD&C Act does not define what constitutes an "advertisement," but FDA regulations provide several examples, including, but not limited to, materials "in published journals, magazines, other periodicals, and newspapers; and advertisements broadcast through media such as radio, television and telephone communication systems" (21 CFR 202.1(l)(1)).

III. GENERAL CONSIDERATIONS

All submissions of promotional materials should meet a set of criteria in order to be reviewed by the Agency. Firms should ensure that the following considerations are met when submitting promotional materials, regardless of the format in which the materials are submitted:

- Include the appropriate NDA, ANDA, or BLA number.
- Use the most specific material type (from Form FDA 2253) to describe the promotional material that is the subject of the submission (e.g., do not use the code "promotional labeling" when another code is available that gives a more specific description of the promotional material).
- Submit different types of promotional material submissions separately (e.g., do not submit materials on Form FDA 2253 pursuant to the requirement in 21 CFR 314.81(b)(3)(i)) together with a request for advisory comments on launch materials).
- Submit ads and promotional labeling separately from other types of submissions (i.e., submissions not related to promotional materials).
- Submit promotional materials directed to healthcare professionals separately from submissions of promotional materials directed to consumers.

Occasionally, promotional materials may be directed both to consumers and healthcare professionals. In those circumstances, firms should identify the audience type based on the end-user for the bulk of the information. For example, press releases should be submitted as consumer-directed materials unless they are specifically intended for healthcare professionals. Websites with distinct sections for healthcare professionals and consumers should be divided into two separate submissions. If the website does not have distinct sections for each audience and it is not intended to be directed solely to healthcare professionals, firms should submit the entire website as a consumer submission.

In cases where a company that holds the application collaborates with another firm in order to promote the drug (e.g., a collaborative marketing agreement where another firm that is not the application holder disseminates and submits promotional materials based on a contractual agreement with the application holder), the application holder should send a general correspondence submission to OPDP or APLB describing the agreement. In addition, the business relationship should be indicated in subsequent submissions of promotional materials.

IV. CONTENT FOR SPECIFIC TYPES OF SUBMISSIONS[7]

This section describes the content of various types of submissions to the Agency relating to promotional materials. The advertising and promotional labeling submissions described in this section represent the types of submissions that FDA currently receives.

A. Promotional Materials Submitted in Fulfillment of the Postmarketing Reporting Requirements (Form FDA 2253 Submissions)

Under the FD&C Act and FDA's regulations implementing postmarketing reporting requirements, applicants must submit specimens of mailing pieces and any other labeling or advertising devised for promotion of the drug product at the time of initial dissemination of the labeling and at the time of initial publication of the advertisement for a prescription drug product. Each submission is required to be accompanied by a completed transmittal Form FDA 2253 (Transmittal of Advertisements and Promotional Labeling for Drugs for Human Use), and is required to include a copy of the product's current professional labeling (21 CFR 314.81(b)(3)(i) and 21 CFR 601.12(f)(4)).[8]

This section provides details on submitting promotional materials in fulfillment of postmarketing reporting requirements. OPDP and APLB have different procedures, so firms should pay careful attention to the following information.

Please include the following:

- Form FDA 2253: Transmittal of Advertisements and Promotional Labeling for Drugs and Biologics for Human Use. (For OPDP submissions, this form should be submitted with ***final*** promotional materials only.) Firms should use the most current version of Form FDA 2253.

- On Form FDA 2253, Box 14 titled "For CBER Products Only:"

---

[7] Please refer to section VI on how to submit promotional materials in module 1 of the eCTD using *us-regional-v3-3.dtd* or higher. Note that complaints should not be submitted using this process.

[8] For more information, see FDA's January 2014 draft guidance for industry entitled *Fulfilling Regulatory Requirements for Postmarketing Submissions of Interactive Promotional Media for Prescription Human and Animal Drugs and Biologics*. When final, the guidance will represent the FDA's current thinking on this topic.

- OPDP: Do NOT check the "Draft" or "Final" boxes
- APLB: Check the "Final" box only for Final postmarketing submissions

- For cases where promotional materials mention multiple products, please note the lead application number on Form FDA 2253 and include an attachment which identifies the other referenced products (e.g., application type and number, trade name, established name).

- Promotional material(s).

- Current product labeling.

Firms are also encouraged to submit annotated versions of the promotional material(s) cross-referenced to the product labeling and references, if applicable.

Professional and consumer materials should be submitted separately and should not include a cover letter or correspondence. For 2253 submissions to OPDP, if a drug has multiple approved indications that are covered by different reviewers in OPDP,[9] firms should submit (when possible) promotional materials that only promote one indication separately from promotional materials that promote only another indication.

B. Presubmission of Promotional Materials for Accelerated Approval Products

Applicants whose drug products are approved under the accelerated approval framework, FD&C Act section 506(c), 21 CFR 314 (subpart H) and 21 CFR 601 (subpart E), and other products where such submissions are required for approval, must submit promotional materials to OPDP and APLB as required under FD&C Act section 506(c)(2)(B), 21 CFR 314.550 and 21 CFR 601.45. Under section 506(c)(2)(B) of the FD&C Act, the Secretary of Health and Human Services may grant accelerated approval of a drug product on the condition, among others, that the sponsor submit copies of all promotional materials related to the product during the preapproval review period and for such period thereafter as the Secretary determines to be appropriate, at least 30 days prior to dissemination of the materials. Additionally, there may be other situations when the Secretary may establish presubmission conditions on promotional materials similar to those in place for accelerated approval products (e.g., section 564(e)(4)(A) of the FD&C Act); in such situations, sponsors will be required to use the format for electronic submission outlined in section V of this draft guidance, no earlier than 24 months after it is finalized.

According to 21 CFR 314.550 and 21 CFR 601.45, unless otherwise informed by the Agency, applicants being considered for accelerated approval must submit to the Agency, during the preapproval review period, copies of all promotional materials, including both promotional labeling and ads, intended for dissemination or publication within 120 days following marketing approval (launch). Pursuant to the same regulatory provisions, after 120 days following marketing approval, unless otherwise informed by the Agency, the applicant must submit

[9] For information about OPDP reviewer assignments based on therapeutic area, refer to: http://www.fda.gov/AboutFDA/CentersOffices/OfficeofMedicalProductsandTobacco/CDER/ucm154886.htm.

promotional materials at least 30 days prior to the intended time of initial dissemination of the labeling or initial publication of the advertisement (non-launch).

The submission should include:

- Correspondence stating that it is a presubmission of promotional material(s) for an accelerated approval product (please refer to section VI.E. for additional details on what to include in the correspondence).

- A clean version of the draft promotional material(s) that does not include annotations to the label or references.

- An annotated copy of the proposed promotional material that clearly identifies the source of support for each claim (e.g., specific page and lines of the FDA-approved full prescribing information (PI) or specific page and column/paragraph from other references).

- The most current FDA-approved PI and, if applicable, the FDA-approved patient labeling or Medication Guide with annotations cross-referenced to the proposed promotional material.

- If applicable, annotated references to support product claims not contained in the PI, cross-referenced to the proposed promotional material.

- If applicable, annotated references to support disease or epidemiology information, cross-referenced to the proposed promotional material.

For draft promotional materials submitted to APLB under 21 CFR 601.45, use Form FDA 2253 with line 14 checked as "Draft." Do ***not*** use Form FDA 2253 for submissions of promotional materials for accelerated approval products to OPDP under 21 CFR 314.550 or 21 CFR 601.45.

C. Promotional Materials Submitted Pursuant to Section 503C of the FD&C Act

On September 27, 2007, the President signed into law the Food and Drug Administration Amendments Act of 2007 (FDAAA) (Public Law No. 110-85). FDAAA authorizes FDA to "require the submission of any television advertisement for a drug . . . not later than 45 days before dissemination of the television advertisement."[10] FDA intends to notify firms when television ads for a drug are subject to this submission requirement. Please refer to the draft guidance *Direct-to-Consumer Television Advertisements—FDAAA DTC Television Ad Pre-*

[10] FDAAA section 901(d)(2). This provision was initially designated as section 503B of the FD&C Act, and codified at 21 U.S.C. 353b. On November 27, 2013, the Drug Quality and Security Act [of 2013] (DQSA), Public Law 113-54, was enacted. Section 102(a) of the DQSA redesignated section 503B as section 503C of the Act, codified at 21 U.S.C. 353c.

Dissemination Review Program for recommendations regarding the components of a pre-dissemination review package.[11]

D. Promotional Materials Submitted Voluntarily for Advisory Comments

Section 21 CFR 202.1(j)(4) provides firms with a voluntary opportunity to submit promotional materials to FDA for advisory comment prior to the dissemination or publication of those promotional materials. Firms may request advisory comments on draft promotional pieces and receive comments in writing from the Agency. Because this process is intended to provide input prior to dissemination or publication, if the Agency learns that the submitted materials, or substantially similar claims or presentations, have been disseminated or published—including after submission for comments—the Agency will generally not review the materials under the advisory process.

1. Requests for Advisory Comments on Draft Promotional Materials Other Than DTC TV Ads Under 21 CFR 202.1(j)(4)

"Launch materials" are draft promotional materials that are voluntarily submitted by a firm to OPDP or APLB during the launch phase (i.e., the first 120 days that an FDA-approved product, indication, delivery system, formulation, dosage form, dosing regimen, strength, or route of administration is marketed to the public) for review and comment prior to dissemination or publication.

Requesting advisory comments on promotional materials prior to launch is encouraged. Review of core launch materials is a high priority for Agency reviewers. Core launch materials generally include:

- One comprehensive promotional labeling piece directed toward professionals (e.g., sales aid, visual aid, detail aid, or exhibit panel (if there is a major conference within the launch phase)), limited to 12 or fewer pages.

- One advertisement directed toward professionals (e.g., journal ad), limited to four or fewer pages, not including the PI or brief summary.

- One comprehensive direct-to-consumer (DTC) labeling piece (e.g., patient brochure), limited to 12 or fewer pages.

- One DTC advertisement (e.g., magazine ad), limited to four or fewer pages, not including the brief summary.

---

[11] The draft guidance *Direct-to-Consumer Television Advertisements—FDAAA DTC Television Ad Pre-Dissemination Review Program* is available on the OPDP Regulatory Information webpage. The draft guidance is not for implementation. When final, it will represent the Agency's current thinking on section 503C.

- A professional and/or DTC product website (limited to 12 printed pages each) or electronic sales aid if it is a derivative (i.e., contains similar claims and/or presentations) of a comprehensive labeling piece that is also submitted for advisory comment.

Launch materials other than those listed above (e.g., slide kits and materials longer than the page limits listed above) are considered non-core launch materials. Non-core launch materials are a lower priority than core launch materials. The Agency recommends that firms apply the Agency's comments on the core materials to non-core materials.

Non-launch materials consist of draft promotional materials that a firm voluntarily submits to OPDP or APLB for review and comment prior to their first use in the public domain but after the launch phase—i.e., after the first 120 days that an FDA-approved product, indication, delivery system, formulation, dosage form, dosing regimen, strength, or route of administration is marketed to the public.

In general, the submission should include:

- Correspondence stating that it is a request for advisory comments (please refer to section VI.E. for additional details on what to include in the correspondence).[12]

- A clean version of the draft promotional material(s) that does not include annotations to the label or references.

- An annotated copy of the proposed promotional material(s) that clearly identifies the source of support for each claim (e.g., specific page and lines of the PI or specific page and column/paragraph from other references).

- The most current FDA-approved PI and, if applicable, the FDA-approved patient labeling or Medication Guide with annotations cross-referenced to the proposed promotional material.

- If applicable, annotated references to support product claims not contained in the PI, cross-referenced to the promotional material.

- If applicable, annotated references to support disease or epidemiology information, cross-referenced to the promotional material.

When submitting draft promotional materials other than TV ads for advisory comments:

---

[12] For draft promotional materials submitted voluntarily to APLB for advisory comment, please use Form FDA 2253 with the box in line 14 checked as "Draft." Please do ***not*** use Form FDA 2253 for submissions of draft promotional material submitted voluntarily to OPDP.

- Draft promotional materials submitted for advisory comment should be consolidated together into one submission for each intended audience (i.e., one submission with professional materials and one submission with consumer materials).

- It is also suggested that draft core launch materials be consolidated into a single submission for each intended audience rather than sending the materials piecemeal in several submissions over the course of a few days or weeks.

- In cases when the firm intends to submit professional and consumer launch core materials at around the same time, it is suggested that both submissions be sent on the same day.

- Likewise, it is suggested that draft non-core launch promotional materials be consolidated into single submissions for each intended audience to the extent possible.

- Submissions of draft DTC TV ads should not be included in submissions with other types of materials (see below for how to submit).

2. *Requests for Advisory Comments on Proposed DTC TV Ads Under 21 CFR 202.1(j)(4)*

The submission should include:

- Correspondence stating it is a request for advisory comments on a proposed TV ad (please refer to section VI.E. for additional details on what to include in the correspondence).

- A clean version of the storyboard of the proposed TV ad that does not include annotations to the label or references.

- An annotated version of the storyboard of the proposed TV ad highlighting which references support which claims.

- The most current FDA-approved PI and, if applicable, the FDA-approved patient labeling or Medication Guide with annotations cross-referenced to the storyboard.

- Other appropriate documentation if any of the following apply:

    - Annotated references to support product claims not contained in the PI, cross-referenced to the storyboard.

    - If the advertisement identifies a person as an actual patient (e.g., a spokesperson) or actual healthcare professional, a signed statement by that person verifying that he or she has in fact used or prescribed the drug product for the advertised indication, and is not merely an actor or model.

    - Verification, in the form of a signed statement by the translator, that an official translation of a foreign-language TV ad is accurate.

- Annotated references to support disease or epidemiology information, cross-referenced to the storyboard.

- Optionally, submissions for advisory review may include a video or animatic of the proposed TV ad. If included, the video or animatic should be in an acceptable file format.[13]

Materials unrelated to a proposed TV ad being submitted for advisory review should not be included in the review package. However, more than one TV ad proposal for a particular indication for a product may be submitted in the same review package.

E. Resubmissions

After FDA has responded to a request for advisory comments or commented on an accelerated approval presubmission, firms may revise and resubmit draft materials.

In general, the resubmission should include:

- Correspondence stating that it is a request for advisory comments on a revised submission (please refer to section VI.E. for additional details on what to include in the correspondence).

- A clean version of the draft promotional material(s) that does not include annotations to the label or references.

- An annotated copy of the proposed promotional material that clearly identifies the source of support for each claim (e.g., specific page and lines of the PI or specific page and column/paragraph from other references).

- The most current FDA-approved PI and, if applicable, the FDA-approved patient labeling or Medication Guide with annotations cross-referenced to the proposed promotional material.

- If applicable, annotated references to support disease or epidemiology information, cross-referenced to the proposed promotional material.

- If applicable, annotated references to support product claims not contained in the PI, cross-referenced to the proposed promotional material.

F. General Correspondence

---

[13] The specification for industry *Specifications for File Format Types Using eCTD Specifications* is available at http://www.fda.gov/downloads/Drugs/DevelopmentApprovalProcess/FormsSubmissionRequirements/ElectronicSubmissions/UCM347471.pdf.

General correspondence includes any correspondence submitted to FDA that may or may not reference a specific drug product application, and that does not fall into one of the other categories (e.g., 2253 submission, request for advisory comments). Please note that complaints should not be submitted under the category of "general correspondence." Examples of types of correspondence to submit under this category include the following:

- Letters in which a firm informs OPDP or APLB of an error that occurred in its promotional piece(s) or activities for its drug product(s).

- Safety update letters in which a firm informs OPDP or APLB that it will promptly revise all of its promotional materials for a particular drug(s) to be consistent with new safety information added to the product labeling.[14]

- General responses to comments from FDA provided in response to advice (advisory or general) when no revised materials are included and there is no further request from the firm to FDA for advisory comments (include Marketing & Advertising (MA) number).[15]

- Notifications from a firm to FDA that it plans to disseminate or publish promotional materials for accelerated approval products previously submitted as required under 21 CFR 314.550 or 601.45 prior to receipt of comments by FDA (e.g., after 30 days for a non-launch presubmission, or after application approval for a launch submission).

- Notifications from a firm regarding agreements with other companies for the promotion of the product.

- Notifications from a firm regarding a change in contact information.

The submission should include:

- Correspondence stating that it is a general correspondence (please refer to section VI.E. for additional details on what to include in the correspondence).

G. Amendments (Submission of Previously Missing or Rejected Materials)

If a previous request for advisory comments or 2253 submission to FDA is missing one or more promotional materials, these materials should be submitted as amendments.

For requests for advisory comments, the submission should include:

---

[14] This type of correspondence is not necessary if the firm notifies FDA in another correspondence (e.g., a presubmission for accelerated approval products) that it intends to comply with 21 CFR 314.70(a)(4) or 21 CFR 601.12(a)(4).

[15] The MA number is the tracking number that CDER uses to identify a submission. CBER uses the *CBER secondary number*. When the term *MA number* is used in this guidance, it refers to both the MA number and CBER secondary number, as applicable.

- Correspondence stating that it is an amendment that includes accompanying materials that were previously missing (please refer to section VI.E. for additional details on what to include in the correspondence).

- Promotional materials that were omitted from a previous submission to FDA.

- Annotated copy of the promotional materials that were omitted from a previous submission to FDA.

- The most current FDA-approved PI and, if applicable, the FDA-approved patient labeling or Medication Guide with annotations cross-referenced to the proposed promotional material.

- If applicable, annotated references to support disease or epidemiology information, cross-referenced to the proposed promotional piece that was previously omitted from a submission to FDA.

- If applicable, annotated references to support product claims not contained in the PI, cross-referenced to the proposed promotional material.

If FDA notifies a firm that promotional materials are missing from a previous 2253 submission that was submitted in paper or non-eCTD format, the firm should resubmit the entire 2253 submission rather than submitting an amendment. In these situations, if part of a 2253 submission is rejected (e.g., a video does not play), the entire 2253 submission should be resubmitted.

If the 2253 submission was in eCTD format, the firm should submit an amendment and include the following:

- Correspondence stating that it is an amendment that includes accompanying materials that were previously missing or rejected (please refer to section VI.E. for additional details on what to include in the correspondence).

- Promotional materials that were missing or rejected from a previous submission to FDA; the firm does not need to resubmit the entire 2253 submission.

  Example: A firm submits a request for advisory comments on launch promotional materials using eCTD. The correspondence file states that three promotional materials are included in the submission along with annotated copies and references. However, upon receipt, FDA notes that the actual submission only includes two promotional materials with annotated copies and references. FDA contacts the firm to notify it that one promotional material is missing from the submission and provides the MA number. The firm should then submit the missing promotional material and the annotated copy and references as an amendment using eCTD. The subject line of the correspondence should note that the submission is an amendment and include the MA number.

H. Withdrawal Requests

A firm may request to withdraw a previous submission to FDA. No materials are submitted with such a request.

Because submission of promotional materials for accelerated approval products is required under 21 CFR 314.550 and 601.45, firms should only use a withdrawal request for such materials if the firm does not plan to disseminate/publish the promotional materials.

The submission should include:

- Correspondence stating that it is a withdrawal request (please refer to section VI.E. for additional details about what to include in the correspondence).

  Example 1: A firm submits draft promotional materials for advisory review for its product (not approved under the accelerated approval regulations at 21 CFR 314.510 or 601.41) and later decides to disseminate the promotional materials without waiting for FDA advisory comments. The firm should notify FDA of its intent to withdraw the advisory request. The subject line of the correspondence should note that the submission is a withdrawal request and include the date of the advisory request or MA number.

  Example 2: A firm submits draft promotional materials for advisory review for its product (not approved under the accelerated approval regulations at 21 CFR 314.510 or 601.41) and later decides not to disseminate the promotional material. The firm should notify FDA of its intent to withdraw the request for advisory comments. The subject line of the correspondence should note that the submission is a withdrawal request and include the date of the advisory request or MA number.

  Example 3: A firm submits draft non-launch promotional materials for its product approved under the accelerated approval regulations at 21 CFR 314.510 or 601.41 and, two weeks later, decides that it does not intend to disseminate the promotional material. The firm should notify FDA of its intent to withdraw the submission. The subject line of the correspondence should note that the submission is a withdrawal request and include the date of the submission or MA number.

I. Response to Untitled Letter or Warning Letter

A response to an untitled letter or a warning letter is a correspondence type that includes a firm's initial response or additional correspondence pertaining to an untitled letter or warning letter from FDA regarding promotion.

The submission should include:

- Correspondence stating that it is a response to an untitled letter or warning letter. This response may include the firm's initial or subsequent responses. (Please refer to section VI.E. for additional details on what to include in the correspondence.)

- Corrective piece(s), if applicable.

J. Response to Information Request

FDA may issue a letter of inquiry to firms when investigating potentially violative activity. The firm's response to a letter of inquiry is considered a *response to an information request*. FDA will notify the firm when a response should be considered a response to information request. The correspondence should state that it is a response to an information request (please refer to section VI.E. for additional details on what to include in the correspondence). The correspondence should include the firm's response to the questions and issues raised in FDA's letter of inquiry, including any materials FDA has requested.

K. Reference Document

Reference documents are annotated references or annotated promotional materials that were missing from a previous submission to FDA. New promotional materials should not be included in this type of submission.

The submission should include:

- Correspondence stating that it is a reference document submission and the specific information regarding what is in the submission (i.e., annotated references, annotated promotional materials, and/or annotated labeling). Please refer to section VI.E. for additional details on what to include in the correspondence.

- Annotated references, annotated promotional materials, and/or annotated labeling.

  Example: A firm submits a request for advisory comments for non-launch materials that includes two clean copies of promotional materials. However, the submission does not include annotated copies of the promotional materials or annotated references. FDA notifies the firm and provides the MA number. The firm should submit the missing materials as a reference document. The subject line of the correspondence should note that it is a reference document submission and include the MA number.

L. Complaints

Please note that complaints about prescription drug promotion are not accepted in eCTD, and they should only be submitted as paper hard copies.[16] Please submit complaints regarding professional and consumer materials separately. A duplicate copy of the submission should be provided. Please do not include Form FDA 2253 or Form FDA 356h.[17]

---

[16] If applicable, an electronic copy of a TV or radio ad in an acceptable file format (e.g, a CD containing a .wmv or .wma file) may be included with a complaint.

[17] Form FDA 356h is an Application to Market a New or Abbreviated New Drug or Biologic for Human Use.

Please include the following:

- Correspondence stating that it is a complaint. Please include the drug, manufacturer, and specific regulatory concerns in the correspondence. In addition, the correspondence should include the contact name, title, address, phone, fax, and email of the person that the Agency should contact about issues related to the submission.

- Supporting information or documentation, if available.

V. FORMAT FOR SUBMISSION OF PROMOTIONAL MATERIALS IN PAPER HARD COPY

Paper copies of all promotional submission types will be accepted up until 24 months following publication of the final version of this guidance. Beginning 24 months after this guidance is finalized, paper copies will no longer be accepted for postmarketing submissions made pursuant to the requirements in 21 CFR 314.81(b)(3)(i) or 21 CFR 601.12(f)(4) and submissions of promotional materials for accelerated approval products and other products where such submissions are required for approval (see section VI for further discussion). If paper hard copy materials are submitted, please use tables 1 and 2 to determine the number of paper hard copy materials to submit for each submission type. Please note that complaints are not accepted in eCTD and they should only be submitted as paper hard copies. If a submission is submitted electronically in eCTD, paper copies should not also be submitted, unless specifically requested.

Table 1: Number of Paper Hard Copies for Various Submission Types Based on Recipient

Type of Submission	Number of Paper Hard Copies	
	If Recipient is OPDP	If Recipient is APLB
Voluntary advisory submission (not a TV ad)	3	2
Voluntary advisory submission of a TV ad	10*	2*
Presubmission of promotional materials for accelerated approval products	3	2
503C TV ad	12*	2*
Resubmission	3	2
General correspondence	2	2
Amendment	3	2
Withdrawal request	2	2
Response to notice of violation or warning letter	2	2
Response to information request	2	2
Reference document	3	2
Complaint	2	2

* If a video is provided, only one copy of the video is necessary.

Table 2: Number of Paper Hard Copies of Promotional Materials to Submit in Fulfillment of the Postmarketing Reporting Requirements (Form FDA 2253 Submissions)*

2253 Submissions	Number of Paper Hard Copies
If the promotional material(s) mentions a single product	2
If the promotional material(s) mentions multiple products	3

** The number of copies is the same for OPDP and APLB. Note that beginning 24 months after this guidance is finalized, pursuant to section 745A(a) of the FD&C Act, firms will no longer be able to submit these promotional materials in paper hard copy.*

A. Submitting Hard Copy Promotional Materials to OPDP

Please send paper hard copies to the following address:

Office of Prescription Drug Promotion
Food and Drug Administration
5901-B Ammendale Road
Beltsville, MD 20705-1266

For time-sensitive materials, please confirm receipt of the submission with a phone call to the OPDP project manager at (301) 796-1200 or by email at CDER-OPDP-RPM@fda.hhs.gov.

For promotional materials other than 503C TV advisories,[18] OPDP suggests applying an "OPDP" sticker or other prominent directional notation to the exterior of packages submitted to OPDP to help avoid misdirection of promotional materials. If it is not possible to add this notation to the exterior of the package, OPDP recommends adding a prominent directional notation (e.g., sticker, rubber stamp, etc.) to the cover letter itself.

B. Submitting Hard Copy Promotional Materials to APLB

Please send paper hard copies to the following address:

Advertising and Promotional Labeling Branch, HFM-602
Food and Drug Administration
Center for Biologics Evaluation and Research
Document Control Center
10903 New Hampshire Ave.
WO71 – G112
Silver Spring, MD 20993-0002

[18] The draft guidance *Direct-to-Consumer Television Advertisements—FDAAA DTC Television Ad Pre-Dissemination Review Program* provides recommendations specific to 503C TV ads. The draft guidance is not for implementation. When final, it will represent the Agency's current thinking on section 503C.

Any questions for APLB may also be addressed to APLB by phone at (240) 402-9158.

VI. FORMAT FOR SUBMISSION OF PROMOTIONAL MATERIALS ELECTRONICALLY

This section provides information on specific aspects of how to submit promotional labeling and advertising materials to FDA electronically in eCTD format.[19] As discussed in section I, there are two types of submissions related to promotional materials that are "submissions under subsection (b), (i), or (j) of section 505 of [the FD&C] Act or subsection (a) or (k) of section 351 of the Public Health Service Act," and are, therefore, subject to the mandatory electronic submission requirement in section 745A(a) of the FD&C Act. The two types of submissions are: (1) postmarketing submissions of promotional materials using Form FDA 2253 (required by 21 CFR 314.81(b)(3)(i) and 21 CFR 601.12(f)(4)), and (2) submissions of promotional materials for accelerated approval products (required by FD&C Act section 506(c)(2)(B), 21 CFR 314.550 or 21 CFR 601.45) and other products where such submissions are required for approval. Therefore, beginning no earlier than 24 months after publication of the final version of this guidance, which, along with the eCTD Revised Draft Guidance, specifies the electronic format for those submission types, firms will be *required* to submit them electronically. As of that date, paper hard copies will no longer be accepted for such submissions.

While the other types of submissions related to promotional materials discussed in this guidance are not subject to the mandatory electronic submission requirement in section 745A(a), firms may—and are strongly encouraged to—make such submissions electronically. However, paper hard copies will still be accepted for submission types that do not fall under section 745A(a). We note that if firms do choose voluntarily to submit other materials electronically, CDER is currently only able to accept them in eCTD format using *us-regional-v3-3.dtd*.[20] Once a firm submits an application-related document in eCTD format, including but not limited to the types of documents described in this guidance, paper copies related to that application should no longer be submitted, unless specifically requested by the Agency.

In some cases, the company that holds the application for a drug collaborates with another company to promote the drug. If the company handling promotion of the drug wants to submit to OPDP or APLB using eCTD, the company should work with the application holder to ensure that both companies are using the same version of the *us-regional- backbone* file. If the submission is for OPDP, both companies will need to use the same version (for example, *us-regional-v3-3.dtd*). In addition, both companies should work together to come up with a system for generating sequence numbers in order to avoid the use of duplicate sequence numbers that will result in a rejection of one of the submissions. For example a company could choose to assign a block of numbers to a particular vendor (e.g., start promotional submissions with sequence 5000).

---

[19] For eCTD module 1 specifications that are discussed in this section see http://www.fda.gov/Drugs/DevelopmentApprovalProcess/FormsSubmissionRequirements/ElectronicSubmissions/ucm253101.htm.

[20] CBER is able to accept eCTD submissions using previous versions of the *us-regional-backbone* file until 24 months after publication of the final version of this guidance.

Please note that the eCTD format accommodates a wide range of applications and related submission types other than submissions of promotional materials. Therefore, a specific submission may not use all of the possible section-heading elements in each module. The following sections describe specific procedures for submitting promotional labeling and advertising to FDA in eCTD format, including submissions made pursuant to section 745A(a) of the FD&C Act.

A. Submission-Description Element

FDA recommends including the *submission-description* element to provide a high-level description of the purpose of the submission and to help differentiate similar types of submissions. The *submission-description* element should include the description of the type of submission and materials, the date of the submission[21], and the MA number (if the MA number has been provided in a previous communication with FDA) or CBER secondary number.

Some examples of helpful submission descriptions are listed below:

- Request for professional launch advisory for website, print ad, and sales aid 20140501
- Withdrawal request 20140405 for print ad MA61 submitted on 20140115
- Response to untitled letter 20140301 MA456
- Reference documents for professional launch advisory for print ad 20140302 MA31
- Consumer 2253 submission 20140915

B. Submission-Type and Submission-Sub-Type

For all promotional materials submitted to FDA via eCTD (including promotional materials submitted in fulfillment of the postmarketing reporting requirements), use the *submission-type* "Promotional Labeling Advertising." If promotional materials are submitted in eCTD without specifying "Promotional Labeling Advertising" as the *submission-type*, the submission may not get appropriately routed to OPDP or APLB and, as a result, there may be a delay in processing and responding to the submission.

The attribute *submission-sub-type* is used to further clarify the purpose of the submission. The following are the current valid *submission-sub-type* codes for the *submission-type* "Promotional Labeling Advertising:"

- *Original.* Use this *submission-sub-type* for all promotional materials submitted in fulfillment of the postmarketing reporting requirements (2253 submissions) and for materials that do not have a submission history with FDA. This includes original promotional materials such as requests for advisory on launch materials, requests for advisory on non-launch materials, presubmission of promotional materials for accelerated approval products, and materials submitted pursuant to 503C. Also use this code for responses to untitled/warning letters,

[21] The date format to be used is yyyymmdd (four-digit year, two-digit month, and two-digit day).

responses to information requests, and other general correspondence if no submission history with the FDA exists for the materials.

- *Resubmission.* Use this *submission-sub-type* for requests for advisory comments and presubmissions of revised promotional materials that were previously submitted as an "original" submission.

- *Amendment.* Use this *submission-sub-type* for a submission that contains additional supportive material to augment information previously submitted, e.g., the submission of promotional material that was previously missing or rejected, withdrawal requests, and submissions of annotated references. In addition, use this *submission-sub-type* for responses to untitled/warning letters, responses to information requests, and general correspondence if there was an original submission to FDA in eCTD format.

Table 3 summarizes the submission process and the *submission-sub-type* code for new submissions.

Table 3: Submission Process and Coding

Submission History[22]	**Action**	**Code for *Submission-sub-type***
Has no prior FDA submission history	Submit to eCTD with the same *submission-id* as the sequence number	• "Original"
All promotional materials submitted in fulfillment of the postmarketing reporting requirements (2253 submissions)	Submit to eCTD with the same *submission-id* as the sequence number	• "Original"
Already has an associated eCTD promotional submission	Submit to eCTD with the same *submission-id* as the original promotional submission	• "Resubmission" for resubmissions • "Amendment" for amendments; withdrawal requests; reference documents; responses to untitled letters/warning letters and information requests; and general correspondence
Has a paper hard-copy submission history only	Do not submit to eCTD	• Submit using paper hard-copy process

[22] The submission history is defined by the format through which the original submission was made. For example, if a 2253 submission was received in paper format, the entire submission is considered to be "paper" and all amendments to that submission should be made in paper. If a submission is received in eCTD format, all amendments to the submission should be made in eCTD format.

C. Form Element

For promotional materials submitted in fulfillment of the postmarketing reporting requirements, use *form-type* Form FDA 2253 (Transmittal of Advertisements and Promotional Labeling for Drugs and Biologics for Human Use) and submit this form in section 1.1. For cases where promotional material(s) mention multiple products,[23] include the attachment listing the other referenced products as a leaf with Form FDA 2253 in section 1.1.

D. Promotional Audience Type

When providing information in module 1.15, reference the leaves at the lowest heading elements. For example, the *m-1-15-promotional-material* heading element needs an attribute of *promotional-material-audience-type.* When a leaf is referenced in any subsection of module 1.15, provide the attribute as a coded value from its corresponding attribute list (promotional-material-audience-type.xml). The current valid codes for *promotional-material-audience-type* are:

- *Consumer*, for promotional materials directed to consumers; and
- *Professional*, for promotional materials directed to healthcare professionals.

E. Correspondence Related to Promotional Materials (Section 1.15.1)

Submit the correspondence relating to promotional materials as an individual portable document format (PDF) file in the appropriate subsection of 1.15.1. Firms will need to submit a correspondence for all submission types listed in section 1.15.1. A separate cover letter should not be submitted in section 1.2. Please note that firms should not submit a correspondence or a cover letter with 2253 submissions.[24] In some cases, the correspondence may be the actual response and the only file necessary for the submission (e.g., response to untitled letter, response to an Agency communication, or a general correspondence). Correspondences submitted to section 1.15.1 should include the following:

- Subject line describing the reason for the submission, the NDA/ANDA/BLA number, proprietary name/established name (dosage form), and the name of the TV ads (if applicable). Examples of acceptable descriptions to be included in the subject line include the following:

    - Request for Advisory Comments on Launch Materials
    - Request for Advisory Comments on Non-Launch Materials
    - Presubmission of Launch Promotional Materials for Accelerated Approval Product
    - Presubmission of Non-Launch Promotional Materials for Accelerated Approval Product
    - Promotional Materials Submitted Pursuant to Section 503C
    - Response to Untitled Letter

---

[23] Please refer to section VI.J. regarding submitting promotional materials that reference more than one application.
[24] If, however, a firm is withdrawing a Form FDA 2253 submission, it must submit a correspondence withdrawing the submission in section 1.15.1.9.

  - Response to Warning Letter
  - Response to Information Request
  - Amendment
  - Withdrawal Request
  - Submission of Annotated References
  - General Correspondence

The body of the correspondence should include the following information:

- Regulatory description of the submission.

- Statement that the submission is virus free with a description of the software (name, version, and company) used to check the files for viruses.

- A list of all promotional materials included in the submission with the material type, material ID, and description for each item listed.

- A concise description of use of the promotional material(s), if applicable.[25]

- Whether the submission is for a "launch" or "non-launch."

- If the submission is for a launch, whether the promotional materials are "core" or "non-core."

- Whether the submission is subject to 21 CFR 314.550, 601.45 regulations, or section 503C of the FD&C Act.

- Whether the submission is a TV ad.

- If the submission is the initial response to an untitled letter or warning letter, a list of all promotional materials (with the 2253 submission date) for the drug product(s) that contain violations similar to those described in the letter.

- Whether the submission contains healthcare professional-directed materials or consumer-directed materials.

- Where applicable, whether the Agency has previously commented on the promotional material(s); the comment date; and the Marketing, Advertising and Communications Management Information System (MACMIS), MA number, or CBER secondary number.

- The name, title, address, phone, fax, and email of the individual the Agency should contact about issues related to the submission. If there are separate regulatory and technical points of contact, please include this information for both individuals.

---

[25] Please refer to section VII.C. for additional details.

F. Materials (Section 1.15.2)[26]

1. Attributes

Submit promotional labeling and advertising materials as individual files in an approved file format in section 1.15.2. When providing information in a subsection of module 1.15.2 materials, three attributes are needed: *promotional-material-doc-type*, *promotional-material-type*, and *material-id*. An additional optional attribute, *issue-date*, should only be provided when the *promotional-material-doc-type* is a promotional 2253 submission. The attribute *promotional-material-doc-type* indicates the purpose of the promotional submission and needs to be provided with the *m1-15-2-materials* heading element. Provide the attributes as coded values from their corresponding attribute list (promotional-material-doc-type.xml). Table 5 shows the current valid codes for *promotional-material-doc-type*.

Table 5: Promotional Material Document Types and Descriptions

Promotional Material Document Type	Description
Promotional 2253	Form and materials required from submitter at initial dissemination of labeling as well as initial publication of an advertisement.
Request for Advisory Launch	Voluntary submission of launch promotional materials for FDA review and comment sent prior to dissemination/publication.
Request for Advisory Non-Launch	Voluntary submission of non-launch promotional materials for FDA review and comment sent prior to dissemination/publication.
Presubmission Accelerated Launch	Promotional materials intended to be used in the first 120 days after approval that are submitted to FDA prior to dissemination/publication as required by 21 CFR 314.550 and 601.45.
Presubmission Accelerated Non-Launch	Promotional materials intended to be used after the 120-day post-approval period that are submitted to FDA prior to dissemination/publication as required by 21 CFR 314.550 and 601.45.
Pre-Dissemination Review of Television Ads	TV ads submitted to FDA for pre-dissemination review in compliance with section 503C of the Federal FD&C Act.

The attribute *promotional-material-type* indicates the type of media/delivery method of the promotional material and should be provided with the *m-1-15-2-1 material* heading element.

[26] If including multiple promotional materials in one submission, please refer to section VI.I. If submitting promotional materials that reference more than one application, see section VI.J.

Provide the attributes as coded values from their corresponding attribute list (promotional-material-type.xml).[27]

The *material-id* attribute may consist of letters, numbers, or both, and should not exceed 30 characters. The *issue-date* attribute, if applicable, should follow the date format as yyyymmdd (four-digit year, two-digit month, and two-digit day).

2. *Clean Version of Submitted Materials (Section 1.15.2.1.1)*

For draft promotional materials submitted (1) voluntarily for advisory comment, (2) as required under section 503C of the FD&C Act, or (3) under 21 CFR 314.550 or 601.45, submit clean versions of the promotional materials (i.e., versions not including annotations to the label or references) in section 1.15.2.1.1.

Clean versions of corrective pieces should also be submitted in section 1.15.2.1.1 using the eCTD "replace" operation.

For promotional materials submitted in fulfillment of the postmarketing reporting requirements, clean final versions of the promotional materials without any annotations must be submitted in section 1.15.2.1.1.

3. *Annotated Version of Promotional Materials (Section 1.15.2.1.2)*

For draft promotional materials submitted (1) voluntarily for advisory comment, (2) as required under section 503C of the FD&C Act, or (3) under 21 CFR 314.550 or 601.45, submit annotated versions of the promotional materials (i.e., versions that are cross-referenced to the product labeling and, if applicable, references) in section 1.15.2.1.2.

Annotated versions of corrective pieces should also be submitted in section 1.15.2.1.2 using the eCTD "replace" operation.

For promotional materials submitted in fulfillment of the postmarketing reporting requirements, firms may choose to submit annotated versions of the promotional materials in section 1.15.2.1.2 that are cross-referenced to the product labeling and, if applicable, references. References improve the efficiency of review.

Firms should highlight and annotate the materials with a cross reference to the product labeling or references. When product labeling or other references are used to support a claim or presentation in proposed promotional materials, hypertext links should be provided in the annotated promotional material to the page/specific lines that contain the supporting information.

---

[27] The current codes for *promotional-material-type*, as well as the codes for other attributes, are available on the FDA website: http://www.fda.gov/Drugs/DevelopmentApprovalProcess/FormsSubmissionRequirements/ElectronicSubmissions/ucm253101.htm.

G. Product Labeling (Section 1.14.6 and Section 1.15.2.1.3)

1. Product Labeling Accompanying Form FDA 2253 Submissions (Section 1.14.6)

Form FDA 2253 specifies that the most current product labeling accompany the submission. Firms must submit the most current product labeling, as required in 21 CFR 314.81(b)(3)(i), to section 1.14.6. For promotional labeling pieces, this is the PI that accompanies the promotional materials. The required format for the PI is PDF.[28]

2. Annotated Product Labeling (Section 1.15.2.1.3)

For draft promotional materials submitted (1) voluntarily for advisory comment, (2) as required under section 503C of the FD&C Act, or (3) under 21 CFR 314.550 or 601.45, include the annotated product labeling in section 1.15.2.1.3.[29] Firms should highlight and annotate, with a cross-reference to the promotional materials, the sections of the product labeling that are referred to in the promotional materials. When product labeling is used to support a claim or presentation in proposed promotional materials, hypertext links should be provided to the page/specific lines that contain the supporting information.

For promotional materials submitted in fulfillment of the postmarketing reporting requirements, firms may choose to provide the annotated product labeling with hypertext links.[30]

H. Annotated References (Section 1.15.2.1.4)

If references are provided, submit each reference as an individual PDF file and place it in section 1.15.2.1.4. Firms should highlight and annotate, with a cross reference to the promotional materials, the sections of the full reference that are referred to in the promotional materials. When a reference is used to support a claim or presentation in proposed promotional materials, firms should provide, in the annotated promotional material, hypertext links to the page and the specific lines of the reference that contains the supporting information.

For promotional materials submitted in fulfillment of the postmarketing reporting requirements, firms may choose to provide references with hypertext links. References improve the efficiency of review.

---

[28] Firms may choose to submit the current product labeling with each 2253 submission. Alternatively, once product labeling is submitted to section 1.14.6 with a 2253 submission, firms may cross reference the current product labeling within the XML backbone. If firms choose to reference the current product labeling within the XML backbone, they should ensure that the version of the product labeling that is referenced is correct and that the leaf title is revised with each 2253 submission to be informative for Agency reviewers (e.g., include the date of submission). Refer to section VI.K. for recommendations regarding leaf titles.

[29] Even if the submission does not include annotations to the label or a part of the label, firms should still include the entire label in section 1.15.2.1.3.

[30] Annotated labeling submitted in fulfillment of the postmarketing reporting requirements must be included as a PDF file in section 1.15.2.1.3. The current product labeling must still be submitted in section 1.14.6.

I. Including Multiple Promotional Materials in One Submission

For draft promotional materials voluntarily submitted for advisory comment or submitted as required under 21 CFR 314.550 or 601.45, if multiple promotional materials are included in one submission, each of these materials is to be submitted with its own clean version, annotated version, annotated labeling, and annotated references. The following example shows how to submit multiple promotional materials in one submission in section 1.15 for advisory comments.

1.15 Promotional material (Professional)
1.15.1 Correspondence relating to promotional materials
1.15.1.1 Request for advisory comments on launch materials
Request for professional launch advisory for sales aid and print ad 20140501
1.15.2 Materials (Request for Advisory Launch)
1.15.2.1 Material (Sales Aid)(65NO35482)
1.15.2.1.1 Clean version
Sales aid 65NO35482 Considerations for treatment 20140501 CLEAN
1.15.2.1.2 Annotated version
Sales aid 65NO35482 Considerations for treatment 20140501 ANNOTATED
1.15.2.1.3 Annotated labeling version
PI annotated to sales aid
1.15.2.1.4 Annotated references
Reference 1 Smith et al. for sales aid
1.15.2.1 Material (Print Ad)(77UY6788)
1.15.2.1.1 Clean version
Print ad 77UY6788 A new option 20140501 CLEAN
1.15.2.1.2 Annotated version
Print ad 77UY6788 A new option 20140501 ANNOTATED
1.15.2.1.3 Annotated labeling version
PI annotated to print ad
1.15.2.1.4 Annotated references
Reference 1 Murray et al. for print ad
Reference 2 Shoon et al. for print ad

For promotional materials submitted in fulfillment of the postmarketing reporting requirements, if multiple promotional materials are included in one submission, submit clean versions of each promotional piece in section 1.15.2.1.1. The following example shows how to submit multiple promotional materials in one submission in section 1.15.

1.1 Forms
Form FDA 2253: Transmittal of Advertisements and Promotional Labeling for Drugs And Biologics for Human Use
Form FDA 2253 Professional website and print ad 20140105
1.15 Promotional material (Professional)
1.15.2 Materials (Promotional 2253)
1.15.2.1 Material (www-website)(68443439)(20130105)
1.15.2.1.1 Clean version

Website 68443439 Challenges to treatment 20140105 CLEAN
1.15.2.1 Material (Print Ad)(3945730)(20140105)
1.15.2.1.1 Clean version
Print a d 3945730 A new treatment 20140105 CLEAN

J. Submission of Promotional Materials Referencing More Than One Application (Grouped Submissions)

Firms may submit promotional pieces that promote more than one product (i.e., a multiple-product submission) as a grouped submission.[31] However, only one application type can be used in a grouped submission. Therefore, should a promotional piece apply to more than one application type (e.g., a BLA and NDA), submit the promotional piece as a separate submission for each application type (i.e., there would be two separate submissions—one for the BLA application and one for the NDA application).

K. Leaf Titles

Appropriately named "leaf titles" allow FDA reviewers to navigate through submissions and distinguish one submission from another in the eCTD viewer. A leaf title should include the MA number if it has been provided in a previous communication with FDA.

The format of the leaf title for the actual form for Form FDA 2253 submissions (placed in section 1.1) should be informative for Agency reviewers. For example, the leaf title "Form FDA 2253 Consumer print ad 20140105" is more informative and searchable than a leaf title of "2253Form." Although both examples identify the submission by type, in the first example the Agency reviewer will know the audience for the promotional material (consumer), the material type code, and the date of the submission—all without having to open the file itself.

In addition, the leaf title for the correspondence related to promotional materials (placed in section 1.15.1) should help the Agency reviewer identify the incoming submission by type. A leaf title of "Response to untitled letter 20140105 MA37" is more informative than a leaf title of "Response to untitled letter" because the former example identifies the type of correspondence, the letter date of the submission, and the MA number.

Leaf titles for each promotional piece (placed in section 1.15.2) should also be informative. For example, a healthcare professional-directed sales aid with the leaf title "Sales Aid 65NO35482 Considerations for treatment 20140102" is more informative than the leaf title "promotional piece.pdf." When displayed in the eCTD viewer, the first example immediately identifies the material type code, the material identifying number of the piece (if applicable), a description of the piece, and the date of the submission. All of this information is useful to the Agency reviewer.

---

[31] For instructions on assembling grouped submissions, please see http://www.fda.gov/downloads/Drugs/DevelopmentApprovalProcess/FormsSubmissionRequirements/ElectronicSubmissions/UCM163552.pdf.

L. Use of Operator Attributes

When using lifecycle operations:

- For resubmissions, use the "replace" operator attribute to replace the previously submitted files with the resubmission's updated files. If a firm is only resubmitting part of the original submission, the operator for the correspondence file should be "new."

- For withdrawals, submit the withdrawal request and use the "delete" operator attribute on all leaves that are affected by the withdrawal request. The operator for the correspondence file should be "new."

VII. PRESENTATION ISSUES

Because electronic images may not adequately convey the net impression of the promotional piece or the details of the intended promotional message within the piece, firms should follow the guidelines below to facilitate review by the Agency.

A. General Presentation Considerations

In general, the presentation considerations below encompass the appearance, layout, format, and visible impression of promotional materials submitted for all promotional submission types and audiences. Optimally, Agency reviewers should be able to use or view each promotional piece submitted to the Agency in the same manner as the end-user audience. In rare instances when this is not possible, firms are to submit electronic promotional materials in a manner for which the net impression is clear and legible; likewise for the individual representations in each promotional piece.

Provide each promotional piece submitted to the Agency in electronic format as an individual file in an approved file format. If the current list of approved file formats does not allow the firm to submit a fully functional piece, the submission needs to provide the ability to view all interactive selection options as still images with annotations or notes that clearly describe the functionality of the piece.

Please note that promotional materials submitted with Form FDA 2253 to OPDP must include a representation of the actual piece that is disseminated rather than solely a proof or galley copy of the promotional piece. However, a proof or galley copy of the promotional piece may also accompany the actual piece as part of the submission in order to demonstrate layout or size presentation elements. Proof or galley copies of the promotional piece should be submitted within section 1.15.2.1.2 of module 1. This recommendation does not apply to APLB submissions.

B. Visibility of Text and Images

Promotional materials should present clear and legible text and images regardless of the format (electronic and/or physical media). While the Agency recognizes that electronic images and text may require magnification on computer screens during the review process, the majority of images and text within each electronic file should not require excessive magnification in order to obtain the net impression of the piece or an understanding of the individual claims.

C. Concise Description of Use

Each promotional piece should include a concise description of use. The description may include, but should not be limited to, the purpose of the piece, setting of use for the piece, and/or an explanation of additional materials that will be used in conjunction with the piece. The concise description of use may be presented on Form FDA 2253 under "Comments" as a comment on the electronic version of the promotional piece, as a comment on an optional proof or galley piece, and/or within the correspondence of an advisory request. A concise description of use is particularly important in situations where additional context is necessary, such as when:

- The purpose of the promotional piece is not self-evident after looking at an image of the piece or reading its title (e.g., a journal ad may be designed with an appearance similar to a booth panel).

- The promotional piece is designed for use only in conjunction with other specific promotional pieces.

- The promotional piece is designed for use in a very specific setting.

- The promotional piece (with the same material ID number) is designed for multiple uses in different and unique settings.

Concise descriptions of use may include, but should not be limited to, language such as:

- Booth panel A will be used only in conjunction with booth panels B, C, and D
- For use as a journal ad and a physician leave-behind
- Item 1 of 5 of kit
- For one-time use during [Conference Title, Month/Year]

D. Layout Indicators

Firms should submit promotional materials with clear and legible indicators for navigating through each promotional piece, as applicable. Indicators describing location and navigation elements in the piece should be presented on each electronic page or image and should not obstruct the image of the promotional materials. Indicators may include, but should not be limited to, the following:

- Front cover, back cover, inside front cover, inside back cover
- Bottom of piece or page, top of piece or page
- Front of piece, back of piece
- Page numbers
- Inserts

- Pockets and pocket content
- Tabs or section dividers
- Folds
- Blank pages or panels
- Annotations to references
- Actual size
- Clarifying the PI position

Indicators may be presented as symbols or text. A key should be provided if symbols are presented as indicators within a submission.

E. Websites, Electronic Interactive Programs, and Electronic Detail Aids

Electronic promotional material submissions including, but not limited to, websites, electronic interactive programs, and electronic detail aids should clearly display and communicate how the promotional piece will look and convey messages to the end user. Preferably, the submission should allow FDA reviewers to view and interact with the piece in the same manner as the end user. For example, still electronic images may not adequately convey how complex interactive promotional pieces convey promotional messages. Such promotional submissions may also be accompanied by a video showing manipulation of the promotional program or application.

In general, in order to comply with the postmarketing requirement for promotional materials in 21 CFR 314.81(b)(3)(i), a firm must submit its entire product website at the time of first use. If the firm then updates one page or section of the website, the firm need only submit the updated page or section with a cross-reference to the original submission of the website noted on Form FDA 2253, including the date of the original submission. If the website is substantially revised, the firm must submit the revised website in its entirety.[32]

F. Materials Requiring Physical Manipulation by the End User

Promotional materials requiring physical manipulation by the end user in order to obtain the net impression of the promotional message (and/or the details of the promotional message) should be submitted in a format that allows the Agency to view all aspects of the promotional piece. For example, the electronic submission of a lenticular refrigerator magnet may display one image if tilted left and an alternate image if tilted right. Representations for both images should be submitted in this case.

G. Three-Dimensional Promotional Pieces or Materials

Electronic submission of three-dimensional promotional objects should provide sufficient detail to allow FDA to view the promotional material from all possible views. In addition, images

[32] For detailed information regarding fulfilling regulatory requirements for postmarketing submissions of interactive promotional media, refer to the draft guidance *Fulfilling Regulatory Requirements for Postmarketing Submissions of Interactive Promotional Media for Prescription Human and Animal Drugs and Biologics*. When final, this guidance will represent the FDA's current thinking on this topic.

should provide adequate information to allow Agency reviewers to determine the size of the object (e.g., point size, dimensions). In rare situations, it may not be possible to accurately represent the promotional piece in an electronic format. In these situations, the best possible electronic image should be submitted electronically and a courtesy copy of the promotional piece can also be sent for the reviewer. The courtesy copy of the promotional piece should be submitted as a general correspondence and should include a reference to the electronic submission and sequence number.

H. Multi-Page Spreads[33]

Promotional materials that include text or images that span more than one page or for which the promotional message may be interpreted as spanning more than one page (e.g., a two- or three-page brochure spread) should include a clear image or representation of the entire spread within a single view. All possible spreads of a given promotional piece should be presented. In addition, electronic images of print materials and electronic materials should be presented in a manner and sequence as they would appear to the end user.

I. Kits

Electronic submission of kits should clearly indicate the components of the kit. Components of the kit that are not intended for distribution apart from the kit should be labeled as such. The accompanying Form FDA 2253 must include the material ID number or identifier for the kit, as well as the material ID number or identifier for each individual component of the kit.

J. Dimensions

All images of physical materials should include dimensions. Images of three-dimensional pieces should be identified as such in the descriptions and provide information adequate to determine height, width, and depth dimensions.

Dimensions should be presented with standard units of measure.

K. Examples of Appropriately Submitted Promotional Materials

Although not exhaustive, the following examples illustrate appropriate electronic submissions of promotional materials in terms of presentation issues:

> *Example 1:* A firm creates a website for a new product that includes links and videos. As part of its postmarketing requirements, the firm must submit an electronic version of the product website under cover of Form FDA 2253. The website should allow the FDA reviewer to click on links within the website and view videos or other animations as an end

[33] In this guidance, the term *spread* is used to refer to adjacent pages of promotional material with related matter or connecting elements extending across the fold.

user will experience while using the site.[34] If the firm is unable to provide active links within the electronic submission, the firm should provide electronic images of each webpage in conjunction with videos.

Example 2: A firm is disseminating an electronic version of a promotional labeling piece containing a healthcare professional-directed quiz. As part of its postmarketing requirements, the firm should submit an electronic working version of the quiz under cover of Form FDA 2253. If the firm is unable to provide a working version of the quiz, the submission must include images that convey the results of selecting correct answers as well as the images resulting from incorrect answers.

Example 3: A firm submits, for advisory comments, an electronic image of a promotional mug that displays a product logo, a frequently used tagline, and a graphic that appears on the mug when hot liquid is added. The submission should include images of the front, back, inside, bottom, and sides of the mug regardless of whether any particular view contains a promotional claim or representation. In addition, the submission should also include images of the mug when hot liquid is added along with an explanation of when the images appear. Such a submission would benefit from layout indicators such as "front," "back," and "intentionally left blank," in addition to measurement indicators.

Example 4: A firm submits, for advisory comments, an electronic image of a trifold branded print brochure. The firm should present, in the following order, images of: (1) the front cover of the brochure, (2) all possible two-page spreads when the brochure is partially opened, (3) the single three-page spread when the brochure is completely opened, and (4) the back cover of the brochure. Such a submission would benefit from layout indicators such as "front panel," "rear panel," "2-panel spread," and "3-panel spread," in addition to measurement indicators.

Example 5: A firm is developing a kit for use that includes consumer-directed promotional materials that are exclusive to the kit to be submitted for advisory comments. For each piece of material included in the kit, the firm should provide a concise description for use. For example, a promotional piece that is intended only for distribution within the kit would include the following description: "Intended for distribution in consumer-directed sample kit only."

Example 6: A firm is developing a Form FDA 2253 submission for an electronic banner used within an exhibit booth. The firm should submit a working version of the banner. However, if a working version of the banner cannot be submitted, the firm should submit a video of the banner in conjunction with screen shots. This is preferable to a submission consisting only of static screen shots. For example, the submission should include a video of the banner along with screen shots that convey how the message will scroll, the time lapse for the complete scroll of the message, and any variation in the rate that the message is scrolled across a screen.

[34] A fully functional website should be submitted in an accessible format whenever possible. Firms should not send links to websites—even if they are password-protected.

Example 7: A firm is developing a Form FDA 2253 submission for a consumer-directed branded video game that is embedded within a standard website. If a working version of the game cannot be submitted using an acceptable file format, the firm should submit a video of the game being played in addition to electronic still images of the game. If the game will also be available to consumers within a conference exhibit setting, the firm should include a concise description of use disclosing this additional unique setting.

Appendix I.

Draft Guidance on Television Commercial Pre-dissemination Review

Guidance for Industry Direct-to-Consumer Television Advertisements — FDAAA DTC Television Ad Pre-Dissemination Review Program

DRAFT GUIDANCE

This guidance document is being distributed for comment purposes only.

Comments and suggestions regarding this draft document should be submitted within 60 calendar days of publication in the *Federal Register* of the notice announcing the availability of the draft guidance. Submit comments to the Division of Dockets Management (HFA-305), Food and Drug Administration, 5630 Fishers Lane, rm. 1061, Rockville, MD 20852. All comments should be identified with the docket number listed in the notice of availability that publishes in the *Federal Register*.

For questions regarding this draft document contact (CDER) Marci Kiester at 301-796-1200, or (CBER) the Office of Communication, Outreach, and Development at 301-827-1800 or 800-835-4709.

U.S. Department of Health and Human Services
Food and Drug Administration
Center for Drug Evaluation and Research (CDER)
Center for Biologics Evaluation and Research (CBER)

March 2012
OPDP

Guidance for Industry Direct-to-Consumer Television Advertisements — FDAAA DTC Television Ad Pre-Dissemination Review Program

Additional copies are available from:

Office of Communications
Division of Drug Information
Center for Drug Evaluation and Research
Food and Drug Administration
10903 New Hampshire Avenue, Bldg. 51, room 2201
Silver Spring, MD 20993-0002
(Tel) 301-796-3400
http://www.fda.gov/Drugs/GuidanceComplianceRegulatoryInformation/Guidances/default.htm

and/or

Office of Communication, Outreach, and Development (HFM-40)
Center for Biologics Evaluation and Research
Food and Drug Administration
1401 Rockville Pike
Rockville, MD 20852-1448
(Tel) 301-827-1800 or 800-835-4709
http://www.fda.gov/BiologicsBloodVaccines/GuidanceComplianceRegulatoryInformation/default.htm

U.S. Department of Health and Human Services
Food and Drug Administration
Center for Drug Evaluation and Research (CDER)
Center for Biologics Evaluation and Research (CBER)
March 2012
OPDP

Table of Contents

Guidance for Industry[1]
Direct-to-Consumer Television Advertisements — FDAAA DTC Television Ad Pre-Dissemination Review Program

This draft guidance, when finalized, will represent the Food and Drug Administration's (FDA's) current thinking on this topic. It does not create or confer any rights for or on any person and does not operate to bind FDA or the public. You can use an alternative approach if the approach satisfies the requirements of the applicable statutes and regulations. If you want to discuss an alternative approach, contact the FDA staff responsible for implementing this guidance. If you cannot identify the appropriate FDA staff, call the appropriate number listed on the title page of this guidance.

I. INTRODUCTION

This guidance is intended to assist sponsors of human prescription drugs, including biological drug products approved under section 351 of the Public Health Service Act, by describing how FDA plans to implement the requirement for the pre-dissemination review[2] of direct-to-consumer television advertisements (TV ads) according to section 503B of the Federal Food, Drug, and Cosmetic Act (the FD&C Act). The guidance describes the types of TV ads that FDA intends to be subject to this provision, explains how FDA will notify sponsors that an ad is subject to the requirement of review under section 503B, and describes the general and Center-specific procedures sponsors should follow to submit their TV ads to FDA for pre-dissemination review in compliance with section 503B of the FD&C Act.

FDA's guidance documents, including this guidance, do not establish legally enforceable responsibilities. Instead, guidances describe the Agency's current thinking on a topic and should be viewed only as recommendations, unless specific regulatory or statutory requirements are cited. The use of the word *should* in Agency guidances means that something is suggested or recommended, but not required.

II. BACKGROUND

On September 27, 2007, the President signed into law the Food and Drug Administration Amendments Act of 2007 (FDAAA) (Public Law No. 110-85). FDAAA gives FDA the authority to ". . . require the submission of any television advertisement for a drug . . . not later than 45 days before dissemination of the television advertisement" (section 901(d)(2), codified at 21 U.S.C. 353b).

---

[1] This guidance has been prepared by the Office of Prescription Drug Promotion (OPDP) in the Center for Drug Evaluation and Research (CDER) in cooperation with the Advertising and Promotional Labeling Branch (APLB) in the Center for Biologics Evaluation and Research (CBER) at the Food and Drug Administration.

[2] The term "pre-dissemination review" is used throughout the guidance to refer to review under section 503B of the FD&C Act, which is entitled "Prereview of Television Advertisements."

In conducting a review of a TV ad under this section, FDA may make recommendations with respect to information included in the label of the drug on:

- changes that are necessary to protect the consumer good and well-being, or that are consistent with prescribing information for the product under review; and
- statements for inclusion in the advertisement to address the specific efficacy of the drug as it relates to specific population groups, including elderly populations, children, and racial and ethnic minorities, if appropriate and if such information exists.

21 U.S.C. 353b(b)(1) and (2).

FDA is issuing this guidance to communicate the categories of TV ads it generally intends to require sponsors to submit under this provision, to explain how it will notify sponsors that FDA is requiring review under section 503B for ads for a particular drug or group of drugs, and to provide sponsors with recommendations for the information they need to properly submit these ads to the Agency for pre-dissemination review.

III. CATEGORIES OF TV ADS SUBJECT TO PRE-DISSEMINATION REVIEW

The Agency intends to require sponsors to submit TV ads for pre-dissemination review in the following categories:

Category 1: The initial TV ad for any prescription drug or the initial TV ad for a new or expanded approved indication for any prescription drug

Category 2: All TV ads for prescription drugs subject to a Risk Evaluation and Mitigation Strategy (REMS) with elements to assure safe use (see section 505-1(f) of the FD&C Act)

Category 3: All TV ads for Schedule II controlled substances

Category 4: The first TV ad for a prescription drug following a safety labeling update that affects the Boxed Warning, Contraindications, or Warnings & Precautions section of its labeling

Category 5: The first TV ad for a prescription drug following the receipt by the sponsor of an enforcement letter (i.e. a Warning or untitled letter) for that product that either cites a TV ad or causes a TV ad to be discontinued because the TV ad contained violations similar to the ones cited in the enforcement letter

Category 6: Any TV ad that is otherwise identified by FDA as subject to the pre-dissemination review provision

These categories reflect a risk-based approach that will enable the Agency to leverage its limited resources to best protect the public health by ensuring that certain high risk and high impact TV ads accurately and effectively communicate key information about advertised products, including their major risks and indications. Specifically, these categories allow the Agency to review and provide comments on TV ads for prescription drugs with particularly serious risks, and to review and provide comments on TV ads at times when feedback on the risk and indication communication in the ad is particularly critical, including when a product is first advertised on TV and after a product has received a significant safety labeling update or a new or expanded indication.

Category # 1: FDA intends to review and comment on the first TV ad for a prescription drug or the first TV ad for a new or expanded indication for an already-approved product. This will allow us to provide feedback on the *major statement* (i.e., the presentation of risk information in a broadcast ad), which sponsors can apply to both the initial ad and future ads. FDA can also identify any issues with the presentation of the product's indication and, where applicable, the product's specific efficacy in population subgroups, and provide feedback relevant to both current and future ads.

Categories # 2 and # 3: FDA intends to review all TV ads for certain prescription drugs with particularly serious risks relative to benefits — specifically, products with REMS with elements to assure safe use and products that are Schedule II controlled substances. FDA believes it is critically important that the risks associated with such products be appropriately communicated in all promotion, and intends to review all TV ads for such products to help ensure that this occurs.

Category # 4: FDA intends to review and comment on the first TV ad for a prescription drug following a significant safety labeling update to the product's FDA-approved prescribing information (PI). This will allow us to provide feedback on the "major statement" for that product to help ensure that new risk concepts are communicated appropriately in the submitted ad and in future ads for the product. FDA understands that certain safety labeling supplements can be submitted as "Changes Being Effected" supplements (CBE supplements), and that sponsors may begin distribution of the product using the modified labeling contained in the supplement upon receipt of the CBE supplement by FDA.[3] If a sponsor chooses to disseminate a TV ad while such a CBE supplement is pending review and approval by FDA, FDA encourages the sponsor to submit the TV ad under the voluntary advisory review process to the appropriate group (OPDP or APLB). Once FDA has approved the CBE supplement (resulting in a significant safety update to the product's *FDA-approved* labeling), FDA intends to require the sponsor to submit its next TV ad for the product to FDA for pre-dissemination review, even if the same or a substantially similar TV ad was submitted voluntarily prior to the FDA approval of the CBE supplement, to ensure that the ad remains consistent with the labeling as approved.

Category # 5: FDA intends to review and comment on the first TV ad for a prescription drug after a sponsor receives an enforcement letter from FDA for its promotion of that product that either cited a TV ad or caused a TV ad to be discontinued because the TV ad contained violations similar to the ones cited in the enforcement letter. In either of these cases, FDA intends to review the next TV ad for the product before it is publicly aired to ensure that the ad is not false or misleading and that the ad does not contain violations that are the same or similar to those cited in the enforcement letter.

[3] See 21 CFR 314.70(c)(6) and 601.12(f)(2).

Category # 6

In addition, FDA may notify a sponsor that a TV ad for a product is subject to the pre-dissemination review provision in the FD&C Act if such pre-dissemination review is deemed necessary from a public health perspective. This would be done on a case-by-base basis after considering the risks associated with particular products. In such a case, a sponsor will be notified in writing of our decision to apply this provision to its product and of the length of time that the pre-dissemination review requirement will be in effect for its product.

Generally, sponsors have the option of submitting any proposed prescription drug television ad to FDA for advisory review before publicly disseminating the ad (see 21 CFR 202.1(j)(4)). In this way, sponsors can benefit from FDA's input on whether or not ads are accurate, balanced, and nonmisleading before they disseminate the ads. This voluntary submission process also gives sponsors an opportunity to address any problems before the TV ads are shown to the public, improving the quality of the ads. This voluntary submission process is still available to sponsors. However, if a sponsor has been notified that a TV ad for one of its products is subject to the pre-dissemination review provisions in section 503B of the FD&C Act, it will be required to submit this TV ad for pre-dissemination review.

FDA understands that sponsors subject to the 503B pre-dissemination review provision may revise their TV ads after receiving comments from the Agency, but before disseminating the ads. FDA does not expect a sponsor to resubmit its draft TV ad for pre-dissemination review if the revisions made to the ad are in response to the Agency's comments and do not introduce new claims, concepts, or creative themes into the TV ad. If a sponsor does wish to request additional comments on such a TV ad, it should do so under the voluntary advisory submission process.[4] However, if a sponsor revises a draft TV ad following pre-dissemination review under section 503B to add new claims, concepts, or creative themes into the TV ad, the sponsor will be required to resubmit the TV ad to the Agency for pre-dissemination review following the procedures outlined in this guidance.

IV. HOW WILL FDA NOTIFY SPONSORS OF THE REQUIREMENT TO SUBMIT A TV AD FOR PRE-DISSEMINATION REVIEW?

FDA intends to notify drug sponsors of the requirement to submit their TV ads for pre-dissemination review in several different ways. For drugs approved in the future and for approved drugs for which an expanded indication is approved in the future (Category 1), for approved drugs that fall under Categories 4 and 5 as described in this guidance, and for any other drugs for which FDA determines pre-dissemination review of TV ads is required (Category 6), FDA intends to notify sponsors in the letter approving the application or supplement, in the approval of the labeling update, in the enforcement letter, or in other correspondence. For drugs already approved prior to the issuance of this guidance that fall under Categories 1, 2, and 3,

[4] Visit http://www.fda.gov/AboutFDA/CentersOffices/OfficeofMedicalProductsandTobacco/CDER/ucm090159.htm and www.fda.gov/BiologicsBloodVaccines/DevelopmentApprovalProcess/AdvertisingLabelingPromotionalMaterials/ucm164120.htm for current information regarding the advisory review submission process.

FDA intends to publish a notice in the *Federal Register* notifying sponsors that their products will be subject to pre-dissemination review in accordance with section 503B of the FD&C Act. However, if a sponsor is developing a TV ad for a product that falls into one of the categories described above and has not yet received written notification, we recommend that the sponsor submit the TV ad for pre-dissemination review as described in this guidance.[5]

V. CONTENTS OF A COMPLETE PRE-DISSEMINATION REVIEW PACKAGE

For FDA to meaningfully review and provide recommendations on TV ads submitted under the section 503B pre-dissemination review provision, the Agency should receive certain information and materials in addition to the ad itself, such as the advertised product's current approved labeling and any references a sponsor is relying on to support claims made in an ad. This section of the guidance outlines what should be included in a sponsor's pre-dissemination review package. Complete pre-dissemination review packages should be sent to either CDER or CBER, depending on which Center regulates the product the TV ad addresses. The following recommendations apply to ***all pre-dissemination review packages*** for TV ads sent to FDA. Specific details regarding submissions to CDER and CBER are provided in the Appendix.

A. What materials should I include in a pre-dissemination review package?

A sponsor should include the following in all pre-dissemination review packages for a TV ad:

1. A cover letter that:
    - Provides the following subject line: Pre-Dissemination Review Package for a Proposed TV Ad for [Proprietary Name/Established Name (dosage form) (for drugs), or Trade name/Proper name (for biologics)] Subject to 503B of the FD&C Act
    - Includes the NDA or STN number
    - Provides the name of the proposed TV ad
    - Lists the contents of the pre-dissemination review package and the number of copies provided of each item contained in the pre-dissemination review package (see Appendix for details on the number of copies to submit to each Center)
    - Provides a sponsor contact's name, title, address, phone, fax, and email
2. Annotated storyboard of the proposed TV ad to show which references support which claims

[5] For current contact information for OPDP, visit http://www.fda.gov/AboutFDA/CentersOffices/OfficeofMedicalProductsandTobacco/CDER/ucm090142.htm. For current contact information for APLB, visit www.fda.gov/BiologicsBloodVaccines/DevelopmentApprovalProcess/AdvertisingLabelingPromotionalMaterials/ucm164120.htm.

3. The most current FDA-approved prescribing information (PI) and, if applicable, the FDA-approved patient labeling or Medication Guide with annotations cross-referenced to the storyboard

A sponsor should also include other appropriate documentation, if any of the following apply:

4. Annotated references to support product claims not contained in the PI, cross-referenced to the storyboard

5. Verification that a person identified in a TV ad as an actual patient or health care practitioner is an actual patient or health care practitioner and not a model or actor; and/or

   Verification that a spokesperson who is represented as a real patient is indeed an actual patient; and/or

   Verification that an official translation of a foreign language TV ad is accurate

6. Annotated references to support disease or epidemiology information, cross-referenced to the storyboard

7. A video of the TV ad in an acceptable format,[6] if available. FDA cannot provide final comments on the acceptability of a TV ad without viewing a final recorded version in its entirety. FDA understands that some sponsors may wish to receive comments from the Agency before producing a final recorded version of the ad. In such situations, sponsors can submit a pre-dissemination review package without a final recorded version of the ad, but once the final recorded version is produced, it will need to be submitted to the Agency for pre-dissemination review.

B. What should ***not*** be included in a pre-dissemination review package?

Materials unrelated to a proposed TV ad being submitted for pre-dissemination review should **not** be included in the pre-dissemination review package. For example, do **not** include other draft promotional materials in the pre-dissemination review package. In addition, only one proposed TV ad should be submitted per pre-dissemination review package.

C. How are incomplete pre-dissemination review packages handled?

Pre-dissemination review packages that are missing any of the elements in section V(A) above or that fail to follow the specific details for submissions to CDER or CBER as provided in the Appendix are considered incomplete. If FDA receives an incomplete package, we will:

- Inform the sponsor that the submission is incomplete
- Provide the reason(s) that the package is incomplete
- Request a submission package that contains the missing materials

---

[6] Visit http://www.fda.gov/AboutFDA/CentersOffices/OfficeofMedicalProductsandTobacco/CDER/ucm090159.htm and www.fda.gov/BiologicsBloodVaccines/DevelopmentApprovalProcess/AdvertisingLabelingPromotionalMaterials/ucm164120.htm for current information regarding acceptable formats.

Note that the 45-day review time frame (see below) does not begin until a **complete** pre-dissemination review package is received.

VI. FREQUENTLY ASKED QUESTIONS AND ANSWERS

A. How long does FDA have to review a television ad under section 503B and when does the clock start?

Under section 503B, FDA may require that a TV ad be submitted to FDA for review not later than 45 days before the sponsor intends to disseminate the ad (21 U.S.C. 353b(a); see also 21 U.S.C. 333(g)(3)(C)). The 45-day review clock for proposed DTC TV ads subject to the pre-dissemination review provision begins when CDER or CBER has received a complete pre-dissemination review package from a sponsor.

B. What happens if FDA is not able to complete its review within the 45-day time frame?

FDA will notify the sponsor if the Agency is not able to provide comments within the 45 calendar day time frame. FDA's notification will include an estimate of the date on which FDA expects to provide its comments. In such situations, the sponsor should determine whether it will wait for FDA's comments before disseminating the TV ad or whether it will disseminate the TV ad without waiting for FDA's comments. The sponsor should notify FDA of its decision. Once the 45-day review time has elapsed, there is no specific legal consequence resulting from disseminating the proposed TV ad without waiting for FDA's comments see section VII.A). However, once an ad is disseminated, the sponsor is at risk of enforcement action if the ad violates the FD&C Act and implementing FDA regulations.

C. Will FDA continue its review if I decide to disseminate my TV ad before receiving FDA comments, but after the clock has run?

No. If a sponsor decides to disseminate the proposed TV ad before receiving FDA's comments, but after the 45-day clock has run, FDA will discontinue its 503B review. As noted above, if the ad is disseminated, the sponsor is at risk of enforcement action if the ad violates the FD&C Act and implementing FDA regulations.

VII. ENFORCEMENT

A. What happens if I do not submit a TV ad for review that is required under section 503B or submit a TV ad for review and disseminate the ad before the 45-day comment period ends, without waiting for comments from FDA?

Under section 301(kk) of the FD&C Act (21 U.S.C. 331(kk)), dissemination of a television advertisement without complying with section 503B is a prohibited act. This prohibited activity can be enjoined (21 U.S.C. 332(a)) and be subject to criminal penalties (21 U.S.C. 333(a)). In addition, if the Agency assesses civil monetary penalties to the sponsor because the TV ad is false or misleading (21 U.S.C. 333(g)), in determining the civil monetary penalty amount, FDA will take into account the fact that the sponsor failed to submit a TV ad for pre-dissemination review that was required to be submitted under section 503B (21 U.S.C. 333(g)(3)(B)), and will take into account the fact that the sponsor, after submitting the ad, disseminated the ad before the end of the 45-day comment period (21 U.S.C. 333 (g)(3)(C)). FDA may also take into account the fact that the sponsor failed to submit the TV ad for pre-dissemination review or disseminated it after submission but before the 45-day comment period without waiting for comments from FDA if it decides to issue an untitled letter or Warning letter to the sponsor for the TV ad.

B. What happens if I disseminate my TV ad without incorporating the Agency's comments?

As previously noted, under section 301(kk) of the FD&C Act (21 U.S.C. 331(kk)), dissemination of a television advertisement without complying with section 503B is a prohibited act. Under section 503B(e), FDA may require specific disclosure of a serious risk listed in the labeling of a drug, and may require the ad to include the date of the product's approval for a period of up to 2 years after that approval, where the absence of either of these pieces of information would render the ad false or misleading. Failure to incorporate these specific required disclosures is a prohibited activity under section 301(kk) that can be enjoined (21 U.S.C. 332(a)) and be subject to criminal penalties (21 U.S.C. 333(a)).

As a result of its review, in addition to requiring disclosures as described above, FDA may also provide comments indicating other elements of the TV ad that it believes would result in the ad being false or misleading, or otherwise violating the FD&C Act or implementing regulations. If the Agency assesses civil monetary penalties to the sponsor because it has disseminated a TV ad that is false or misleading (21 U.S.C. 333(g)), in determining the civil monetary penalty amount, FDA will take into account the fact that the sponsor disseminated the TV ad without incorporating the Agency's comments (21 U.S.C. 333(g)(3)(D)). FDA may also take into account the fact that the sponsor disseminated the TV ad without incorporating the Agency's comments if it decides to issue an untitled or Warning letter.

APPENDIX: CENTER-SPECIFIC SUBMISSION PROCEDURES

CDER

1. Forms

No specific form is to be used. Please submit the materials in accordance with the recommendations in this guidance.

2. Number of Copies

How many copies should I submit?

For CDER OPDP pre-dissemination reviews, submit the following number of copies in pre-dissemination review packages for a proposed TV ad:

- If a video is being provided, 2 copies in an acceptable format
- 12 copies ***of all other materials*** discussed in V(A)(2)-(6)

As an alternative, all materials discussed above can be submitted on a CD.

3. Address

For products regulated in CDER (OPDP), submit proposed DTC TV ads (pre-dissemination review packages and amendment packages) to:

Project Manager
Office of Prescription Drug Promotion
Food and Drug Administration
5901-B Ammendale Road
Beltsville, MD 20705-1266

It is very important to specify on both the ***outer*** package and the cover letter that the contents concern a pre-dissemination review package subject to section 503B of the FD&C Act. Follow the recommendations discussed in section V(A) of this guidance for the cover letter. Include a large type reference line on the outer package that indicates the package is a 503B pre-dissemination review package, such as the following:

- OPDP Pre-Dissemination Review Package as Required by Section 503B of the FD&C Act

Any questions for OPDP may also be addressed to an OPDP project manager by phone at 301-796-1200.

CBER

1. **Forms**

For pre-dissemination review packages for biologics under the purview of CBER (sent to APLB), include the most current version of Form FDA 2253, with Line 13 checked as "Part 1/Draft." Note that this form is **not** to be included with CDER submissions (see above).

2. **Number of Copies**

For CBER APLB pre-dissemination reviews, submit the following number of copies in each pre-dissemination review package for a proposed TV ad:

- If a video is being provided, 2 copies in an acceptable format
- 2 copies ***of all other materials*** discussed in V(A)(2)-(6)

3. **Address**

For products under the purview of CBER (APLB), submit proposed TV ads (pre-dissemination review packages and amendment packages) to:

Advertising and Promotional Labeling Branch, HFM-602
Center for Biologics Evaluation and Research
Food and Drug Administration,
1401 Rockville Pike, suite 200N
Rockville, MD 20852

It is very important to specify on both the ***outer*** package and the cover letter that the contents concern a pre-dissemination review package subject to section 503B of the FD&C Act. Follow the recommendations discussed in section V(A) of this guidance for the cover letter. Include a large type reference line on the outer package that indicates the package is a 503B pre-dissemination review package, such as the following:

- APLB Pre-Dissemination Review Package as Required by Section 503B of the FD&C Act

Any questions for APLB may also be addressed to APLB by phone at 301-827-3028.

Appendix J.

Draft Guidance on Responding to Unsolicited Requests for Off-label Information

Guidance for Industry
Responding to Unsolicited Requests for Off-Label Information About Prescription Drugs and Medical Devices

DRAFT GUIDANCE

This guidance document is being distributed for comment purposes only.

Comments and suggestions regarding this draft document should be submitted within 90 days of publication in the *Federal Register* of the notice announcing the availability of the draft guidance. Submit comments to Division of Dockets Management (HFA-305), Food and Drug Administration, 5630 Fishers Lane, Rm. 1061, Rockville, MD, 20852. All comments should be identified with the docket number listed in the notice of availability that publishes in the *Federal Register*.

For questions regarding this draft guidance document, contact (CDER) Jean-Ah Kang at (301) 796-1200; (CBER) Office of Communication, Outreach and Development at 800-835-4709 or 301-827-1800; (CVM) Dorothy McAdams at (240) 276-9300; or (CDRH) Deborah Wolf at (301) 796-5732.

U.S. Department of Health and Human Services
Food and Drug Administration
Center for Drug Evaluation and Research (CDER)
Center for Biologics Evaluation Research (CBER)
Center for Veterinary Medicine (CVM)
Center for Devices and Radiological Health (CDRH)

December 2011

Guidance for Industry

Responding to Unsolicited Requests for Off-Label Information About Prescription Drugs and Medical Devices

Additional copies are available from:

Office of Communications, Division of Drug Information Center for Drug Evaluation and Research Food and Drug Administration 10903 New Hampshire Ave., Bldg. 51, rm. 2201 Silver Spring, MD 20993-0002 Tel: 301-796-3400; Fax: 301-847-8714; E-mail: druginfo@fda.hhs.gov http://www.fda.gov/Drugs/GuidanceComplianceRegulatoryInformation/Guidances/default.htm	*Communications Staff (CVM) Center for Veterinary Medicine Food and Drug Administration 7519 Standish Place, HFV-12 Rockville, MD 20855 Tel: 240-276-9300; E-mail: AskCVM@fda.hhs.gov http://www.fda.gov/AnimalVeterinary/GuidanceComplianceEnforcement/GuidanceforIndustry/default.htm*
Office of Communication, Outreach and Development (HFM-40) Center for Biologics Evaluation and Research Food and Drug Administration 1401 Rockville Pike, Suite 200N Rockville, MD 20852-1448 Tel: 800-835-4709 or 301-827-1800; E-mail: ocod@fda.hhs.gov http://www.fda.gov/BiologicsBloodVaccines/GuidanceComplianceRegulatoryInformation/default.htm	*Division of Small Manufacturers, International and Consumer Assistance (DSMICA) Office of Communication, Education and Radiation Programs Center for Devices and Radiological Health Food and Drug Administration 10903 New Hampshire Ave., Bldg. 66, rm. 4613 Silver Spring, MD 20993-0002 Tel: 800-638-2041 or 301-796-7100; Fax: 301-847-8149; E-mail: dsmica@fda.hhs.gov http://www.fda.gov/MedicalDevices/DeviceRegulationandGuidance/GuidanceDocuments/default.htm*

U.S. Department of Health and Human Services
Food and Drug Administration
Center for Drug Evaluation and Research (CDER)
Center for Biologics Evaluation Research (CBER)
Center for Veterinary Medicine (CVM)
Center for Devices and Radiological Health (CDRH)

December 2011

TABLE OF CONTENTS

Guidance for Industry

Responding to Unsolicited Requests for Off-Label Information About Prescription Drugs and Medical Devices

This draft guidance, when finalized, will represent the Food and Drug Administration's (FDA) current thinking on this topic. It does not create or confer any rights for or on any person and does not operate to bind FDA or the public. You may use an alternative approach if the approach satisfies the requirements of the applicable statutes and regulations. If you want to discuss an alternative approach, contact the FDA staff responsible for implementing this guidance. If you cannot identify the appropriate FDA staff, call the appropriate number listed on the title pages of this guidance.

I. INTRODUCTION

This draft guidance is intended to describe the Food and Drug Administration's (FDA or Agency) current thinking about how manufacturers and distributors (firms) of prescription human and animal drug products (drugs) and medical devices (devices) can respond to unsolicited requests for information about unapproved or uncleared indications or conditions of use (off-label information) related to their FDA-approved or cleared products.[1,2] This draft guidance updates and clarifies FDA's policies on unsolicited requests for off-label information, including those that firms may encounter through emerging electronic media.

---

[1] This draft guidance has been prepared by the Office of Prescription Drug Products (OPDP) in the Center for Drug Evaluation and Research (CDER) in consultation with the Center for Biologics Evaluation Research (CBER), the Center for Devices and Radiological Health (CDRH), and the Center for Veterinary Medicine (CVM).

[2] The recommendations in this draft guidance also apply to biological products that are approved for marketing under section 351 of the Public Health Service Act (PHS Act). Because each biological product also meets the definition of "drug" or "device" under the Federal Food, Drug, and Cosmetic Act (FD&C Act), it is also subject to regulation under provisions of the FD&C Act applicable to drugs or devices, as well as the regulations implementing these provisions, except that a biological product licensed under section 351 of the PHS Act is not required to have an approved new drug application under section 505 of the FD&C Act. (See PHS Act section 351(j), 42 U.S.C. 262(j).)

In addition, the term "approved or cleared product" in this draft guidance encompasses devices that are legally marketed for a specific intended use without an individual product approval or substantial equivalence determination (clearance). This includes class I and class II devices marketed for uses that make them exempt from premarket notification, in accordance with sections 510(l) or (m) of the FD&C Act (21 U.S.C. 360(l) & (m)). As a result, with regard to such products, a request for "off-label information" refers to any request for information regarding a new use for which approval or clearance would be required. This draft guidance does not address devices solely intended for use in animals.

This draft guidance does not address requests for information about approved or cleared indications or conditions of use (on-label information) for FDA-regulated medical products. It also does not address requests for information about medical products that are not currently approved or cleared for any purpose.

FDA's guidance documents, including this draft guidance, do not establish legally enforceable rights or responsibilities. Instead, guidances describe the Agency's current thinking on a topic and should be viewed only as recommendations, unless specific regulatory or statutory requirements are cited. The use of the word *should* in Agency guidances means that something is suggested or recommended, but not required.

II. BACKGROUND

The Federal Food, Drug, and Cosmetic Act (FD&C Act) and FDA's implementing regulations prohibit manufacturers and distributors (firms) from introducing new drugs, new animal drugs, and most Class III medical devices into interstate commerce for any intended use that FDA has not determined to be safe and effective. The FD&C Act and FDA's implementing regulations also prohibit device firms subject to premarket notification requirements under section 510(k), which includes most class II and some class I devices, from introducing such devices into interstate commerce for any intended use that is outside FDA's substantial equivalence determination (clearance) for such devices.[3] Statements that promote a drug or medical device for uses other than those approved or cleared by FDA may be used as evidence of a new intended use. Introducing a product into commerce for such a new intended use without FDA approval or clearance would, under these requirements, generally violate the law. However, once a drug or medical device has been approved or cleared by FDA, generally, health care professionals can lawfully use or prescribe that product for uses or treatment indications that are not included in the product's approved labeling[4] (or, in the case of a medical device cleared under the 510(k) process, in the product's statement of intended uses). FDA recognizes that these off-label uses or treatment regimens may be important therapeutic options and may even constitute a medically recognized standard of care.

Scientific or medical departments within drug or medical device firms often maintain a large body of information about their products. This information typically includes data and other information consistent with the approved or cleared indications or conditions of use for their products, but may also include off-label information for their products. As noted, although dissemination of off-label information can be used as evidence of new intended uses for products in distribution, such information may also be of use to individuals seeking information about a

---

[3] See e.g., sections 505(a), 501(a), 301(d), 501(f)(1)(B) and 502(o) of the FD&C Act; 21 U.S.C. 355(a), 351(a), 331(d), 351(f)(1)(B) and 352(o).

[4] See sections 512(a)(4) and (a)(5) of the FD&C Act and this Agency's regulations at 21 CFR part 530 for specific provisions related to the off-label (or extra-label) use of approved animal and human drugs in animals.

medical product for themselves, patients, family members, or friends. These individuals sometimes submit non-public requests for off-label information directly and privately to firms.

The rapid growth of the Internet, including social media tools and other emerging technologies, has made it easier for both consumers and health care professionals to quickly seek information about medical conditions and treatments.[5] Many firms have also used emerging electronic media to disseminate product information. As a result, firms may encounter requests for off-label information about their products through product websites, discussion boards, chat rooms, or other public electronic forums that they maintain and over which they have full control. In addition, third-party sites (i.e., websites and other venues that are either entirely independent of a firm's control and influence or not fully controlled by a firm) also may reveal questions about off-label uses of a firm's products. These questions about off-label uses are typically directed to users of the site at large, rather than directly and privately to firms. Such posted information is likely to be available to a much broader audience than just the original requester, especially because communication threads (i.e., questions and replies) are often available for an indefinite period of time.

This draft guidance provides FDA's recommendations to firms wishing to respond to unsolicited requests for off-label information, including both requests made directly and privately to firms and requests made in public forums, including through emerging electronic media. FDA recognizes that firms are capable of responding to requests about their own named products in a truthful, non-misleading, and accurate manner. Furthermore, as these firms are regulated by FDA and have robust and current information about their products, FDA recognizes that it can be in the best interest of public health for a firm to respond to unsolicited requests for information about off-label uses of the firm's products that are addressed to a public forum, as other participants in the forum who offer responses may not provide or have access to the most accurate and up-to-date information about the firm's products.

If a firm responds to unsolicited requests for off-label information in the manner described in this draft guidance, FDA does not intend to use such responses as evidence of the firm's intent that the product be used for an unapproved or uncleared use. Such responses would also not be expected to comply with the disclosure requirements related to promotional labeling and advertising. Firms may choose to respond to unsolicited requests for information about off-label uses of their approved or cleared products in a manner other than that recommended in this draft guidance. Such activity would not constitute a per se violation of the law, but could potentially be introduced as evidence of a new intended use.[6]

---

[5] For example, the public is able to obtain information on certain clinical trial results from www.ClinicalTrials.gov. This may include information related to off-label uses. This information may generate questions directly to a firm.

[6] This draft guidance is not intended to suggest that receiving an unsolicited request is the only circumstance in which a firm can disseminate information about unapproved uses of its FDA-regulated products without such dissemination being used as evidence of the firm's intent that the product be used for an unapproved use. For example, FDA has developed separate guidance that addresses manufacturer-initiated distribution of reprints regarding off-label uses. See *Good Reprint Practices for the Distribution of Medical Journal Articles and Medical or Scientific Reference*

III. DETERMINING WHETHER A REQUEST IS UNSOLICITED OR SOLICITED

This draft guidance addresses how to respond to ***unsolicited requests*** for off-label information about drugs and medical devices. To illustrate the difference between unsolicited and solicited requests, this section describes these two categories of requests and presents a number of examples of both types of requests.

A. Unsolicited Requests

Unsolicited requests are those initiated by persons or entities that are completely independent of the relevant firm. (This may include many health care professionals, health care organizations, members of the academic community, and formulary committees, as well as consumers such as patients and caregivers). Requests that are prompted in any way by a manufacturer or its representatives are not unsolicited requests. Two types of unsolicited requests are addressed in this draft guidance: non-public unsolicited requests and public unsolicited requests. Responses to unsolicited requests can likewise be non-public (private) or public.

- Non-public unsolicited requests

A non-public unsolicited request is an unsolicited request that is directed privately to a firm using a one-on-one communication approach.

Example 1: An individual calls or e-mails the medical information staff at a firm seeking information about an off-label use. In this case, neither the request nor the response would be visible to the public.

- Public unsolicited requests

A public unsolicited request is an unsolicited request made in a public forum, whether directed to a firm specifically or to a forum at large.

Example 2: During a live presentation, an individual asks a question, directed to a firm's representative but heard by other attendees, regarding off-label use of a specific product. This request is a public request. Similarly, a response by the firm that is conveyed to the same audience as the original question would be considered a *public response*.

Example 3: An individual posts a question about off-label use of a specific product on a firm-controlled website (or a third-party discussion forum) that is visible to a broad audience. The request could be directed to a firm specifically or posed to users of a discussion forum at large.

Publications on Unapproved New Uses of Approved Drugs and Approved of Cleared Medical Devices, available at http://www.fda.gov/RegulatoryInformation/Guidances/ucm125126.htm.

This request is a public online request. Similarly, a response by the firm that is visible to the same audience as the original question would be considered a *public online response*.

B. Solicited Requests

FDA considers requests for off-label information that are prompted in any way by a manufacturer or its representatives to be solicited. Such solicited requests may be considered evidence of a firm's intent that a drug or medical device be used for a use other than that specifically approved or cleared by FDA. Although not exhaustive, the following examples illustrate what FDA generally considers to be solicited requests for off-label information[7]:

Example 4: If a firm's sales representative mentions a use of a product that is not reflected in the product's approved labeling and invites a health care professional to request more information, resulting requests would be considered solicited requests.

Example 5: If a representative of a firm, such as a medical science liaison or paid speaker (e.g., key opinion leader), presents off-label use data at a company-sponsored promotional event (e.g., a dinner) and attendees then ask or submit requests for more information, these requests would be considered solicited requests.

Example 6: If a firm issues to health care professionals business reply cards that are intended for use in requesting off-label information, presents statements or contact information in promotional pieces in a manner that solicits requests for off-label medical or scientific information (e.g., "Product X continues to be evaluated in more than 50 trials in a broad range of conditions and patients" and "Call 1-800-... for more information"), or displays a commercial exhibit panel suggesting a new indication (e.g., a sign that reads "Coming Soon, a new use for Product X"), requests made in response to these types of prompts would be considered solicited requests.

Example 7: If a firm provides a phone number, e-mail address, uniform resource locator (URL), or username that is a word, alpha phrase, or alpha representation implying the availability of off-label information for its product, requests using this phone number, e-mail address, URL, or username would be considered solicited requests.

Example 8: A firm asks or otherwise encourages users to post videos about their own uses of its product on third-party video-sharing sites (e.g., YouTube), which may result in video postings about an off-label use of its product. If the firm's initial request for posting of videos results in any questions about off-label uses, or if any off-label video posting made in response to the firm's encouragement of video postings results in questions about the product's off-label use, these questions would be considered solicited requests.

[7] The focus of this draft guidance is unsolicited requests for off-label information, not compliance with provisions of FDA's advertising and labeling regulations for drugs. We note, however, that in some of the following examples, a firm's activities that serve to solicit the requests for off-label information may themselves give rise to specific regulatory violations.

Example 9: If a firm sends out packets of information to known bloggers or online consumer reviewers and encourages them to write about an off-label use of its product on third-party sites and this then provokes a discussion about that off-label use, any requests inquiring about the product's off-label use as a result of these blogs, whether posted as comments to the third-party site or directed to the firm, would be considered solicited requests.

Example 10: If a firm announces results of a study via a microblogging service (e.g., Twitter) and suggests that an off-label use of its product is safe and effective, any comments and requests received as a result of the original message about the off-label use would be considered solicited requests.

Example 11: If a firm sets up a website that enables viewers to read prepared standard responses for the firm's products that are generated from prefixed pull-down menus naming various disease states, including any standard responses related to off-label uses for the firm's product, resulting requests for off-label information would be considered solicited. Moreover, if this website makes it possible to use search terms to generate standard responses that go beyond the scope of the product information being requested, including off-label use information, resulting requests for and responses to such a search would be considered solicited requests.

IV. OVERVIEW OF FDA'S POLICY ON RESPONDING TO UNSOLICITED REQUESTS FOR OFF-LABEL INFORMATION

FDA has long taken the position that firms can respond to unsolicited requests for information about FDA-regulated medical products by providing truthful, balanced, non-misleading, and non-promotional scientific or medical information that is responsive to the specific request, even if responding to the request requires a firm to provide information on unapproved or uncleared indications or conditions of use. If responses to unsolicited requests fall within these parameters, FDA has not expected those responses to meet regulatory requirements for promotional labeling or advertising and has not considered these responses as evidence of intended use. This draft guidance sets forth FDA's current thinking on this topic, consistent with the Agency's past policy statements about responding to unsolicited requests.[8,9] Regardless of whether the initial

[8] This policy was articulated in a letter to industry in 1982 and has been restated on many occasions. See _Position on the Concept of Solicited and Unsolicited Requests_ (April 22, 1982) ("[T]he Division of Drug Advertising and Labeling will not regulate as labeling any and all unsolicited requests received from outside the company for information about a drug manufactured, distributed, or repacked by the company. These types of legitimate requests from scientists/individuals for drug information will be regarded and treated as a personal communication between the requestor and firm."); 59 Fed. Reg. 59820, 59823 (November 18, 1994) (stating that manufacturers may respond to unsolicited requests for information with "responsive, nonpromotional, balanced scientific information, which may include information on unapproved uses, without subjecting their products to regulation based on the information"). FDA's current views (expressed in this draft guidance) remain consistent with these past policy statements.

[9] In addition, section 557(a) of the FD&C Act, which expired on September 30, 2006, provided that "nothing in section 551 [of the Act] shall be construed as prohibiting a manufacturer from disseminating information in response to an unsolicited request from a health care practitioner." 21 U.S.C.360aaa-6

unsolicited request for off-label information was made in a non-public or public forum, a firm that chooses to respond should provide the final response containing the requested off-label information about its product only to the specific individual who requested the information as a private, one-on-one communication.

Section V explains in detail FDA's recommendations for firms that choose to respond to non-public unsolicited requests for off-label information, and Section VI addresses FDA's recommendations for firms that choose to respond to public unsolicited requests for off-label information, including those that are encountered through emerging electronic media.

V. RESPONDING TO NON-PUBLIC UNSOLICITED REQUESTS FOR OFF-LABEL INFORMATION DIRECTED TO DRUG OR MEDICAL DEVICE FIRMS

This section of the draft guidance makes recommendations about responding to non-public unsolicited requests for off-label information about prescription human and animal drugs (drugs) and medical devices (devices) specifically directed to firms privately through one-on-one communications. For example, an individual might call or correspond directly with a firm concerning the use of its product for an unapproved or uncleared indication or condition of use. The firm could receive the request by mail, e-mail, telephone, or through a firm-controlled website that enables individuals to privately submit a request directly to the firm so that the request is *not* available to the public.

FDA makes the following recommendations to a firm that is responding to a ***non-public*** unsolicited request for off-label information about its product that was specifically directed to the firm privately through a one-on-one communication.

1. Information distributed in response to an unsolicited request should be provided only to the individual making the request directly to the firm as a private, one-on-one communication.

2. Information distributed in response to an unsolicited request should be tailored to answer only the specific question(s) asked.

A firm should ensure that all pertinent background data are obtained to be able to determine what information is being requested before providing a response. If an unsolicited question is broad in nature, the firm should appropriately narrow the question. In other words, the level of specificity of the question posed is important to ensure that the firm's response is tailored to the request.

Example 12: An individual requests information on the use of a drug or device for one particular disease or condition that is considered off-label for that drug or device (e.g., use of Drug X during pregnancy in patients with diabetes). Generally, a firm should provide information pertaining only to that disease or condition (i.e., the firm should provide a response tailored only to the use of Drug X during pregnancy in patients with diabetes).

However, if there is information about known or suspected _risks_ associated with other diseases or conditions that is also relevant to the disease or condition for which information was requested, the firm should provide such information to ensure a complete and accurate presentation of the risk issues associated with the requested use (e.g., Drug X is known to cause fetal harm when used in pregnant patients with arthritis, and this risk information should be disclosed as part of the response about use of Drug X during pregnancy in patients with diabetes).

3. Information distributed in response to an unsolicited request should be truthful, non-misleading, accurate, and balanced.[10]

A response should provide non-biased information or data relating to the particular off-label use that is the subject of the request, including applicable data that are not supportive or that cast doubt on the safety or efficacy of that use. For example, when conclusions of articles or texts that are disseminated have been specifically called into question by other articles or texts, a firm should disseminate representative publications that reach contrary or different conclusions regarding the use at issue. The response should include complete copies of scientific reprints, technical literature, or other scientific and medical information responsive to the request, not just summary documents or abstracts prepared by the firm. The response can include unpublished data on file if they are responsive to the specific request (either supporting or casting doubt on the safety or efficacy of the off-label use). However, to the greatest extent possible, a firm should rely on published peer-reviewed journal articles, medical texts, or data derived from independent sources. To the extent the response consists of published reprints from journals, those reprints should be from journals that have a publicly stated policy, to which the organization adheres, of full disclosure of any conflict of interest or biases for all authors, contributors, or editors associated with the journal or organization.

4. Information distributed in response to an unsolicited request should be scientific in nature.

When responding to an unsolicited request for information, a firm should respond with material that is scientific in tone and presentation. The material should not be promotional in tone or presentation. Furthermore, the responsive material should not be distributed along with other material or information that is promotional in nature or tone.

5. Responses to unsolicited requests for information should be generated by medical or scientific personnel independent from sales or marketing departments.

FDA recommends that questions or requests about off-label uses be referred to the firm's medical or scientific representative or department. FDA recommends that medical or scientific personnel have specialized backgrounds in responding to unsolicited requests for information, including

[10] Evaluating evidence of intended use may also involve considering the context in which manufacturer communication about an off-label use occurs. For this reason, FDA's recommendations in this draft guidance for responding to unsolicited requests for information by third parties are not identical to its recommendations regarding the spontaneous manufacturer-initiated activity of distributing reprints, as addressed in other FDA guidance.

important training, such as appropriately narrowing questions, tailoring responses only to the specific questions being asked, providing unbiased responses, and properly documenting responses.

By contrast, because sales and marketing personnel are focused by training and experience on promoting a firm's products, FDA recommends that sales and marketing personnel have no input on the content of responses to unsolicited questions or requests for off-label information.

6. Information distributed in response to an unsolicited request should be accompanied by the following:

    - A copy of the FDA-required labeling, if any, for the product (e.g., FDA-approved package insert and, if the response is for a consumer, FDA-approved patient labeling or, for new animal drugs, FDA-approved client information sheet)
    - A prominent statement notifying the recipient that FDA has not approved or cleared the product as safe and effective for the use addressed in the materials provided
    - A prominent statement disclosing the indication(s) for which FDA has approved or cleared the product
    - A prominent statement providing all important safety information including, if applicable, any boxed warning for the product
    - A complete list of references for all of the information disseminated in the response (e.g., a bibliography of publications in peer-reviewed medical journals or in medical or scientific texts; citations for data on file, for summary documents, or for abstracts)

7. A firm should maintain the following records:

    - The nature of the request for information, including the name, address, and affiliation of the requestor
    - Records regarding the information provided to the requestor
    - Any follow-up inquiries or questions from the requestor

If a firm responds to non-public unsolicited requests for off-label information in the manner described above, FDA does not intend to use such responses as evidence of the firm's intent that its product be used for an unapproved or uncleared use. Such responses also would not be expected to comply with the disclosure requirements related to promotional labeling and advertising.

VI. RESPONDING TO PUBLIC UNSOLICITED REQUESTS FOR OFF-LABEL INFORMATION, INCLUDING THOSE ENCOUNTERED THROUGH EMERGING ELECTRONIC MEDIA BY DRUG OR MEDICAL DEVICE FIRMS

This section of the draft guidance makes recommendations about responding to public unsolicited requests for off-label information about prescription human and animal drugs (drugs) and medical devices (devices), including those that are encountered through emerging electronic media.

The Internet has revolutionized communication, information-sharing, information exchange among systems, and collaboration, enabling consumers to become more proactive about their health and safety. Consequently, the Internet has become a widely used medium for manufacturers and distributors of FDA-regulated medical products to disseminate information. The Internet has also spawned a variety of social media tools that host online content primarily created and published by users other than the intellectual property owner or product manufacturer. In some cases, this online content may not be accurate. Because consumers increasingly use the Internet to search for information about medical conditions and treatments, firms may receive public requests for off-label information about their products through, for example, product websites, discussion boards, chat rooms, or other public electronic forums that they maintain and over which they have full control. Firms may also encounter requests for off-label information on third-party sites (i.e., websites and other venues that are either entirely independent of a firm's control and influence or not fully controlled by a firm). Questions about off-label use may be directed to the website users at large, rather than specifically to a firm.

As previously stated in Section II, FDA recognizes that firms are capable of responding to requests about their own named products in a truthful, non-misleading, and accurate manner. Moreover, because firms usually have robust and current information about their products, it can be in the best interest of public health for a firm to respond to unsolicited requests for information about off-label uses of the firm's products that are made in public forums, especially since other responders may not provide or have access to the most accurate and up-to-date medical product information.

However, because product information posted on websites and other public electronic forums is likely to be available to a broad audience and for an indefinite period of time, FDA is concerned that firms may post detailed public online responses to questions about off-label uses of their products in such a way that they are communicating unapproved or uncleared use information about FDA-regulated medical products to individuals who have not requested such information. In this circumstance, communications to persons who have not requested information may promote a product for a use or condition for which FDA has not approved or cleared. FDA is also concerned about the enduring nature of detailed public online responses to off-label questions because specific drug or device information may become outdated (e.g., new risk information may become available).

FDA makes the following recommendations to a firm that chooses to respond to ***public*** unsolicited requests for off-label information about its product(s), including those encountered through emerging electronic media.

1. If a firm chooses to respond to public unsolicited requests for off-label information, the firm should respond only when the request pertains specifically to its own named product (and is not solely about a competitor's product).

The level of specificity of the question posed in a public forum is important in determining the appropriateness of a firm responding to the unsolicited request.

Example 13: An individual poses the specific question "Can Drug/Device X be used for Condition Y" in a public forum (and this question is not prompted by or on behalf of the firm). It may be appropriate for the firm to respond as outlined below because the question is unsolicited and specific to the firm's named drug or device.

However, if an individual poses the non-specific question "What drug/device can be used for Condition Y" in a public communication thread and the firm manufactures or distributes Drug/Device X, which is not FDA-approved or cleared for Condition Y, the firm should not respond to the request because the question is ***not*** specific to Drug/Device X.

2. A firm's ***public*** response to public unsolicited requests for off-label information about its named product should be limited to providing the firm's contact information and should ***not*** include any off-label information.

    - The firm's public response should convey that the question pertains to an unapproved or uncleared use of the product and state that individuals can contact the medical/scientific representative or medical affairs department with the specific unsolicited request to obtain more information.
    - The firm's public response should provide specific contact information for the medical or scientific personnel or department (e.g., e-mail address, telephone number, facsimile) so that individuals can follow up independently with the firm to obtain specific information about the off-label use of the product through a non-public, one-on-one communication.

After an individual has privately contacted a firm for more information regarding an off-label use of the firm's product, the firm should provide a detailed response and maintain records following the parameters outlined in Section V of this draft guidance. Therefore, any substantive communication about off-label uses for the product, in response to the original unsolicited off-label question, should occur solely between the firm and the individual who made the request. Regardless of the fact that the original, unsolicited off-label question may have been available to a very broad audience, the firm should not make its detailed response with off-label information publicly available within the same forum. For example, after the requestor has contacted the firm and provided a personal e-mail address to obtain an answer to the off-label question, the firm's detailed off-label response, within the parameters outlined in Section V of this draft guidance, should be e-mailed to the requestor since this resulting communication will occur solely between the firm and the specific individual making the unsolicited request for the off-label information.

3. Representatives who provide public responses to unsolicited requests for off-label information should clearly disclose their involvement with a particular firm.

FDA recommends that a representative who responds to a public request clearly disclose in his/her public response that he/she is a particular firm's representative and inform the requestor of the name of the firm representative or department to contact should the individual choose to follow up directly with the firm in a non-public forum for detailed information about the unsolicited request for off-label information.

4. Public responses to public unsolicited requests for off-label information described in numbers 2 and 3 should not be promotional in nature or tone.

In addition to a firm's contact and disclosure information, a public response should include a mechanism for providing readily accessible current FDA-required labeling, if any, for the product (e.g., FDA-approved package insert and, if the response is for a consumer, FDA-approved patient labeling or, for new animal drugs, FDA-approved client information sheet). The public response should *not* provide any promotional information. For example, a public online response should include a direct link to the current FDA-required labeling, if any, but should *not* include links to any other information (e.g., product websites, product promotional materials, firm websites, third-party websites). Furthermore, the uniform resource locator (URL) or web address where viewers are directed to obtain the FDA-required labeling, if any, should *not* itself be promotional in tone or content (e.g., should not be www.bestcancercure.com).

If a firm responds to public unsolicited requests for off-label information, including those encountered through emerging electronic media, in the manner described above, FDA does not intend to use such responses as evidence of the firm's intent that its product be used for an unapproved or uncleared use. Such responses also would not be expected to comply with the disclosure requirements related to promotional labeling and advertising.

www.ingramcontent.com/pod-product-compliance
Lightning Source LLC
Chambersburg PA
CBHW081125180926
51611CB00004B/57
9781935065852